Applications and
Trends in Fintech I
Governance, AI, and Blockchain Design Thinking

Global Fintech Institute - World Scientific Series on Fintech

Print ISSN: 2737-5897
Online ISSN: 2737-5900

Series Editors: David LEE Kuo Chuen *(Global Fintech Institute, Singapore &*
Singapore University of Social Sciences, Singapore)
Joseph LIM *(Singapore University of Social Sciences, Singapore)*
PHOON Kok Fai *(Singapore University of Social Sciences, Singapore)*
WANG Yu *(Singapore University of Social Sciences, Singapore)*

In the digital era, emerging technologies such as artificial intelligence, big data, and blockchain have revolutionized people's daily lives and brought many opportunities and challenges to industries. With the increasing demand for talents in the fintech realm, this book series serves as a good guide for practitioners who are seeking to understand the basics of fintech and the applications of different technologies. This book series starts with fundamental knowledge in finance, technology, quantitative methods, and financial innovation to lay the foundation for the fundamentals of fintech, and understanding the trending issues related to fintech such as regulation, applications, and global trends. It is a good starting point to the fintech literature and is especially useful for people who aspire to become fintech professionals.

Published:

Vol. 4 *Applications and Trends in Fintech I: Governance, AI, and Blockchain Design Thinking*
edited by David LEE Kuo Chuen, Joseph LIM, PHOON Kok Fai and WANG Yu

Vol. 3 *Fintech for Finance Professionals*
edited by David LEE Kuo Chuen, Joseph LIM, PHOON Kok Fai and WANG Yu

Vol. 2 *Finance for Fintech Professionals*
edited by David LEE Kuo Chuen, Joseph LIM, PHOON Kok Fai and WANG Yu

Vol. 1 *Foundations for Fintech*
edited by David LEE Kuo Chuen, Joseph LIM, PHOON Kok Fai and WANG Yu

More information on this series can also be found at https://www.worldscientific.com/series/gfiwssf

(Continued at end of book)

Global Fintech Institute - World Scientific
Series on Fintech : 4

Applications and Trends in Fintech I

Governance, AI, and Blockchain Design Thinking

Editors

David LEE Kuo Chuen
Global Fintech Institute, Singapore
Singapore University of Social Sciences, Singapore

Joseph LIM
Singapore University of Social Sciences, Singapore

PHOON Kok Fai
Singapore University of Social Sciences, Singapore

WANG Yu
Singapore University of Social Sciences, Singapore

Published by

World Scientific Publishing Co. Pte. Ltd.
5 Toh Tuck Link, Singapore 596224
USA office: 27 Warren Street, Suite 401-402, Hackensack, NJ 07601
UK office: 57 Shelton Street, Covent Garden, London WC2H 9HE

and

Global Fintech Institute Ltd.
80 Robinson Road, #08-01, Singapore 068898

Library of Congress Cataloging-in-Publication Data
Names: Lee, David (David Kuo Chuen), editor. | Lim, Joseph, editor. |
    Phoon, Kok Fai, editor. | Wang, Yu, editor.
Title: Applications and trends in fintech I : governance, AI, and blockchain design thinking / editors,
    David Lee Kuo Chuen (Global Fintech Institute, Singapore, Singapore University of
    Social Sciences, Singapore), Joseph Lim (Singapore University of Social Sciences, Singapore),
    Phoon Kok Fai (Singapore University of Social Sciences, Singapore),
    Wang Yu (Singapore University of Social Sciences, Singapore).
Description: Singapore ; Hackensack, NJ : World Scientific Publishing Co., [2022] |
    Series: Global Fintech Institute - World Scientific series on fintech, 2737-5897 ; vol. 4 |
    Includes bibliographical references.
Identifiers: LCCN 2022000595 | ISBN 9789811247965 (hardcover) |
    ISBN 9789811249297 (paperback) | ISBN 9789811247972 (ebook) |
    ISBN 9789811247989 (ebook other)
Subjects: LCSH: Finance--Technological innovations.
Classification: LCC HG173 .A754 2022 | DDC 332--dc23/eng/20220112
LC record available at https://lccn.loc.gov/2022000595

British Library Cataloguing-in-Publication Data
A catalogue record for this book is available from the British Library.

For any available supplementary material, please visit
https://www.worldscientific.com/worldscibooks/10.1142/12578#t=suppl

Desk Editors: Balasubramanian Shanmugam/Yulin Jiang

Typeset by Stallion Press
Email: enquiries@stallionpress.com

Printed in Singapore

Preface

Just a few years ago, the word "Fintech" did not mean much to members of the public. Some associated it with cryptocurrency while others thought of payment systems using the phone. However, over the past five years, the adoption of Fintech in the mainstream public life has increased in pace. Fintech startups have also proliferated as the low interest rate environment provided cheap and more easily available financing. Adoption of Fintech applications has also been accelerated by the changes in working and living brought about by the Covid-19 pandemic restrictions.

The fast pace of developments in Fintech has fostered a demand for professionals to work in this field. The problem is that someone who aspires to work in this field has little idea about the requisite knowledge and skills. It is to this end that the Global FinTech Institute (GFI) was established.

The Global FinTech Institute aims to serve as a hub for the following initiatives:

- A forum for Fintech professionals to meet and collaborate to develop best practices for the industry and serve as a focal point to advocate for the industry.
- A professional society to develop standards and governance frameworks.
- A center to share insights and advance knowledge through the promotion of research.
- A professional body to organize the Fintech body of knowledge, and promote Fintech education.

- A fiduciary to certify knowledge and proficiency in Fintech through the Chartered Fintech Professional (CFtP) designation.

The CFtP program is designed to equip the candidate with a set of tools and a body of knowledge to practice as a Fintech professional. The program starts with building the foundation to understand finance and computer technology through tools like statistics, quantitative methods, programming, and fundamentals of blockchain and cryptocurrency. These tools are used to facilitate the fundamental building blocks of finance, computing, and technology. Finally, the program ends with the application of the concepts learned earlier. A more detailed description of what the program covers is given in what follows, in the listing of the CFtP courses. The CFtP designation is attained by passing a series of exams as well as satisfying the relevant work experience requirement and attestation of good character. The CFtP exams are organized as follows:

- Level 1AB – Foundation
  o Ethics and governance; statistics; quantitative methods; financial innovations; blockchain and cryptocurrency
- Level 1A – Finance
  o Economics; financial statement analysis, financial management; investment management
- Level 1B – Fintech
  o Data structure, algorithms, and Python programming; big data and data science; artificial intelligence and machine learning; computer network and network security
- Level 2 – Applications and Professional Practice
  o Ethics and governance; machine learning and deep learning in Finance; blockchain design and programming; cloud computing, cyber security, and quantum computing; compliance and risk management; global Fintech trends

This book is the first volume of a set of materials used for the CFtP Level 2 exams. While the book is geared toward the body of knowledge for the CFtP Level 2 exams, nevertheless, it can serve as a quick guide and summary of the issues pertaining to the areas of Fintech related to ethics and governance, machine and deep learning, and blockchain design.

About the Editors

Professor David LEE Kuo Chuen is a professor at the Singapore University of Social Sciences and Adjunct Professor at the National University of Singapore. He is also the founder of BlockAsset Ventures, the Chairman of Global Fintech Institute, Vice President of the Economic Society of Singapore, Co-founder of Blockchain Association of Singapore, and Council Member of British Blockchain Association. He has 20 years of experience as a CEO and an independent director of listed and tech companies and is a consultant and advisor to international organizations on food supply chain, blockchain, fintech, and digital currency.

Associate Professor Joseph LIM is with the Singapore University of Social Sciences where he teaches finance. He has also taught at the National University of Singapore and the Singapore Management University. Joseph obtained his MBA from Columbia University and PhD from New York University. In between his stints in academia, he worked in various advisory positions in the areas of private equity and valuation. Joseph, who is a CFA charter holder, has served in various committees at the CFA Institute and as President of CFA Singapore. In addition, he was on the board and committees of various investment industry associations. In the non-profit sector, he was on the board of a pension fund and several endowment funds. He is a coauthor of several popular college finance textbooks.

Associate Professor Kok Fai PHOON teaches finance at the School of Business, Singapore University of Social Sciences (SUSS). He received his PhD in finance from Northwestern University, MSc in Industrial Engineering from the National University of Singapore, and BASc in Mechanical Engineering (Honours) from the University of British Columbia. His research interests focus on the use of technology in portfolio management, wealth management, and risk and complexity of financial products. In addition to his current position at SUSS, Kok Fai has taught at other universities in Singapore and at Monash University in Australia. He has worked at Yamaichi Merchant Bank, at GIC Pte Ltd, and as Executive Director at Ferrell Asset Management, a Singapore hedge fund. He has published in academic journals including the *Review of Quantitative Finance and Accounting* and the *Pacific Basin Finance Journal* as well as practice journals like the *Financial Analyst Journal*, the *Journal of Wealth Management*, and the *Journal of Alternative Investments*.

Ms Yu WANG (Cheryl) is a fintech research fellow at the Singapore University of Social Sciences FinTech and Blockchain Group. Her main research interests are fintech, machine learning, and asset pricing. Prior to SUSS, she worked at the National University of Singapore, Business School as a research associate on corporate governance and sustainability. She graduated with an MSc in Applied Economies from Nanyang Technological University and BSc in Financial Engineering from Huazhong University of Sciences of Technologies. She has multiple journal papers, including an empirical study on sustainability reporting and firm value published on an SSCI journal, *Sustainability*, and one investigating cryptocurrency as a new alternative investment published on *Journal of Alternative Investments* that has been cited for over 200 times and recommended by *CFA Institute Journal Review*. She also serves as referee for various journals such as *Singapore Economic Review*, *Quarterly Review of Economics and Finance*, and *Journal of Alternative Investments*.

Contents

Part A: Ethics and Governance

Note to the candidate:
Ethics and governance is an area which few of you know much. It is not taught in school and much of it is learned on the job. However, this area is one which you should take seriously. Compliance with the ethical codes and governance requirements is necessary for one to be a competent professional. Violation of the codes and governance requirements has grave consequences for the professional's reputation and even ability to practice. Even if a violation does not result in some penalty, trust in the professional may be eroded and their professional standing diminished.

The scope of this module is very wide. To keep the material manageable, we have focused on the fundamentals. Candidates interested in particular areas or topics can use the references to expand their knowledge and understanding.

Examples of specific regulations are shown in separate "notes" indicated in brackets.

Ethics and governance is crucially important in corporate affairs. Any violations of proper ethical conduct or governance procedures can have adverse implications for the firm as such breaches can be easily revealed through social media. Yet, this important area is seldom taught in schools. A professional, such as the CFtP charter holder, cannot plead ignorance of ethical and governance concerns. For this reason, the CFtP program strongly emphasizes a thorough knowledge of the issues as well as good understanding in order to apply the ethical and governance principles appropriately.

The candidate may find this topic in the curriculum somewhat daunting as there is seldom any prior exposure or training in their experience. One can easily get lost as it is often difficult to see the forest for the trees. We advise the candidate to focus on the principles as these would provide the foundation for understanding the often complex ethical and governance problems in the workplace. Failure to comply with governance guidelines can potentially have adverse implications such as legal outcomes.

In the context of the CFtP curriculum, ethics and governance is about behavior, as well as incentives, whether at the personal or corporate realms. We can observe the behavior but may not know the motivation behind the action. Ethics is about ensuring that the actions undertaken by the professional have the correct motivation.

What is governance? It is a framework of policies and procedures that a company establishes to govern the conduct of corporate affairs so that actions taken by the company and its employees are aligned to the goals of the company, comply with the laws and regulations of the state, and do not subject the company to unnecessary risk. Failure to observe corporate governance requirements can potentially have adverse outcomes leading to legal issues, financial harm, and loss of reputation and goodwill.

While poor governance could result in negative consequences, good governance can provide benefits through inspiring stakeholders' trust and confidence in the firm's policies and decisions, yielding dividends through lower financing and transaction costs. The firm's reputation for good governance can also give it the competitive edge in securing business.

Society does not rely only on social norms and personal ethical beliefs to regulate behavior. In order for a society to function in an orderly fashion and fulfill the needs of its members, rules and regulations are needed to prescribe minimal standards of behavior or even to proscribe certain unwanted behavior. It is incumbent on the professional to understand the rules and regulations that govern her area of work as non-compliance may give rise to legal penalties as well as tarnish the reputation of the firm and the profession. Consequently, we have a section discussing common principles that regulators adopt to help them draw up the rules and regulations. Major rules and regulations pertaining to Fintech will be discussed. This will be complemented by specific examples of how those rules and regulations apply in various jurisdictions.

For the whole module of Ethics and Governance, we draw on work done by two premier associations representing the finance industry and the IT industry, namely, the CFA Institute and the Association of Computer Machinery (ACM).

The CFA Institute is well known for the rigor of the CFA program, as well as being a thought leader in the investment management industry. Its Code of Ethics and Standards of Professional Conduct are a well-regarded set of principles for ethical and professional conduct which quite a few professional organizations have used as a model. The Code and Standards espouse ethical behavior and professional conduct that are sometimes at a level beyond the requirements of the ethics and regulation curriculum required in licensing exams that finance practitioners have to take before they are allowed to practice in the finance industry.

In the area of IT, the ACM can be considered the most highly respected association for practitioners. The ACM Code of Ethics and Professional Conduct is a comprehensive guide to practitioners navigating the issues of ethics and professional conduct in IT. The importance and significance of the ACM code cannot be overemphasized as IT practitioners are often not required to be licensed, unlike their finance counterparts. Further, the importance of ethics for IT practitioners is recognized by institutions like Harvard University which has embedded ethics in its Computer Science courses.[1] However, CFtP holders should be aware that FinTech is more complicated than purely IT as other technologies and related human impact are involved. Certain basic ethics and moral principles should guide decision making.

---

[1]Grosz, B. J., Grant, D. G., Vredenburgh, K., Behrends, J., Hu, L., Simmons, A., and Waldo, J. (2019). Embedded ethiCS: Integrating ethics across CS education. *Communications of the ACM*, 62(8), 54–61.

Chapter 1

Ethical Framework and Principles

1.1 Introduction

What are the hallmarks of a true professional? Ethical behavior and competence. Ethical behavior inspires trust and confidence in the public that the professional will render her service with the utmost integrity. Competence gives assurance that the work or service is rendered to the highest standards of practice in the profession.

We lay the foundation for a discussion on ethics by providing a framework to think about the issues and challenges confronting ethical behavior. Then we discuss various ethical principles which can help guide us in making ethical decisions. Behaving ethically comes from the belief of the professional in doing the "right thing" which benefits her clients, her coworkers, and society at large. Integrity is infused in all aspects of the professional's works.

Beyond behaving ethically, the professional has also to live up to the expectations of the public regarding professional conduct. This pertains to the quality of work and services the professional renders. How a professional conducts herself not only projects competence but also promotes trust from the public. It is always good for the professional to benchmark her work against best practices as she is often the best critic of her professional performance.

1.2 The Ethical Framework

1.2.1 *Introduction*

What is ethical behavior depends on the ethical standards or principles through which we judge behavior. For our purposes, behavior is confined to the professional realm. How a person behaves outside the work environment can have implications on professional reputation. However, issues of behavior in a non-professional setting go beyond the scope of how we expect professionals to behave, as they may entail moral and other values judgments.

Ethical judgments can be difficult and complex. Knowledge about ethics is not enough. What we need is a framework which presents, in a systematic manner, a process for incorporating ethical issues in decision making.

Learning Objectives
• Understand the ethical framework.

Main Takeaways

Main Points
• Recognizing that ethical issues in a situation requires familiarity with ethical principles and their application to real world situations.
• Getting the relevant facts is crucial to making an informed decision.
• One should not be wedded to a particular course of action but should be open to alternative courses.
• It is important to test the decision and consider how fellow professionals would view it.
• Implementing the decision must be done thoughtfully.

(a) Framework for Ethical Decision Making[2]
There are six steps in this framework:

1. recognize an ethical issue;
2. get the facts;
3. understand the technology.

---

[2]This section is adapted from "A framework for ethical decision making" developed by the Markkula Center for Applied Ethics at Santa Clara University.

4. evaluate alternative actions;
5. make a decision and test it;
6. act and reflect on the outcome.

(1) Recognize an ethical issue

Recognizing that there could be an ethical issue in a situation requires that the professional be familiar with ethical principles as well as how they are applied to various situations. While one may learn the principles in courses or programs like the CFtP, facility in applying the principles can only come through practice. Learning vicariously through case studies allows the professional to encounter more situations and improve the ability to identify a potential ethical issue early. As in any skill, lack of usage will dull the skill. Therefore, ethics will be a regular feature of CFtP continuing education.

A main difficulty for this first step in the framework is that ethical issues go beyond legal and regulatory stipulations and prohibitions. Laws and regulations make clear what cannot be done or what must be done. However, the demarcation between what is ethical and what is not is not clear-cut for many situations. One way to resolve this is to consider the following:

- Could the decision or situation be disadvantageous to another party?
- Does the technology give rise to a good and intended outcome?
- What are the possible choices? Is it between a good and a bad choice, or between two "bad" or two "good" choices?
- Would the situation or issue go beyond the legal requirements?
- Is it a question of efficiency?

(2) Get the facts

Relevant facts are important inputs for analyzing a situation or issue. Decisions based on facts tend to have greater objectivity, credibility and acceptance by the parties to the decision. Some of the questions that need to be asked are:

- Are the facts sufficient to make a decision? What more needs to be known?
- What are the interests of the parties to the situation or issue? Are certain interests more important?
- What are the options for acting? Have the issues been discussed with all the relevant parties?

(3) Understand the technology
The individual must understand the technology that is being used. Decisions should only be made after acquiring a certain level of knowledge or expertize, bearing in mind that nascent technology is dynamic and changing. These technologies may involve hardware and software, and the technology risks may not be fully understood. Some of the questions that need to be asked are:

- Are humans governing the technology or codes?
- Are technology or codes governing human behavior?
- How are computer codes governing the technology?
- What behavior can be expected from the technology governing model?
- Are the codes audited and have the intended outcomes?
- What good and harm will the technology bring?

(4) Evaluate alternative actions
After marshaling the facts, the professional has to come up with various proposals to resolve the issue or situation. It is important for the professional not to be wedded to a particular option or design, but be open to alternatives. In proposing the alternatives the following bear consideration:

- Which option or design is fair to the parties?
- What is the trade-off, if any, between doing good and harm?
- Does the option chosen consider other stakeholders beyond the parties directly involved in the situation or issue?

(5) Make a decision and test it
Selecting the best course of action is not easy as it is often not obvious which option is best. Whichever the option that best resolves the situation or issue at hand, the chosen option should not conflict with ethical principles. A good way to test the soundness of the decision is to consider how your fellow professionals would view the option you have chosen.

(6) Act and reflect on the outcome
Making a good decision but implementing it poorly may not lead to the desired effect. The concerns of the stakeholders must be taken into

account as ultimately it is their perception of fairness that determines, to a large extent, whether the implementation is satisfactory.

It is always good for the professional to reflect on the decision taken and the outcome of the decision so that lessons can be drawn from the experience. Ideally, the professional does not keep the lessons learned to herself but endeavors to share them with the wider body of professionals. This is especially important for FinTech areas where there are other expertise needed, such as code auditing, hardware expertise, platform economics, game theory perspectives and regulatory consequences. Sharing the experience would help the profession progress to higher standards of ethical practice and justify the public's trust in them.

(b) Principal-Agent Relationships and Distributed Governance
Underlying many of the relationships in the workplace is the principal-agent relationship. An employee is an agent of the firm which is the principal. This has important ramifications as the employee, through the authority conferred upon him by the firm, is empowered to establish legal relations on the principal's behalf. Any contract made by the employee with a third party is legally binding on the firm and the third party.

Where a client is concerned he is the principal, and the person who provides the service and acts on his behalf is the agent. Stretching the concept, somewhat, all of us can be considered agents of the society or community we live in.

The key issue in principal-agent relationships arises from the conflict of interests between the two parties. Note that while an agent may act in his own best interest there is a duty to act in the best interest of the principal. This issue will be discussed later under the ethical standards of integrity and duty of care. Further, loyalty to the principal is an important and treasured element in the relationship between the employee and the firm. Agents must act with prudence and care as though a particular transaction involves their own money.

A simple example illustrates this issue. An employee is tasked with an assignment. The effort put into finishing the assignment is often unobservable. The employee can improve on the finished product which is satisfactory but the extra effort comes at the expense of the employee's alternative use of the time needed.

Here is another example. A visitor to the firm looks a bit lost. Many employees who notice the visitor will just go on their way and not offer help as they view offering help as not part of their responsibilities and, further, it may take effort and time. However, from the perspective of the firm, helping the visitor would benefit the firm as the visitor may be a prospective client who may form a good impression of the firm based on the conduct of its employees.

At the level of the individual there may be some mechanisms to align the principal's and agent's interests, for example profit sharing arrangements or the grant of stock options to top management. However, where those mechanisms are not available, it is the strong sense of ethical conduct and professionalism of the individual that ameliorates the conflict of interest between the two parties.

In a societal context, the issue of conflict of interests between the individual and society is exemplified by the "tragedy of the commons" which describes a situation where many individuals share a common resource. For example, to prevent overfishing, the authorities regulate the amount of fish that can be caught in a particular area of the sea. Without regulation, each fishing trawler will try to catch as much of the fish as possible. However, if every fishing trawler were to do the same, then the stock of fish would be depleted to a level insufficient to produce enough offspring to replenish the stock of fish. If fishing continued at the same rate as before, the quantity of each catch brought in would dwindle and everyone would be worse off for that. Unless the conflict of interest between the individual and the collective is managed, everyone loses in the end.

When it comes to the common good, regulation and technology may help, for example in blockchain governance and anti-pollution laws. However, when it comes to green initiatives like cutting waste or recycling, the situation here is similar to the situation described in the example above of the visitor to an office. Some individuals feel that playing their part would not make much of a difference. In this instance, what causes individuals to play their part is their embrace of the value of sustainability. Similar to ethical values which spur ethical behavior, the concern about future generations, which is the essence of sustainability, serves to play a role similar to the moral compass for ethical behavior, and guides the thoughts and behaviors in issues like climate change.

As far as technology is concerned, it is essential that the design thinking behind the technology aligns the interests of all parties. With distributed ledger technology such as tokenization and smart contracts, both offline and online governance can help reduce the conflicts of interest and distribute the trust to ensure tragedy of the commons situations will be minimized or avoided as much as possible. There is an interaction between the human and technology. The issue of who governs who, who governs what, what governs who, and what governs what must be clearly understood. For example, technology may govern human behavior and vice versa. We may even have situations where technology will govern technology. These are challenging and essential issues in principle-agent and distributed governance models. There is a duty to ensure that the design or emergence of third-party trust will not lead to rent-seeking behavior. For example, individuals will need to be discerning to ensure that the new Fintech agent or intermediary acting as a trusted third party has the basic or higher ethical standards. As a CFtP holder, these issues must be discussed and considered upfront.

1.3 Ethical Principles — CFtP Code of Ethics

1.3.1 *Introduction*

The CFtP Code of Ethics is a set of ethical principles that all CFtP charter holders must uphold. These principles inform the charter holders' decisions when they have to make difficult decisions when conflicting interests are involved. Making the right decision calls for a solid knowledge of the principles as well as the facility to apply them in complex situations.

Learning Objectives
- Discuss the four ethical principles and their implications.

Main Takeaways

Main Points
- Integrity is the foundation and basis for trust in the work of a professional.
- Fairness requires that the actions and decisions of the professional are inclusive and not restricted to a favored few.
- In performing their work, professionals should exercise duty of care to avoid adverse outcomes due to oversight.
- Professionals who respect the rights of others do not abuse their advantages due to their position or access to privileged information.

(a) Integrity

(1) Honest and trustworthy
A professional has integrity when she acts honestly, is trustworthy, and is guided by strong morals of right and wrong.[3] Her behavior is consistent and she is not easily swayed by appeals, arguments, or threats antithetical to her ethical values.

A professional possesses knowledge and skills that often puts her in an advantageous position over her clients. To ensure that she works and renders service with integrity, the professional should "place the integrity of the profession and the interests of the clients above their own personal interests".[4] In this regard, the professional should disclose any conflicts of interests "that could reasonably be expected to impair their independence and objectivity or interfere with respective duties to their clients, prospective clients, and employer".[5] Even though transparency and trust elements of integrity may be delegated to technology for enforcement, the human responsibility for deciding whether it is "right or wrong" must not be diminished. CFtP holders must be mindful of any harmful consequences of using a specific technology, given the element of trust in cyberspace, so that trust is not misplaced.

(b) Fairness

(1) No discrimination
The principle of fairness incorporates "values of equality, tolerance, respect for others and justice".[6] This principle requires that the professional embraces inclusiveness and does not discriminate, putting aside her personal preferences and predispositions. Concerning clients, the professional must "deal fairly and objectively ... in professional activities".[7]

Fintech professionals should be mindful of the impact of information and technology on either creating or perpetuating inequities. The design

---

[3]ACM Code of Ethics and Professional Conduct section on General Ethical Principles, Clause 1.3.

[4]CFA Institute Code of Ethics and Professional Conduct: The Code of Ethics.

[5]CFA Institute Standards of Professional Conduct: Conflicts of Interest, A. Disclosure of Conflicts.

[6]ACM Code of Ethics and Professional Conduct section on General Ethical Principles, Clause 1.4.

[7]CFA Institute Standards of Professional Conduct: Duties to Clients, Clause B. Fair Dealing.

of systems should factor in inclusiveness and not allow them to be used for purposes of discrimination or rent-seeking.

(c) Duty of Care

(1) Avoiding harm

(i) *Negative consequences*
In the performance of their work, the professional should exercise the duty of care. It is expected that a professional is competent and the work rendered is of a high standard. By not exercising care in the course of fulfilling the work, the professional may end up causing harm.

(ii) *Indirect or unintentional consequences*
The failure to exercise care can have indirect and unintentional consequences. Negligence on the part of the professional can have a direct cost, for example, the loss of a client. The indirect cost is the tarnishing of the firm's reputation.

(Note: From a legal perspective, the tort of negligence is broader than the layman's understanding of negligence or carelessness. It can cover both acts and omissions. In other words, a person can be negligent at law for doing something he should not have done as well as for not doing something when he should have.

The tort of negligence also extends to statements (as opposed to acts or omissions) made negligently. Negligent misstatement often arises when a client claims that his professional adviser has provided sub-standard advice. Bankers, lawyers, doctors, accountants and valuers are among the professional advisers who must ply their services mindful of the risks of being sued for negligent misstatement.)

(2) Duty to report signs of failure or risks that may cause harm
Finally, the duty of care imposes on the professional to report signs of failure or risks that may cause harm.[8] A professional is well-trained and has the knowledge and skills to spot potential risks and failures. Her expertise would serve the firm well as firms typically have a small number of risk specialists.

---

[8]ACM Code of Ethics and Professional Conduct section on General Ethical Principles, Clause 1.2.

(d) Respect for the Rights of Others and Sharing

(1) Respect privacy

An important part of respecting the rights of others is when you respect their privacy. This is highly relevant today when "[t]echnology enables the collection, monitoring, and exchange of personal information ... often without the knowledge of people affected".[9] If privacy protection technology exists, the CFtP holder should explore its potential and regulatory implications.

(2) Respect intellectual property and the contributions of others

Going beyond the personal realm is the respect for the intellectual property and contributions of others. This means that professionals should "credit the creators of ideas, inventions, work, and artifacts, and respect copyrights, patents, trade secrets, license agreements, and other methods of protecting authors' works".[10] At the individual level, if open source leads to the betterment of society, it may be appropriate to share one's invention or creation for the general good via open source, or to consider the act of patenting for public use.

(Note: If a person infringes copyright in some jurisdictions, for example Singapore, that person can be liable for both civil and criminal penalties. For civil sanctions, the court may order a person to pay compensation to the copyright owner in the form of damages and/or to take down all infringing materials. The copyright violator can also be charged with the criminal offense of willful infringes resulting in fines and/or a jail sentence).

(3) Safeguard confidentiality

Having access to private information and put in a position of trust, the professional is required to safeguard the confidentiality of the information she is privy to. An exception to maintaining confidentiality is any requirement to disclose to the appropriate authorities.

(Note: Unless it is a confidentiality agreement with a government agency, a breach of confidentiality in itself will not amount to a criminal

---

[9]ACM Code of Ethics and Professional Conduct section on General Ethical Principles, Clause 1.6.

[10]ACM Code of Ethics and Professional Conduct section on General Ethical Principles, Clause 1.5.

offense. However, a breach of confidentiality means the person could be sued for damages.)

Beyond the professional's immediate sphere of influence, there is a need to be aware of the society at large. The concept of sustainability has taken root in the corporate agenda and respecting the rights of others extends to other stakeholders, whether direct or indirect. For example, the Singapore Exchange introduced sustainability reporting on a "comply or explain" basis in 2016 for companies listed on their exchange. For technology design, it is crucial to have designs to safeguard confidentiality and privacy while balancing the harm of such designs.

1.4 Professional Practice — CFtP Standard of Practice

1.4.1 *Introduction*

Professional practice is concerned with how the professional should go about doing her work. A foundation for good professional practice is competence. Without competence, the standard of work may not be at a level commensurate with the high standards expected of a professional. As the status of a profession is often constituted by the authorities, it is incumbent that the professional be conversant with the laws and regulations governing her area of work. Further, professionals often deal with sensitive information, some of which are of a personal nature. Protecting the information and maintaining confidentiality is another aspect of professional practice. Finally, an area which is not often brought up in discussing professional practice is leadership. As professionals are held in high regard, they are often called upon to exercise leadership at work and in the society at large, and hence the responsibility that leadership entails has to be highlighted.

Learning Objectives
- Discuss the CFtP Standards of Practice and their implications.

Main Takeaways

Main Points
- Competence requires knowledge and skills guided by ethical values to achieve high quality work.

- The professional should be mindful of not doing work outside their realm of expertise and yet not be overly conservative with nascent technology.
- The professional should ensure that those performing the work have the competence to achieve a high standard of work, and to continuously acquire knowledge of technology.
- Knowledge of technology, and applicable laws and regulations is essential to ensure their compliance.
- Through their work, professionals may be in possession of sensitive information that they are bound to keep confidential and ensure the information is kept secure, or to deploy privacy protection technology if appropriate.
- As professionals are responsible for those under their charge, they are to exercise leadership in three areas: the work itself, the welfare and dignity of subordinates, and the implication for the social good of the professional's work.
- Upholding the reputation of the CFtP designation is the responsibility of all charter holders.

(a) Competence

Competent professionals are those who possess the knowledge, skills and ethical values to "achieve high quality in both the processes, [technology], and the products of professional work".[11] They "[m]aintain and improve their professional competence and strive to maintain and improve the competence of their [fellow] professionals".[12]

(1) Knowledge

Knowledge is obtained through a course of study in school, online, or through a certification program like the CFtP. Also, the professional needs to update her knowledge through continuing education given the quick pace of change taking place in the world as a result of new technologies

---

[11]ACM Code of Ethics and Professional Conduct section on Professional Responsibilities, Clause 2.1.

[12]CFA Institute Code of Ethics and Standards of Professional Conduct: The Code of Ethics.

and innovations. The CFtP requires that charter holders continually upgrade their knowledge through its continuing education programs.

(2) Skills
The skills that the professional possesses come from practice in applying the knowledge acquired to solve problems in the professional's sphere of expertise. Skills can be enhanced through offline and online interaction with fellow professionals at conferences and meetings as well as through case studies.

(3) Ethical values
Ethical behavior is discussed extensively in the ethics section of this module. Ethical behavior cannot be overemphasized. Unless the professional is guided by ethical values in using her knowledge and skills in her practice, she cannot be considered a true professional. CFtP holders should pay particular attention to inclusion and sustainability, especially when dealing with nascent technology.

(4) Area of work
CFtP members are also admonished to perform work only in their areas of competence without being too conservative when dealing with innovation. They are to "[evaluate] the work's feasibility and advisability, and [make] a judgement about whether the work assignment is within the professional's areas of competence. If at any time before or during the work assignment the professional identifies a lack of necessary expertise, they must disclose this to the employer or client".[13]

(b) Standard of Work
High standards of work can be achieved through individuals and their team taking responsibility to ensure that they are competent.[14] However, competence is just a prerequisite of high quality work. The professional

---

[13] ACM Code of Ethics and Professional Conduct section on Professional Responsibilities, Clause 2.7.
[14] ACM Code of Ethics and Professional Conduct section on Professional Responsibilities, Clause 2.2.

must be guided by the ethical principles of integrity, fairness and duty of care towards her clients and employer. It is all too easy to produce a quality of work that is satisfactory given the constraints of time and considerations of profitability. However, doing one's best comes from not just a duty of responsibility but a sense of professional pride.

(c) Knowledge of Law and Regulations
In addition to domain knowledge, professionalism requires a knowledge of the law and regulations that govern the sphere of the professional's work. "The professional must understand and comply with all applicable laws, rules and regulations ... [including the CFtP Code of Ethics and Professional Practice] of any government, regulatory organization, licensing agency, or professional association governing their professional activities. In the event of conflict, [members] ... must comply with the more strict law, rule or regulation".[15]

(d) Confidentiality and Security
The professional should be aware of the importance of ensuring proper security over the intellectual property and confidentiality of his work.[16] Any breach can be costly as the professional and her employer may be sanctioned by the authorities or face lawsuits from affected parties. Further, the damage from such a breach could have ramifications on the business of the professional. The affected party's competitors may gain an edge from the confidential information released and the firm's reputation would be tarnished leading to some existing clients leaving due to lack of confidence and trust in the company. Such adverse publicity could also make it difficult to acquire new clients.

Data breaches could violate data protection laws which will be discussed in the section on Governance and Regulations. In the age of the digital and information economy, data is an extremely important resource and should be well protected. This means that "[r]obust security should be a primary consideration when designing and implementing systems ... [and] parties affected by data breaches are notified in a timely and clear

---

[15]CFA Institute Code of Ethics and Standards of Professional Conduct: Standards of Professional Conduct, Section I Professionalism, A. Knowledge of the Law, as well as ACM Code of Ethics and Professional Conduct section on Professional Responsibilities, Clause 2.3.
[16]ACM Code of Ethics and Professional Conduct section on General Ethical Principles, Clause 1.7.

manner providing appropriate guidance and remediations".[17] In dealing with clients there is a need to "keep information about current, former and prospective clients confidential unless the information concerns illegal activities, [or] disclosure is required by law, or the client, or prospective client permits".[18]

The professional should keep up with the knowledge on technology dealing with confidentiality and cybersecurity. Efforts should be targeted at protecting privacy and ensuring a secure technology environment.

(e) Leadership

Beyond the technical realm of work, the professional is also called upon to provide leadership in her organization and the community-at-large. The areas and circumstances where leadership should be exercised are articulated in some detail in the section on professional leadership principles in the ACM Code of Ethics and Professional Conduct. We highlight a few principles here.

(1) Management of personnel

(i) *Quality of working life and promotion of professional growth*

Work-life balance and professional development of the employee are growing concerns which employees expect their employers to address. "Leaders should enhance, not degrade, the quality of working life ... [and] consider the personal and professional development ... and dignity of all workers".[19]

(Note: Harassment in the workplace is recognized by many governments. For example, in Singapore a workplace harasser may be in contravention of a Protection from Harassment Act (POHA) provision. Victims of harassment can apply for a Protection Order (PO) or an Expedited Protection Order (EPO). The victim of harassment can also commence a civil suit against the harasser for monetary damages. It is possible to initiate both criminal and civil actions at the same time.)

---

[17]ACM Code of Ethics and Professional Conduct section on Professional Responsibilities, Clause 2.9.

[18]CFA Institute Standards of Professional Conduct: Duties to Clients, Clause E. Preservation of Confidentiality.

[19]*Ibid*, Clauses 3.3 and 3.5.

(ii) *Social responsibilities*

As a leader, the professional has to ensure that "the public good is the central concern during all professional work"[20] as well as, for the IT professional, to "recognize and take special care of systems that become integrated into the infrastructure of society".[21] Privacy protection, operation continuity, inclusion and sustainability are critical social responsibilities in a cyber world.

(f) Upholding the Reputation of the CFtP Designation and the Profession

The CFtP is a designation that members expend much effort to secure. Any untoward action of a member has the potential to tarnish the image and reputation of the CFtP designation as well as the reputation of the profession in general. It is therefore incumbent on every member to safeguard this reputation as well as report any member whom they have reason to believe is acting in a manner contrary to the Code of Ethics and Professional Practice which could harm the reputation of the CFtP designation as well as the Global Fintech Institute, the awarding body.

As there are many topics in this module and each topic, in itself, has a wide scope, we are only able to discuss the fundamentals. The references here provide the candidates with material that may be relevant to their areas of work and go into greater depth as well as cover the applications, and the laws and regulations in various jurisdictions.

References/Further Readings

Ethical Framework and Principles
Association for Computing Machinery (2018). ACM Code of Ethics and Professional Conduct. Retrieved from https://www.acm.org/code-of-ethics.
CFA Institute (2014). Code of Ethics and Standards of Professional Conduct. Retrieved from https://www.cfainstitute.org/-/media/documents/code/code-ethics-standards/code-of-ethics-standards-professional-conduct.ashx.

---

[20] *Ibid*, Clause 3.1.
[21] *Ibid*, Clause 3.7.

IESBA. (2019). International Code of Ethics for Professional Accountants. Retrieved from https://www.ethicsboard.org/international-code-ethics-professional-accountants.

Indeed (2021). 10 Characteristics of Professionalism. Retrieved from https://www.indeed.com/career-advice/career-development/the-ultimate-guide-to-professionalism.

Markula Center for Applied Ethics at Santa Clara University (2015). A Framework for Ethical Decision-making. Retrieved from https://www.scu.edu/ethics/ethics-resources/ethical-decision-making/a-framework-for-ethical-decision-making/.

National Society of Professional Engineers (NSPE). (2019). NSPE Code of Ethics for Engineers. Retrieved from https://www.nspe.org/resources/ethics/code-ethics.

Vivian, W. (2008). Illinois Institute of Technology Center for the Study of Ethics in the Professions. Retrieved from http://ethics.iit.edu/teaching/professional-ethics.

1.5 Sample Questions

Question 1

Who is least likely to be required to observe the CFtP Code of Ethics and Standards of Practice?

(a) CFtP exam candidate
(b) Associate member of GFI
(c) Subordinate of CFtP charter holder

Question 2

Which is the least likely desirable conduct for CFtP exam candidates?

(a) Acting with integrity when dealing with competitors
(b) Being transparent with clients
(c) Balancing the interests the employer with the need in the profession to act with integrity

Question 3

Tom, a CFtP charter holder, was in charge of multiple projects. For one of the projects, he needed to make a filing with the authorities to satisfy a regulatory requirement. There was no time to consult the expert in this area, and Tom having worked in this area before decided to do the filing himself. Unfortunately, Tom did not know that the regulation had been changed and the firm had to pay a penalty for making the wrong filing. Tom is guilty of violating which CFtP Standard of Practice:

(a) Competence and leadership
(b) Competence and knowledge of laws and regulations
(c) Leadership and knowledge of laws and regulations

Question 4
Many of the staff working under John, a CFtP charter holder, complained about having to work till late evening every day as well as having to work every weekend. Work-life balance is:

(a) The firm's responsibility
(b) The HR department's responsibility
(c) John's responsibility in his exercise of leadership

Question 5
Which principle is the requirement of no discrimination a part of?

(a) Integrity
(b) Fairness
(c) Duty of care

Question 6
Respecting privacy is a component of the following principle:

(a) Integrity
(b) Fairness
(c) Duty of care

Question 7
Which of the following is not part of the responsibilities the CFtP charter holder in exercising leadership?

(a) Ensuring work-life balance
(b) Ensuring no harassment in the work place
(c) Ensuring the employees stay healthy

Solutions

Question 1

Solution: Option **c** is correct.

The CFtP charter holder has to exercise leadership in the organization beyond her professional or job scope to foster ethical behavior. However, the subordinate, unlike the other two persons, has no direct obligation to observe the CFtP Code of Ethics and Standards of Practice.

Question 2

Solution: Option **c** is correct.

While the CFtP exam candidate has an obligation to work for the best interests of the employer, this fact should not compromise the need to act with integrity.

Question 3

Solution: Option **b** is correct.

Tom is acting beyond his level of competence as he is not an expert in the area. He is also guilty of not keeping up with the laws and regulations.

Question 4

Solution: Option **c** is correct.

In the CFtP Standards of Practice, it is stipulated under the standard on leadership that the CFtP charter holder should consider the work-life balance of his subordinates in his exercise of leadership.

Question 5

Solution: Option **b** is correct.

The CFtP charter holder is acting fairly when she does not discriminate against certain groups of people because of their attributes like gender, race, or age, etc.

Question 6

Solution: Option **c** is correct.

Exercising duty of care means that we do not infringe on the rights of others, for example that of privacy.

Question 7

Solution: Option **c** is correct.

While the leader can ensure that the workplace does not pose physical or health hazards, as well as encourage her subordinates to adopt a healthy lifestyle, ensuring the health of the employee is a personal responsibility.

Chapter 2

Governance and Regulation

2.1 Introduction

Regulation is an intervention by the state in a society to require or proscribe conduct. In a society where competing interests exist, the greater good of the society may be affected by the actions of some, whether inadvertently or not. By laying down the rules governing the transactions of corporations and individuals, the economy and society can function more efficiently to cater to the needs of its members.

As the interests of the participants in an economy are diverse, it is impossible to satisfy the needs of everyone. Recognizing this fact, it is evident that regulation is a compromise that serves to ensure that the greater good of society is a key consideration.

Professionals have a role in examining regulations in place or regulations in the making to ensure that they are relevant to society and would benefit society at large. Hence, a knowledge of the aims of regulation as well as the considerations regulators have to take into account in drafting the regulations is important. It is only when professionals understand the regulatory process that they can then set about to comment on and influence policies from a perspective that draws on their specialized knowledge, skills and ethical values.

What about governance? How different is governance from regulation? A simple answer is that governance is much broader than regulation. Given their nature, the sword of laws and regulations has to be sharper than that of governance. For laws and regulations it is a matter of whether they have been violated or not. On the other hand, governance is a matter of degree. We talk of good versus poor governance.

2.2 Governance and Regulatory Framework

The regulation of Fintech consists of two strands — regulation of financial activities and regulation of IT activities. To some extent the two strands operate separately and the legacy of existing regulations results in each strand seldom considering implications of or for the other strand. However, as Fintech becomes more embedded in the economy, regulations would have to adopt a more holistic approach. This has been seen, for example, in crypto currency and payment systems.

For the CFtP program, a holistic approach to regulation will not be attempted. The reason is that many Fintech activities are recent developments and few regulatory and legal issues have been tested in the courts or a strong consensus among stakeholders of how some of those issues ought to be settled has not evolved. Hence, no attempt will be made to unify both strands of regulation. Each would be discussed separately. Further, as local regulations take into account each jurisdiction's unique circumstances and approach, the examples that are cited are meant for illustrative purposes, showing how various jurisdictions have chosen to address some of the issues pertaining to that regulation. However, the underlying principles should be to uphold the highest ethics and moral standards, emphasizing societal interest, especially when there is no regulation.

Learning Objectives
- Understand the key elements of the framework for regulation and governance.

Main Takeaways

Main Points
- The three components of regulation are incentive, deterrence, and enforcement.
- The principle of incentive is to promote desired behavior.
- Enforcement of laws and regulations are less effective or not effective at all outside a country's jurisdiction. The internet is a good example.
- Many cross-border transactions are governed by uniform codes or international conventions.
- Where regulatory regimes have little effect because cross-border transactions are digital, and enforcement is difficult, self-regulation is the only alternative.

(a) General Framework

Regulation relies on the three components of incentive, deterrence, and enforcement. The principle of incentive aims to promote desired behavior while the principle of deterrence aims to deter undesired behavior. However, regulation is ineffective if it is not backed by enforcement through sanctions or penalties against undesired behavior. Enforcement is effective only within a particular jurisdiction where the authorities have legal sway over people and entities domiciled in that jurisdiction. In a globalized world where cross-border transactions are common, the issue of enforcement takes on another dimension as the arm of the law is not long enough to extend beyond the national borders. Introduce the world of the internet and enforcement becomes even more complicated.

Many cross-border transactions in assets, goods or services may be governed by some international convention that counts most countries in the world as signatories. An example is the United Nations Convention on Contracts for the International Sale of Goods which provides a framework for governing international commerce. Where the cross-border transaction is not governed by some uniform code or convention, the parties involved needs to decide on the issue of the applicable governing law and dispute settlement mechanisms.

Where cross-border transactions are of a digital nature, regulation is challenging because of the difficulty of enforcement. When regulatory regimes break down, the only regulation that is effective is self-regulation or governance by technology. This requires a focus on incentive. Some of the developments in the area of digital regulation embed incentive mechanisms in their design.

As the governing law often depends on the domicile of the entity, there is a trade-off between legal and tax considerations, as different domiciles have different legal systems as well as tax regimes.

In the earlier sections on the CftP Code of Ethics and Standards of Practice, we note that violation of the Code and Standards may bring forth sanctions from the professional body. The power of the professional body to sanction a member is quite limited. The most severe sanction is expulsion from the professional body. Unless the professional's ability to practice her specialty is contingent on the person being a member of a professional body, expulsion may not have much force to ensure compliance.

Regulations and laws, however, allow the enforcing authority to impose penalties much more severe than those meted out by a professional body.

That said, it does not mean the professional could view the observance of the code of ethics and standards of conduct lightly. Rather, if the professional embraces both the CFtP Code and the Standards of Practice, and observes them strictly with high moral and ethical standards, it is highly unlikely such a professional would run afoul of the law.

(b) What is Being Governed?

Unlike conventional governance where humans verify compliance, the new world of Fintech introduces a new mode of verification. Technology, especially the blockchain, can be used in the verification process. Not requiring the active hand of human verification, technology is able to streamline the verification process and make it more efficient. An added benefit of monitoring compliance through technology is that verification can be done on a real-time basis. This has tremendous benefits as malfeasance can be spotted early and corrective action taken before much damage can be done.

An illustration of how technology adds a new dimension to verification of compliance is shown in Figure 2.1.

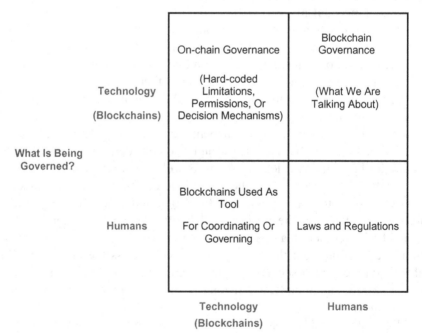

Figure 2.1:   Technology and compliance.

2.3 Governance and Regulatory Principles

Some of the governance and regulatory principles may overlap with the ethical principles on which we base the Code of Ethics and Standards of Practice. Examples of the overlap would be the principle of fairness and the principle of respect for the rights of others. Where the principles have been discussed in the Ethics section, we will only discuss their application from the regulatory viewpoint.

Learning Objectives
• Discuss the CFtP Standards of Practice and their implications.

Main Takeaways

Main Points
• Regulation and governance require that professionals are accountable for performing actions required by regulation as well as refraining from actions prohibited by regulation.
• In the context of IT, equity or fairness requires that the professional considers the potential impact of her work on the wider society, that is, to think beyond the confines of her organization or even the country she works in.
• Showing transparency in the software gains the trust of users.

(a) Accountability
The principle of accountability rests on the notion that an individual is responsible for the performance of certain actions as prescribed by the regulation as well as refraining from performing actions prohibited by the regulation. However, accountability goes beyond the individual's action. Where the professional has people under her charge, she is also accountable for their observance of the regulation.

(b) Equity/Fairness
Fairness was discussed as one of the ethical principles those holding the CFtP charter need to uphold. In the context of IT, systems and software like AI have "pervasive, far-reaching and global implications that are transforming societies, economic sectors and the world of work". Knowing the potential impact on the wider society, fairness implies that the professional should think beyond the confines of the organization or even country she works in.

The principle of equity means that the professional should consider the following:

- The individual
  Concerns of the individual encompass privacy issues as well as inclusiveness. Are the individual's rights part of the decision making process? Is her privacy protected? Are individuals discriminated against because of their status, disability or income?
- Society
  Are there segments of the society that are left out because of their particular circumstances, for example, the less educated, the less IT-literate or those who do not know the language in which the program is written? Do software and systems lead to development and progress of society? Are issues of sustainability factored in?

(c) Transparency
Software and systems are often perceived to be arcane black boxes. Developers hide behind a veil of secrecy to thwart the prying eyes of competitors and other parties. Consequently, users are at the mercy of bugs and hidden features.

The professional who embraces the principle of transparency will disclose as much as possible, subject to the constraint of proprietary intellectual property, to gain the trust of users. Inefficiencies due to asymmetry of information will be greatly reduced through transparency. Open software encapsulates this principle of transparency.

2.4 Areas of Governance and Regulation

2.4.1 *Technology*

The fast pace of technological innovations presents problems for governance and regulation which have to play catch-up. There are several reasons for this:

(a) It takes time for those in charge of governance and regulation to understand the new technology. The technical nature of some of these regulations implies a longer learning curve.

(b) There may not be governance codes and regulations that can be adapted from other areas. Having to draft codes and regulation from scratch requires much discussion and consultation which may require considerable time.

(c) Some implications of the new technology will only surface with more use cases.

The CFtP curriculum will cover four areas of technology, corresponding to the first four letters of the alphabet. They are AI, Blockchain, Cybersecurity, and Data Protection/Privacy.

Fintech regulations are discussed in much greater detail in Module 2.5 Compliance and Risk Management. This section focuses more on the ethics component and touches briefly on some regulations.

A popular regime of Fintech regulation has been the use of the "Regulatory Sandbox". As the name suggests, the sandbox is a place where participants can play and experiment. Sandboxes provide the ability to test services with real customers in a controlled environment without incurring regulatory consequences.

Under this regime, regulators can gain an understanding of the function of the Fintech systems and cooperate with the industry to identify and develop methods for compliance. This would help regulators develop a level of regulation that encourages and enables innovation while ensuring adequate protection for users — and would encourage development of technology solutions (such as electronic identification, authentication, and trust services that mitigate, for example, anti-money laundering and ultimate beneficial ownership concerns).

One challenge of regulatory sandboxes is ensuring they are attractive to start-ups. Sandboxes should encourage innovation and allow for start-ups to grow, rather than merely offering value for the regulator.

As it is labeled a sandbox, users of the products developed in the sandbox will know that regulators have basically been hands-off and they interact and use the products on a "buyer beware" basis.

In the area of technology risk management, the Monetary Authority of Singapore (MAS) has issued a set of guidelines.[1] The areas covered are:

- Technology risk governance and oversight
  - Role of the board of directors and senior management

---

[1] Monetary Authority of Singapore: Technology Risk Guidelines. Available at https://www.mas.gov.sg/-/media/MAS/Regulations-and-Financial-Stability/Regulatory-and-Supervisory-Framework/Risk-Management/TRM-Guidelines-18-January-2021.pdf.

- o Policies, standards and procedures
- o Management of information assets and third party services
- o Competency review
- o Security awareness and training
- Technology risk management framework
  - o Risk identification, assessment and treatment
  - o Risk monitoring, review and reporting
- IT project management and security-by-design
- Software application development and management
  - o Agile software development
  - o Application programming interface development
- IT services management
- IT resilience
  - o System availability and recoverability
  - o System backup and recovery
  - o Data center resilience
- Access control
- Cryptography
- Data and infrastructure security
- Cyber security operations and assessment
- Online Financial services
- IT audit

For our curriculum, we will cover four areas of technology, corresponding to the first four letters of the alphabet. They are:

- AI
- Blockchain
- Cybersecurity
- Data Protection/Privacy.

2.4.2 *Artificial Intelligence*

AI has become more pervasive in our lives. AI has been harnessed and used in various applications like facial recognition, self-driving cars, detection of anomalous transactions, and making recommendations for purchases, videos or services based on the user's engagement and actions on the website. Such widespread use of AI has prompted concerns about the proper use of AI to avoid adverse consequences whether intended or not. There are many highly complex issues regarding the governance of AI. The CFtP curriculum will discuss only the general issues.

Learning Objectives
- Understand the general principles of AI governance.

Main Takeaways

Main Points
- AI governance can be examined at three levels: The individual/organizational, the societal and the operational.
- At the individual/organizational level, there has to be accountability for the AI system put in place.
- AI should be seen as a fair and non-discriminatory system against particular groups of people, whether inadvertent or not.
- The transparency of the AI system inspires trust.
- The professional must consider the impact of AI on society. This means a high regard for people, respecting their rights and privacy.
- A good AI system is transparent and explainable. It is accurate and its workings verifiable. It is also robust, secure and safe.

The general principles to guide AI governance have two strands. First, "[o]rganizations using AI in decision-making should ensure the decision-making process is explainable, transparent and fair." [2] Doing so engenders trust in the decisions made by the AI system. The second strand focuses on the need to ensure that solutions are human-centric. In particular, "the protection of the interests of human beings, including their well-being and safety, should be the primary considerations in the design, development and deployment of AI". [3]

Initiatives for the governance and regulation of AI include the OECD's "Recommendation of the Council on Artificial Intelligence" [4] and

---

[2] Infocomm Media Development Authority and Personal Data Protection Commission, *Model Artificial Intelligence Governance Framework*, Second Edition, 2020.

[3] *Ibid.*

[4] OECD, *Recommendation of the Council on Artificial Intelligence, OECD/LEGAL/0449,* 2020.

Singapore's "Model Artificial Intelligence Governance Framework".[5] These documents lay down various governance principles which we amalgamate and organize into three areas:

Individual/Organizational
1. Accountability
2. Fairness
3. Transparency

Societal
1. Human centricity
2. Privacy
3. Inclusivity
4. Sustainability
5. Human rights alignment

Operational
1. Transparency
2. Explainability
3. Accuracy
4. Auditability
5. Robustness, security and safety

(a) Individual/Organizational Principles
The principles at the individual/organizational level are similar to those discussed in Section 2.2 on Governance and Regulatory Principles.

(b) Societal Principles
(1) Human-centricity
In the area of societal concerns, the first principle of human-centeredness puts human considerations and well-being above other considerations like the organization, or efficiency, or profit. This leads to a more specific principle related to human-centeredness of privacy which is discussed in greater detail below.

---

[5]Infocomm Media Development Authority and Personal Data Protection Commission, *Model Artificial Intelligence Governance Framework*, Second Edition, 2020.

(2) Privacy

In the information age, much data, some of which is of a personal nature, is collected. How the data collected is used, as well as whether the data is made available to third parties, raise concerns about the abuse of the data. As much of an individual's persona can be inferred from personal data, the consequences of improper handling of the data can be severe.

The governance and regulation of privacy is discussed in greater detail in the section on Data Protection/Privacy.

(3) Inclusivity

Moving to the wider area of society, the principle of inclusivity rules out discrimination whether inadvertent or not. Societal concerns does not just include accessibility but the notion of progress must be included, hence the principle of progressiveness which embeds value creation in processes. However, for society to progress over long periods, the sustainability of the various initiatives is important. Finally, alignment with human rights upholds the dignity of an individual as a human being and ensures that the AI systems do not infringe internationally recognized human rights.

(4) Sustainability

Sustainability means the use of resources to meet present needs without compromising the ability of future generations to meet their needs. Sustainability is discussed in greater detail in the topic on ESG (Environmental, Social and Governance) towards the end of this module.

AI has played a big part in the digital transformation of many sectors. Fintech professionals should incorporate sustainability in their solutions. While there may be greater short run profits from ignoring sustainability, the increasing awareness of, and the increasing adoption of sustainability as an important goal in its own right, suggest that any short run competitive advantage will soon dissipate.

(5) Human rights alignment

The ability of AI to analyze big data and the use of AI algorithms in many applications can give rise to potential abuses of human rights. AI may be used to discriminate against certain groups whether inadvertently or not. For example, there have been many instances of discrimination against dark-skinned people in predictive policing where such people were more likely to be identified as suspects than lighter skin people.

(c) Operational Principles

In the operational area, the principles revolve around transparency and integrity in AI systems. This principle of transparency is supplemented by the principle of explainability. While you can see what is going on, you may not be able to understand why. That is why the principle of explainability is crucial.

The next two principles of accuracy and auditability help to provide confidence in the process and in the data. Data accuracy helps to reduce uncertainty. In turn, an audit of the process and the data results in more reliability. In addition, incorporating the principle of auditability facilitates review by third parties and instills confidence in both the process and the data.

The last operational principle pertains to robustness, security and safety. A robust system is one that has built-in mechanisms to enable the system to function despite shocks. Robustness could take various forms like redundancy or alternative mechanisms to provide checks and balances to withstand the effects of attacks or human error. Outside disturbances or attacks could be thwarted by various physical and cyber security measures. The end result is to enhance users' safety.

2.4.3 *Blockchain*

The blockchain or distributed ledger technology does away with a centralized "clearing system". By contrast, transfers and payments in the banking system are mediated through the central bank. The lack of authority or a "leader" in blockchain has implications regarding its governance and its enforcement.

In finance, the decentralized nature of blockchain helps in the financial inclusion of the underserved who have difficulty accessing the traditional financial system. Besides finance, blockchain can be used for establishing ownership of assets through better and more transparent record keeping.

While the benefits from harnessing the power of blockchain are many, there are concerns especially in the area of cryptocurrency where money laundering is an issue. In short, there is a need for rules to govern the blockchain system.

Learning Objectives
- Understand the governance of blockchain technology.

Main Takeaways

Main Points
- The architect of the system must consider how a user is identified, who gets access to the system, and how the identity of the user is protected.
- Proper verification and authentication of the user or of information posted promotes trust in the system.
- Regarding access, digital literacy and the means of accessing must be considered so as to include "disadvantaged" users.
- There are advantages and disadvantages to the distributed structure of the blockchain.
- The distributed storage of data makes data more secure.
- The private–public key system of access gives rise to the possibility of an individual losing their private key, resulting in their inability to access the system.
- The blockchain system, like any other system, could be vulnerable to hacking, resulting in theft.

Transactions within the blockchain system are governed by a set of rules. "Governance includes questions such as who sets up the rules, who maintains the system, how the rules are executed, and how a blockchain system would be closed out."[6] In addition, the "governance structure should also be responsible for ensuring adherence to the guiding principles and design philosophy"[7] of the system.

A governance framework for blockchain considers the following elements:

(a) Identity
This revolves around the nature of an identity. What sort of information or amalgamation of information would serve to give a user a particular

---

[6]Lapointe, C. and Fishbane, L. (2019). The blockchain ethical design framework. *Innovations: Technology Governance, Globalization*, 12(3–4), 50–71, Winter-Sp. This section on the governance of Blockchain draws heavily from this article.
[7]*Ibid.*

identity? How is blockchain used in the granting, usage, access and protection of identity? Essentially, the issue is how to be certain that the claim of a user to a particular identity is true.

(b) Verification and Authentication

It is vital that the information that goes into the open blockchain system is authentic. In particular for transactions relating to digital or non-digital assets, the ownership of the asset has to be verified. Verifying the identity of the owner needs care if people are involved to ensure that their rights and privacy are not compromised.

Designers of blockchain systems could ensure compliance with the legal and regulatory framework by building it into the system. For example, participants could be locked out of the system unless and until they had been through an appropriate anti-money laundering compliance check.

(c) Access

In addition to who gets access the professional should consider whether digital literacy and the means to access the system may prevent certain users from interacting effectively with the system.

(d) Data Ownership

Beyond the ownership of data is the control over the data and its storage. Another issue is who corrects wrong information and how it is done.

(e) Security

A distributed structure is less vulnerable than a centralized system when it comes to data security. The reason is that no data is stored at a central location but data is distributed throughout the system. One issue of security with a distributed system is the potential loss of the private digital key. As a distributed system relies on a private–public key system with no central control, the loss of the private key for the individual implies that she would no longer be able to access the system.

(f) A Note on Accountability Related to the Blockchain

Accountability is a huge issue. In relation to decentralized systems, a key question for regulators is who should be held accountable for breaches of law and regulation. This is similar to the problem of determining accountability on the Internet before the emergence of blockchain. Accountability of the various parties carrying out relevant activities on the Internet has been a vexing problem since its inception. Prior to the Internet, information and other content, such as music and video, could only be published through existing publishers with an established distribution network. Where there were legal issues about content, for instance issues with copyright infringement and defamation, the publisher was clearly accountable.

In the case of C-131/12 *Google Spain v AEPD*, the Court of Justice of the European Union (CJEU) ruled that a search engine could be held accountable for the protection of personal data in respect of third party websites accessible through its service. It was emphasized in this case that the search engine's activities could be clearly distinguished from those of the original publisher of the data. The harm to the data subject was not a result of the publication, but rather from the widespread availability of this information through a search engine.

In a public blockchain system, by contrast, there is no one easily held accountable in the same way as a search engine.

In a private blockchain system, where there is clear ownership and responsibility, regulators might expect those running the system to be accountable for data added to the system by all the network users. The system owner could be seen as enabling the distribution of data through the blockchain in a comparable way to a search engine. It would then be the system owner's responsibility to protect this data, despite not publishing the personal data itself. The owner would likely have to put in place a set of operating conditions on the private blockchain that comply with regulations which all users would in turn agree to comply with.

2.4.4 *Cybersecurity*

Cybersecurity is about protecting the IT systems from attacks and other risks. The governance of cybersecurity requires that there is a framework of accountability as well as oversight so that cybersecurity risks can be mitigated. Governance is needed to ensure compliance with the framework.

Managing cybersecurity risks requires a good understanding of the organization's business and the technology that supports it. In securing the organization from cybersecurity threats, the professional needs to be mindful of the individual and respect their rights as well as protect their privacy. The importance of cybersecurity cannot be overemphasized as any breach or failure in cybersecurity defense will erode public trust and confidence in the organization.

Learning Objectives
- Understand how the risks in the IT system can be mitigated and the measures put in place are complied with.

Main Takeaways

Main Points
- The core of the cybersecurity framework consists of five functions: Identify, protect, detect, respond, and recover.

The cybersecurity framework discussed here is based on the US National Institute of Standards and Technology (NIST) Cyber Security Framework[8] which consists of three frameworks: The Framework Core, the Framework Implementation Tiers, and the Framework Profiles. We focus only on the first framework.

Framework Core: "This is a set of cybersecurity activities, desired outcomes, and applicable references that are common across critical infrastructure sectors."[9] There are five functions comprising the core:

- Identify — This requires an understanding of the cybersecurity risks associated with the systems, assets, data, and people in the organization.
- Protect — This involves having safeguards so critical services can be delivered without interruption or being compromised.
- Detect — This calls for the development of certain activities to identify the occurrence of a cybersecurity event.
- Respond — This is a set of appropriate actions to take upon the detection of a cybersecurity breach.
- Recover — This requires building resilience into the system so the effects of an attack can be ameliorated, as well as a set of actions to restore capabilities after an attack.

(Note: In Singapore, the Cybersecurity Act is a dedicated cybersecurity law that creates a framework for the protection of designated critical

---

[8]Cybersecurity Framework: available at https://www.nist.gov/cyberframework.
[9]*Ibid.*

information infrastructure (CII) against cybersecurity threats; provides for the appointment of the Commissioner of Cybersecurity (the Commissioner) and other officers for the administration of the Cybersecurity Act; authorizes the taking of measures to prevent, manage and respond to cybersecurity threats and incidents in Singapore; and establishes a licensing framework for providers of licensable cybersecurity services in Singapore, specifically, managed security operations centre monitoring services and penetration testing services.

Personal liability may, in certain circumstances, be imposed on certain individuals for offenses committed by their organizations under the Cybersecurity Act. Such offenses may include, among others, the failure of a CII owner to notify the Commissioner of certain cybersecurity incidents within the prescribed period of becoming aware of such occurrence under section 14, and the failure of a CII owner to conduct regular cybersecurity audits and risk assessments under section 15.

Section 36 of the Cybersecurity Act imposes personal liability on officers, members (where the affairs of a corporation are managed by its members) and individuals involved in the management of the corporation who are in a position to influence its conduct for offenses committed by the corporation under the Cybersecurity Act, where such person: "consented or connived, or conspired with others to effect the commission of the offense; is in any other way knowingly concerned or party to the commission of the offense; or knew or ought reasonably to have known that the offence by the corporation would be or is being committed, and failed to take all reasonable steps to prevent or stop the commission of that offense."[10]

In relation to offenses committed by an unincorporated association or a partnership under the Cybersecurity Act, Section 37 of the Cybersecurity Act imposes personal liability on officers of unincorporated associations and members of their governing bodies, partners in a partnership, and individuals involved in the management of the unincorporated association or partnership and who are in a position to influence its conduct in circumstances similar to those set out under Section 36 of the Cybersecurity Act.

The MAS has issued different cyber hygiene notices. The one applicable to licensed financial advisers which sets out cyber security requirements on securing administrative accounts, applying security

---

[10]Cybersecurity Act 2018 (Singapore). Available at https://sso.agc.gov.sg/Acts-Supp/9-2018/#pr36-.

patching, establishing baseline security standards, deploying network security devices, implementing anti-malware measures and strengthening user authentication.)[11]

2.4.5 *Data Protection/Privacy*

In a digital world, data is a valuable resource that should be protected. The ease by which the resource can be transferred once there is a breach in the system highlights the importance of protecting data.

The protection of privacy stems from the value of respect for the individual as well as the fact that certain information that falls into the wrong hands can be abused and used to harm the individual. The legal and medical professions have regulations that confer protection to information obtained through a lawyer-client or doctor-patient relationship. In a world driven by social media, private information needs to be safeguarded and consent is needed before disclosure.

Many countries have enacted laws that protect an individual's privacy. The professional who is involved in the collection, analysis, and storage of information needs to be aware of the responsibilities entrusted to them with regards to privacy. However, be mindful of laws which allow or obligate professionals to override their obligation to protect privacy where there are criminal or national security concerns.

Learning Objectives
- Understand how data and privacy are protected.

Main Takeaways

Main Points
- The key data protection requirements deal with the consent for data collection, the use, the protection, and the transfer of data.

Many countries have enacted legislation to protect data. iSight[12] has a listing of 30 countries with links to their data protection legislations.

---

[11] Available at https://www.mas.gov.sg/-/media/MAS/Notices/PDF/MAS-Notice-FAA-N21.pdf.

[12] iSight, *"A Practical Guide to Data Privacy Laws by Country"* https://i-sight.com/resources/a-practical-guide-to-data-privacy-laws-by-country/.

Singapore's Personal Data Protection Act (PDPA) (2012) referenced supranational organizations and jurisdictions with comprehensive data protection guidelines or laws, such as the OECD, APEC, the EU, UK, Canada, Hong Kong, Australia and New Zealand.

The EU has enacted the General Data Protection Regulation (GDPR). This is discussed in greater detail in Module 2.5 in the section on Global Fintech Regulation.

Elements of data protection include the definition of data as well as the obligations for the data collector. Some of these obligations include:

(a) The need to seek consent to collect the data.
(b) The limitation regarding the use of the data.
(c) The requirement to notify the individual regarding the data collected and its intended use.
(d) The obligation to allow an individual access to her personal data and to make corrections to the data.
(e) The obligation to ensure accuracy of the data in the collection and the dissemination.
(f) The obligation to protect the data.
(g) The requirement not to retain data when the original purpose for doing so is no longer valid.
(h) The restriction on the transfer of data.
(i) The obligation to be held accountable for the data.
(j) The obligation to report a data breach.

Regarding the last point, it is mandatory for an organization to report a data breach, once it has credible grounds to believe that a breach has occurred. When a breach occurs, the organization must take reasonable and expeditious steps to assess whether a data breach meets the criteria for notification.

Organizations which discover a data breach must notify the authorities if the breach (a) is likely to result in significant harm to the individuals whose personal data is affected by the breach; or (b) is of a significant scale (not fewer than 500 individuals).

Organizations must also notify the affected individuals once they have assessed that the breach is one that is likely to result in significant harm to said affected individuals.

(Note: Data security should be taken seriously. A breach of data privacy laws can have severe consequences. Many countries have data protection laws. An example is Singapore's PDPA[13] which includes a "do not call" prohibition that disallows unwanted solicitation to sell products or services through the phone.)

2.4.6 *Finance*

The finance industry is highly regulated given the potential systemic risks it poses and its importance in the national economy. Many of the Fintech innovations have disrupted the finance industry whether intended or not. As Fintech professionals work at the intersection of finance and technology, they need to be aware of some of the financial regulations.

Two key regulations are the Dodd-Frank Act and the MiFID II directive. The first stems from the Great Financial Crisis (GFC) of 2008. It was enacted in the US to regulate lenders and banks so as to protect consumers as well as ensure the soundness of banks and financial institutions. Banks were also required to increase their regulatory capital so that the probability of bank failure is reduced. The capital that banks need to put up has to conform to the Basel III framework which is risk-based, where the amount of capital required depends on the quantity as well as the risk of the assets.

MiFIID II, like the Dodd-Frank Act, was enacted in the aftermath of the GFC to restore confidence in the financial industry. It is an EU framework that covers the trading systems, the assets traded and the profession as well. MiFIID II is discussed in greater detail in Module 2.5 on regulation.

The CFtP curriculum will focus on four aspects of governance in this section.

- Anti-Money Laundering/Combating the Financing of Terrorism (AML/CFT):
  This is highly relevant for Fintech as there are many applications in payments and online investment.
- Corporate Governance.
- Environmental, Social, and Corporate Governance (ESG).
  This encompasses notions of sustainability and fairness.
- Sustainability and Green Finance.

---

[13]A description of the PDPA is available from https://www.pdpc.gov.sg/Overview-of-PDPA/The-Legislation/Personal-Data-Protection-Act.

2.4.7 Anti-Money Laundering/Combating the Financing of Terrorism (AML/CFT)

Money laundering is a crime of trying to conceal money obtained through illegal means, for example, corruption, tax evasion and drug trafficking. Money laundering, as the name suggests, takes "dirty" money and "cleans" it such that the end product is legitimate, and no one would ask questions when the cleaned-up money is spent.

From the economic perspective, money laundering deprives society of resources which could be deployed to benefit all rather than a small group of criminals. Without money laundering the criminals would find it difficult to spend their ill-gotten gains as they would have difficulty justifying the sources of their wealth.

Combating the Financing of Terrorism is an important way to curtail terrorist activities. Large scale terrorist attacks require large amounts of funds. Preventing the transfer of funds to terrorist-related groups helps to curtail terrorist activities.

Learning Objectives
- Understand AML/CFT.

Main Takeaways

Main Points
- Some Fintech innovations like cryptocurrency and payment systems can lend themselves to facilitating money laundering.
- The KYC (Know Your Customer) process is used to screen potential clients before accepting their business.

Fintech professionals involved in payments, taking of deposits, or investments need to be aware of the potential of their system being a conduit for money laundering or terrorism financing. Money laundering is about inserting "dirty money" into the financial system in a process known as placement. The next step is to cover up the money trail in a process known as layering where the funds are moved around such that there is almost no link to the original source. Finally, in the last step called the integration process, the funds are withdrawn to be used for legitimate purposes.

Online payments or online banking make it much easier to move funds in the financial system and launder them compared to using regular banking facilities. Cryptocurrency could also be used because of its perceived anonymous features. Many financial institutions institute the KYC or "Know Your Customer" process before agreeing to on-board or open an account for a customer. This is to prevent the institution from being an unwitting conduit of dirty money.

Hence, potential customers are probed and assessed on the sources of their funds. In addition, particular attention is paid to politically exposed persons (PEPs) who could be either government officials or people related to them. The reason why PEPs are carefully investigated is that in some countries, bribes are paid to government officials for the grant of licenses, to secure contracts, and to obtain permits to operate business activities.

Foreign governments, especially the United States, pay close attention to combating terrorism financing as terrorists operate in the shadows and their attacks can be devastating. Except for the 911 attacks, most terrorist attacks do not cause large numbers of casualties, but the effects can paralyze normal life by creating fear and necessitating costly security checks which disrupt normal movement and economic life.

Generally, the AML/CFT requirements concern:

- risk identification, assessment and mitigation;
- customer due diligence (including KYC for beneficial owners);
- reliance on third parties;
- correspondent accounts;
- record-keeping;
- internal policies, procedures and controls;
- compliance, account review, audit and training.

(Note: Financial institutions regulated by the MAS must observe the MAS AML/CFT requirements, regardless of whether transactions are conducted in fiat or cryptocurrencies. Such financial institutions must put in place robust controls to detect and deter the flow of illicit funds through Singapore's financial system.

Regarding AML/CFT, all persons must also abide by the following:

- Obligations to report suspicious transactions to the Suspicious Transactions Reporting Office, part of the Commercial Affairs Department of the Singapore Police Force under Section 39 of the Corruption, Drug Trafficking and Other Serious Crimes (Confiscation of Benefits) Act (Cap 65A) (CDSA).

- Prohibitions on dealing with or providing financial services to designated individuals and entities under the Terrorism (Suppression of Financing) Act (Cap 325) (TSOFA) and various regulations giving effect to United Nations Security Council Resolutions).

2.4.8 *Corporate Governance*

The development of the modern corporation has enabled firms to tap the vast pool of funds from the public. The rise of public listed companies has allowed modern business to expand and thrive as companies are no longer restricted to borrowing, whether from the banks or others, to grow.

Unlike some corporations which are majority owned by a few individuals, many modern large corporations have diverse shareholder bases with few, if any, shareholder having a substantial proportion of the shares, and the managers of the firm owning relatively few shares. While the firm is owned by the shareholders collectively, shareholders have little say in the affairs of the corporation. Corporate governance addresses this issue. Besides shareholders, there are other stakeholders, for example, employees, suppliers, customers and the society at large. Corporate governance is about balancing the interests of these stakeholders.

In summary, corporate governance goes beyond the traditional goal of a company to maximize the returns for its shareholders. Corporate governance adds another consideration for the company in its pursuit of profits. Besides profits, the company has to consider social goals. We can think of corporate governance as trying to balance economic and social goals.

Learning Objectives
- Understand key concepts of corporate governance.

Main Takeaways

Main Points
- Corporate governance is about the processes to govern the management and control of the company.
- Corporate governance aims to balance the interests of different stakeholders in the company.

Corporate governance consists of rules and processes put in place in the corporation to govern the management and control of the company. As there are many stakeholders and interests in the corporation, corporate governance attempts to balance the interests of the different parties.

To a large extent, corporate governance is about the corporation's board of directors in terms of its composition and roles, and the policies relating to disclosure, independence of non-key office holders, and risk management.

(a) Corporate Governance Practices

Some principles of good corporate governance relate to:
- Board composition
  - Chairperson is an independent director
  - Majority of board consists of independent directors
  - Diversity in the composition of board
- Board roles
  - Define roles of the board versus the management
  - Ensure independence of auditors
  - Ensure processes for management of risk

There are other aspects of corporate governance. We focus on a few.

(b) Conflicts of Interest

It is unrealistic to assume that the interests of all stakeholders in the corporation are aligned. The conflict of interest in the principal-agent relationship was discussed in the ethics section. Mechanisms like profit sharing and stock options have been used to align the interest of the agent to the principal's.

However, there could be other conflicts of interest, for example, at the board level where directors may sit on other boards or even be officers in some. Given the wide scope of activities in many corporations, it is possible that a director may find the intersecting of interests in some of the boards on which she sits. It is in such a circumstance that the corporate governance processes the corporation has instituted would be activated. These processes include measures to limit and disclose conflicts of interest, as well as the means to resolve those conflicts. For example, directors who face a conflict of interests should declare their conflict and recuse themselves from the decision making process.

When there is technology involved, the design thinking should be to ensure the situations of conflict of interest are minimized or that the incentive system should work towards an alignment of interests. For example, using a token as an incentive mechanism may assist in the alignment of interest.

(c) Related-Party Transactions

These are transactions where an officer or director of the corporation is making a decision when she has an interest in the other party to the transaction. Related-party transactions can occur due to weak corporate governance. The board should ensure there is no involvement in the decision making process of directors who are involved in related-party transactions.

(d) Corruption

Many countries have anti-corruption or bribery laws. While bribery appears to be a "normal" way of doing business in some foreign countries, such acts can result in prosecutions in the home country. In the US, the Foreign Corrupt Practices Act (FCPA) has been used against public listed companies whose employees and/or their agents engage in bribery in foreign countries. The law prohibits US citizens and entities from bribing foreign government officials to further their business interests.

(Note: The Code of Corporate Governance (2018), which applies to listed companies in Singapore on a comply-or-explain basis, establishes the principle that the board of directors is responsible for the governance of risk and should ensure that management maintains a sound system of risk management and internal controls to safeguard the interests of the company and its shareholders.

An example of domestic bribery law is the Prevention of Corruption Act (PCA) in Singapore. The Act specifically states that it is illegal to bribe a domestic public official. Both individuals and companies can be held liable for bribery offenses. The various provisions in the PCA and Penal Code set out certain offenses that may be committed by a 'person' if such a person were to engage in certain corrupt behavior. The term 'person' has been defined in the Singapore Interpretation Act to include 'any company or association of body of persons, corporate or unincorporated.)

2.4.9 *Environmental, Social and Governance (ESG)*

Sustainability has been placed at the top of the agenda for corporations. The term "sustainability" has been used in many contexts and has even become a buzzword. For the CFtP curriculum the term embraces the focus on future generations and is aligned to the UN initiative to achieve 17 Sustainable Development Goals (SDG) by 2030.

The concept of ESG goes by the name of social technology in the tech sector. Social technology consists of the different ways technology can be used to achieve ESG goals.

In the investment industry, ESG has been embraced by many funds which incorporate an ESG orientation. ESG is associated with impact investing where investors go beyond getting a good return on their investments to ensure that the investments make an impact by either improving the environment or promoting various social goals like equality, diversity, or creating access to services for the underserved in society. ESG funds have been shown to outperform non-ESG funds in some studies.

While aspects of ESG have been discussed in other sections of this module, this section discusses ESG in greater detail as well as looks into the practical implications of the ESG imperative.

Learning Objectives
• Understand the importance of ESG.

Main Takeaways

Main Points
• ESG encompasses sustainability as well as the governance of corporations to align them with the goals of sustainability.

(a) Environmental
This aspect of ESG is most closely related to climate change and the conservation of resources, which was known as the green movement in the early days of awareness of these issues. This movement propelled efforts which culminated in the singing of the well-known international treaty 'The Paris Agreement' by the United Nations Framework Convention on Climate Change (UNFCC) in December 2015. Adopted by 196 states, the goal of the agreement is to keep the increase in global average temperature to below 2°C (35.6°F). A climate change initiative that predated the Paris Agreement is the Kyoto Protocol that extended the UNFCC. It was signed in 1997 in Kyoto, Japan and came into effect in 2005. This Protocol had the goal of reducing greenhouse gases (GHGs) to reduce global warming.

The implications of environmental concerns are:

• How can the company's business enhance the environment?

- Can waste be reduced and recycling be a consideration in the manufacture of products or delivery of services?
- Can the company help lead the adoption of good environmental practices in society?

(b) Social

For the social aspect of ESG, the emphasis is on the company's relationship with its workforce and the society at large. The company should ensure that its employment policies are not discriminatory in terms of gender, race, and other social factors. While there are employment laws that mandate minimum standards, can the company exceed those standards?

In its business practices the company should be aware of its actions impacting the well-being of society. For example, in the aftermath of fatal shootings in some US cities, Walmart chose not to sell firearms at its stores.

(c) Governance

Governance is about the conduct of corporate affairs. In particular, the company should not place shareholders' interests above all else. Instead, it should consider the interests of other stakeholders as well. As firms operate within an environment comprising of stakeholders, regulators, social media and many others, it has to consider the wider ramifications of its actions. A policy of considering the needs and interests of other parties in this environment pays dividends over the long run as public trust is an asset that takes time to build but can be diminished through some selfish act.

(Note: The Singapore Exchange introduced sustainability reporting on a "comply or explain" basis in June 2016. Sustainability reporting complements the financial reporting that listed issuers are already doing. Statements of financial position and comprehensive income provide a snapshot regarding the firm's condition at a particular date and an account of the business over the past year, respectively, while sustainability reports of environmental, social and governance factors ("ESG factors") show the risks and opportunities within sight. Taken together, the combined financial and sustainability reports enable a better assessment of the firm's financial prospects and quality of management.)

2.4.10 *Sustainability and Green Finance*

Learning Objectives

- Describe environmental, social, and governance factors in investment analysis.
- Distinguish between the different approaches to ESG investing, including the extent to which they focus on economic value versus integrated value.
- Explain differences in ESG ratings from different third-party providers.
- Discuss the key components of a sustainability report.
- Discuss the conditions under which ESG investing can generate outperformance.
- Distinguish between the different ESG-related debt securities.
- State the Green Loan principles.
- Discuss the key considerations for a socially responsible investor.

Main Takeaways

Main Points

- Environmental factors reflect a firm's performance as a steward of the natural environment. Social factors reflect a firm's relationship with its stakeholder. Governance factors reflect the oversight of ESG issues and how stakeholder interests are balanced.
- The different ESG investing approaches, starting from one with a sole focus on economic value and progressively increasing in focus on stakeholder value, are ESG integration, negative screening, engagement, and impact investing.
- The key components of a sustainability report are material ESG factors; policies, practices, and performance; targets; reporting framework; and board statement.
- ESG ratings by different third-party providers, even for the same firm, can differ because of scope, measurement, and weight divergence in their methodologies.
- ESG investing can generate outperformance if markets are inefficient and underestimate either the long-term impact of corporate ESG efforts or the probability and impact of negative ESG events.
- The different ESG-related debt securities are green bonds, green loans, sustainability-linked loans, and social impact bonds (SIBs).
- The green loan principles relate to the use of proceeds, the process for project evaluation and selection, the management of proceeds, and reporting.

- The key considerations for a socially responsible investor are the estimation of costs associated with ESG portfolios, the verification that candidate products truly reflect the investor's values, and the assessment of whether the cost of trade-off to satisfy the investor's ESG preferences is acceptable.

Main Terms

- **Sustainability:** The ability to meet the needs of the current generation while preserving the planet and societal foundations to meet the needs of future generations.
- **Green finance:** The channeling of funds to companies and projects to effect positive environmental outcomes.
- **ESG investing:** The practice of taking into account environmental, social, and governance factors in the investment decision-making process.
- **Sustainability report:** Report that describes a company's practices with regard to specific sustainability components.
- **Green bond:** A fixed-income instrument to raise money that is specifically earmarked for climate and environmental projects.
- **Social impact bond:** A multi-stakeholder pay-for-success contract, in which investors provide funding for a provider of social services to disadvantaged groups, and are paid by the government if the provider achieves pre-agreed, measurable target outcomes.
- **Sustainability-linked loan:** A bank loan with interest rates that are positively linked to the ESG performance of the borrowing company and with proceeds that are not restricted to green projects.

(a) Sustainability

Sustainability refers to meeting the needs of the current generation while preserving the planet and societal foundations to meet the needs of future generations.

Human activities are disrupting the fine balance of the Earth's ecosystems and threatening our ability to continue living on the planet, a situation that is becoming dire with each passing day. The most pressing environmental issue is that of climate change, which is caused by greenhouse gas (GHG) emissions, primarily CO_2, from livestock and the burning of fossil fuels to produce electricity and energy for commercial and residential purposes, industrial production, and transportation.

In the pursuit of economic growth, we have neglected to respect environmental boundaries and societal needs. Sustainable development aims to respect these boundaries and needs.

(b) Sustainability Challenge

Sustainable development is often considered a wicked problem, one that is difficult to solve because (i) the problem is multifaceted and difficult to define because of its complexity; (ii) there is a large number of stakeholders with different priorities involved, yet cooperation is required to solve the problem; (iii) the interconnectedness of conflicting issues imply that potential solutions to some issues can cause new problems for other issues.

For example, besides the requirement that countries cooperate with one another, entities within each country — the government, financial institutions, companies, and individuals — have to establish efficient modes of partnership to achieve the task of solving climate change.

Since business activities are primarily responsible for producing negative environmental and social externalities (e.g., air pollution and child labor), it may seem reasonable to expect companies to solve the problem.

However, when environmental costs generated by companies are borne by society, a relentless pursuit of shareholder value maximization often leads to unsustainable business practices. For example, the widespread underassessment of climate risk may lead to two undesirable economy-wide harms: 1) systemic risk to the financial system and 2) the physical damages stemming from climate change itself, as mispriced equity leads to mis-allocation of investment resources. If investors fail to demand risk assessment from companies, managers may be left unpunished by the market when they build homes and hotels in hurricane prone regions too close to the shore, or build bridges to withstand a "100-year-flood" based on a grossly unrepresentative historical record. This mis-investment imposes costs not just on the company and the investor, but on the communities harmed by collapsing bridges and hotel evacuees.

Focusing only on economic value produces poor societal and environmental outcomes. In light of this understanding, the impact of companies on society and on the earth's systems should be factored into business decision-making.

Expecting senior corporate executives to transition from maximizing shareholder value to maximizing integrated value, which combines economic, social, and environmental values, on their own accord may be a tall order. Unlike shareholders who have control over the company and its management, other stakeholders do not have sufficient clout to exert pressure on the company. Maximizing integrated value will remain a lofty goal as long as negative social and environmental impacts are not reflected in share price and managers are compensated based on share performance.

One possible solution, then, is to internalize the negative externalities, essentially making the shareholders of a company bear some of the societal and environmental costs that the company generates, so that the market can price these costs.

(c) Role of Government

Governments will clearly have to provide the initial impetus for sustainable development. One mechanism to internalize negative environmental externalities created by companies is through a carbon tax: Levying a dollar tax per ton of carbon dioxide equivalent (tCO2e) emitted by a company would incentivize the company to reduce carbon emissions.

Governments can also play a role in social sustainability issues. For instance, they can improve worker health by capping the number of working hours or introduce safety regulations. They can also introduce living wages in low-income countries or tax addictive products such as alcohol and tobacco.

(d) Green Finance

As mentioned above, sustainable development and climate change are issues with different dimensions of problems. Finance is, in no small part, responsible for the current unsustainable state of affairs, but it can also play a large part in solving the problem.

An important role for finance is to allocate funding to its most productive use and to stimulate value creation. While this has not changed, the terms "productive use" and "value creation" need refinement. Specifically, green finance can be defined as the channeling of funds to companies and projects to effect positive environmental outcomes, while sustainable finance includes social outcomes. Of course, the value created has to be broadened beyond economic value to encompass environmental and social value as well.

By incorporating sustainability considerations into their decision-making, financial institutions can catalyze the transition to a sustainable economy. Some governments have also stepped in to encourage corporations to incorporate sustainable finance. For example, the Monetary Authority of Singapore (MAS) has a sustainable bond grant scheme that encourages the issuance of green, social, sustainability and sustainability-linked bonds in Singapore and is open to first-time and repeat issuers. Sustainable finance can, thus, be a powerful force for positive change.

(e) Role of Asset Managers

ESG investing goes by many alternative names, including sustainable investing, responsible investing, and ethical investing, as there is a lack of terminology standardization within the investment community. Another term, socially responsible investing, has traditionally meant the exclusion of investments that are incompatible with an investor's values. As an example, investors with love for peace and diplomacy will not invest in companies which are part of the arms industry in one way or another.

For our purposes, we define ESG investing as the practice of taking into account environmental (E), social (S), and governance (G) factors in the investment decision-making process. Specifically, the environmental factor reflects a firm's performance as a steward of the natural environment, mainly along the lines of climate change, pollution, water scarcity, use of non-renewable resources, disposal of waste, and loss of biodiversity. The social factor reflects a firm's relationship with its stakeholders, including its customers, employees, suppliers, and the broader community within which it operates; common issues include corruption, labor relations, health and safety, diversity and inclusion, child and forced labor across supply chains, and quality of product or service provided to customers. The governance factor, which we do not focus on in this section, involves the oversight of ESG issues, how stakeholder interests are balanced at the board level, and traditional corporate governance matters.

(f) Approaches to ESG Investing

A good framework to classify ESG investing approaches is the extent to which an approach focuses on only economic value versus integrated value, which combines economic with social and environmental values. Between the economic value-based approach and the integrated value-based approach lies a continuum of approaches, which progressively increase the weight placed on stakeholder value, as follows:

(1) ESG integration
Uses ESG factors to supplement conventional financial analysis to identify ESG-related opportunities that can improve returns or reduce risks without sacrificing portfolio returns. For example, funds can identify companies that are expected to be unprofitable in the long-term because of their exposure to material ESG risks and those that are expected to be profitable in the long-term because they are well-positioned to exploit certain ESG opportunities.

(2) Negative screening
Excludes investments that are incompatible with an investor's ESG values. Many Shariah-compliant funds, for example, are required to exclude companies that derive a large proportion of their income from the sale of alcohol, weapons, pork products, gambling, or pornography. Many of these screens use a specific set of standards, such as the Ten Principles of the UN Global Compact, which covers issues on anti-corruption, the environment, human rights, and labor.

(3) Engagement
Actively uses shareholder power and voting rights to engage and influence senior management and boards of companies so that the business can achieve specific ESG objectives in addition to a financial return.

(4) Impact investing
Focuses on making a positive, measurable environmental and social impact rather than a financial gain, typically providing financing to businesses with a distinct social or environmental purpose in order to express a moral or ethical belief.

(g) ESG Information
Although ESG factors were once regarded as intangible or qualitative information, refinements in the identification and analysis of such factors, as well as increased corporate disclosures, have resulted in increasingly quantifiable information. Still, the process of reflecting quantitative ESG-related data in investment analysis is evolving. Two key sources of ESG information include sustainability reports and ESG ratings, which we discuss in this section.

Sustainability reports are disclosures by companies of ESG-related (nonfinancial) information that can potentially impact enterprise value but are not traditionally made available in financial reports.

In Singapore, it is mandatory for companies listed on the Singapore Exchange (SGX) to produce a sustainability report annually. This report must describe the company's practices with regard to specific sustainability components, failing which the company must offer alternative information and explain the rationale for not complying. The sustainability components are as follows:

- Material ESG factors: Sustainability is a broad concept covering a multitude of issues. Given time and resource constraints, it is important to focus on the issues that matter the most, which raises the questions of "to whom?" and "in what context?" A material issue in the technology industry is user data privacy since user data is commonly harvested and sold, whereas what is material in the pharmaceutical and mining industries may be consumer product safety and worker safety, respectively. SGX-listed companies have to identify the material ESG factors, and describe how and explain why they selected these factors.
- Policies, practices, and performance: Measurement of performance relative to targets is important because it allows companies to evaluate the extent to which they are meeting their ESG objectives. SGX-listed companies, therefore, have to provide both qualitative and quantitative information on what they identified as material ESG factors.
- Targets: For each identified material ESG factor, SGX-listed companies have to set targets for the coming year.
- Reporting framework: Transparency in sustainability reporting is important and organizations such as the International Integrated Reporting Council, the Global Reporting Initiative, and the Sustainability Accounting Standards Board have produced global reporting frameworks. Yet companies have been very slow to adopt these frameworks because they do not have an incentive to do so, opting for meaningless reports that are visually appealing and have nice stories instead. SGX-listed companies are recommended to select a globally-recognized reporting framework.
- Board statement: The board of an SGX-listed company has to declare that it has incorporated sustainability considerations in its strategic formulation process, and ascertained which ESG factors are material to its business. It also has to commit to providing oversight in managing and monitoring said factors.

(h) ESG Ratings

ESG ratings are metrics of a firm's ESG performance. They are provided by various rating agencies to help investors choose funds that meet their ESG criteria. The problem with ESG ratings, however, is that different agencies can rate the fund differently based on their own rating methodology. For example, differences in the scope of the factors used to determine compliance with ESG, the manner in which factors are measured, and the weight given to each would give rise to different ratings. Further, agencies are likely not to use identical set of data, resulting in rating differences.

(i) ESG Investing Performance

Do ESG considerations improve investment performance? In order to determine whether ESG data has price-relevant information, we need to consider market efficiency. If markets are informationally efficient, all the opportunities and risks associated with corporate ESG activities would have been priced-in. Since ESG investing is constrained optimization (i.e., maximizing risk-adjusted expected returns, subject to ESG criteria), in an efficient market, investors are worse off with ESG investing because ESG constraints reduce their opportunity set, leading to a suboptimal risk-adjusted return compared to unconstrained optimization.

So, for ESG data to matter, there should be certain market inefficiencies and we consider two possibilities.

First, markets may underestimate the long-term impact of corporate ESG efforts. ESG efforts lead to the creation of intangible assets (e.g., brand equity, employee loyalty) that tend to pay off in the long run, which the market may not fully appreciate, so firms that have strong ESG initiatives are undervalued.

Second, markets may underestimate the probability and impact of negative ESG events, which corporate ESG efforts can help to mitigate. This underestimation is evident during the Global Financial Crisis of 2008, which led to a breakdown of trust in companies, institutions, and markets. During times of market stress, firms with strong ESG initiatives may have greater social capital, which serves to build trust between the firm and its stakeholders. Lins *et al.* (2017) find that companies that engaged in greater corporate social responsibility (CSR) efforts prior to the crisis fared better during the crisis itself. ESG efforts appear to have pricing implications but are ESG ratings data price-relevant? Khan *et al.* (2016) show that, for material sustainability issues, firms with high ratings on those issues outperform firms with low ratings. However, ratings do not seem to affect performance significantly for immaterial sustainability issues.

(j) ESG-Related Debt Securities — Social Impact Bonds (SIBs)

SIBs, which are really a misnomer as these are not publicly traded, are more appropriately called multi-stakeholder pay-for-success contracts. The three main parties are the investors, the social service provider, and the government. The investors, who typically care about making a social impact in addition to a financial return, provide up-front funding for the social service provider, which is typically a non-profit organization that is delivering social services to marginalized or vulnerable people (e.g., homeless individuals). This social service provider is contracted by the government, which specifies certain pre-agreed, measurable target outcomes, which are monitored for progress by an assessment adviser, who may propose course corrections as needed. If the outcomes are achieved, as evaluated by an independent assessor, then the government repays the investor with an investment return ranging from 8% to 12%, on average. Otherwise, the investor loses the interest and, potentially, the principal as well.

The early evidence suggests that SIBs are not delivering on their potential. The biggest challenge may be the lack of private impact investing capital, which means that program outcomes have to be compromised in order to attract more capital, since stipulating more metrics means that the odds of the investors receiving a positive return will be lower. In practice, investors actually have a strong influence over what gets funded and how the programs are designed, even though the government is supposed to set the agenda. Since the investors are well aware that the risk of these programs have been transferred to them, only the safest, proven programs get funded, not the innovative ones, which tend to be of higher risk.

(k) Green Loans

Green loans are similar to green bonds, except that the funds are provided by the bank rather than by investors and they generally follow the Green Loan Principles, a set of guidelines banks use to assess each project before deciding if a project qualifies for the loan. The principles are as follows:

- Use of proceeds: The projects that loans are funding should provide clear environmental benefits. Green projects that can qualify for funding include renewable energy products, sustainable water and wastewater management, and green buildings that are certified to have a positive environmental impact.

- Process for project evaluation and selection: The borrower should provide its lenders information such as the project's environmental sustainability objectives. It is also encouraged to disclose any green standards or certifications that the project seeks to meet.
- Management of proceeds: Green loans should be credited to a dedicated account to maintain the transparency and integrity of the loan. The borrower is also encouraged to establish an internal governance process to track the funds.
- Reporting: Borrowers should readily provide information on how the proceeds will be used, including which green projects the loan is intended for and how much is allocated to each project, as well as the project's expected impact; this information is subject to yearly review.

(l) Role of Companies

It may seem counterintuitive to discuss the role of companies in sustainable development efforts last, considering that companies are responsible for producing much of the negative environmental and social externalities.

The rationale is as follows: Governments can incentivize companies to internalize these externalities via taxation or regulation; asset managers are able to use their financial clout to engage companies in ESG efforts and to produce measurable impact; banks are able to starve unsustainable companies of capital, leading to an increase in their cost of capital; and finally individuals can consume responsibly and invest in a socially responsible way. The hope is that such a coordinated effort will be enough to convince companies that acting in the interest of all stakeholders in turn is beneficial for them. In fact, shareholders, as monitors of corporate management, have the power to amend managerial incentives and director responsibilities in order to strengthen climate risk assessment and response. They should examine the metrics by which executive compensation is determined and remove those that do not incentivize managers to adopt long-term stewardship. Increasing, investors are pushing for the integration of climate-related metrics in executive remuneration.

The key is to reach that inflection point where it is actually good business to operate sustainably. At that point, we enter a virtuous cycle in which there will be a massive exodus by asset managers and banks from companies with carbon-based assets to avoid being stuck with stranded assets, leading to a scale-up in the use of clean energy. At that point, companies will realize that business as usual will not cut it and that they will have to rethink and adapt their business models to be more sustainable.

As there are many topics in this module and each topic, in itself, has a wide scope, we are only able to discuss the fundamentals. The references here provide the candidates with material that are relevant to their areas of work and go into greater depth as well as cover the applications, laws, and regulations in various jurisdictions.

References/Further Readings

Technology

General

Mckie, S. (2018). Blockchain Communities and their Emergent Governance. Retrieved from https://medium.com/amentum/blockchain-communities-and-their-emergent-governance-cfe5627dcf52.

Monetary Authority of Singapore (2020). Consultation Paper on the New Omnibus Act for the Financial Sector. Retrieved from https://www.mas.gov.sg/publications/consultations/2020/consultation-paper-on-the-new-omnibus-act-for-the-financial-sector

AI

Info-communications Media Development Authority (IMDA) and Personal Data Protection Commission (PDPC). (2020). Model Artificial Intelligence Governance Framework (2nd Ed.). Retrieved from https://www.pdpc.gov.sg/-/media/Files/PDPC/PDF-Files/Resource-for-Organisation/AI/SGModelAI-GovFramework2.pdf.

Monetary Authority of Singapore. (2018). Principles to Promote Fairness, Ethics, Accountability and Transparency (FEAT) in the Use of Artificial Intelligence and Data Analytics in Singapore's Financial Sector. Retrieved from https://www.mas.gov.sg/publications/monographs-or-information-paper/2018/FEAT.

OECD. (2019). Recommendation of the Council on Artificial Intelligence. Retrieved from https://legalinstruments.oecd.org/en/instruments/OECD-LEGAL-0449.

World Economic Forum (WEF). (2019). AI Governance: A Holistic Approach to Implement Ethics into AI. Retrieved from https://www.weforum.org/white-papers/ai-governance-a-holistic-approach-to-implement-ethics-into-ai.

World Economic Forum (WEF). (2020). Ethics by Design: An Organizational Approach to the Responsible Use of Technology. Retrieved from https://www.weforum.org/whitepapers/ethics-by-design-an-organizational-approach-to-responsible-use-of-technology.

Blockchain
Lapointe, C. & Fishbane, L. (2019). The blockchain ethical design framework. *Innovations: Technology, Governance, Globalization*, 12(3/4), 50–71. Retrieved from https://www.mitpressjournals.org/doi/pdf/10.1162/inov_a_00275.

Cybersecurity
International Chamber of Commerce (ICC). (2015). ICC Cyber Security Guide for Business. Retrieved from https://iccwbo.org/publication/icc-cyber-security-guide-for-business/.
Monetary Authority of Singapore. (2021). Technology Risk Management Guidelines. Retrieved from https://www.mas.gov.sg/-/media/MAS/Regulations-and-Financial-Stability/Regulatory-and-Supervisory-Framework/Risk-Management/TRM-Guidelines-18-January-2021.pdf.
National Institute of Standards and Technology (NIST). (2018). Cybersecurity Framework. Retrieved from https://www.nist.gov/cyberframework.

Data protection/Privacy
iSight. (2021). A Practical Guide to Data Privacy Laws by Country. Retrieved from https://i-sight.com/resources/a-practical-guide-to-data-privacy-laws-by-country/(2021).
Personal Data Protection Commission Singapore (2012). Singapore Personal Data Protection Act. Retrieved from https://www.pdpc.gov.sg/Overview-of-PDPA/The-Legislation/Personal-Data-Protection-Act.

Finance
Anti-Money Laundering/ Combating the Financing of Terrorism (AML/CFT)
AML-CFT. (2017). 6 Elements of an Effective AML/CFT Compliance Programme. Retrieved from https://aml-cft.net/6-elements-effective-amlcft-compliance-programme/.
International Monetary Fund (IMF) (n.d.). Anti-Money Laundering/ Combating the Financing of Terrorism (AML/CFT). Retrieved from https://www.imf.org/external/np/leg/amlcft/eng/.
International Finance Corporation (IFC). (2019). Anti-Money-Laundering (AML) & Combating the Financing of Terrorism (CFT) Risk Management in Emerging Market Banks. Retrieved from https://www.ifc.org/wps/wcm/connect/e7e10e94-3cd8-4f4c-b6f8-1e14ea9eff80/45464_IFC_AML_Report.pdf?MOD=AJPERES&CVID=mKKNshy.

Corporate Governance
CFA Institute. (2018). The Corporate Governance of Listed Companies (3rd Ed.). A Manual for Investors. Retrieved from https://www.cfainstitute.org/en/advocacy/policy-positions/corporate-governance-of-listed-companies-3rd-edition.

Corporate Finance Institute (CFI). (n.d.). What is Corporate Governance? Retrieved from https://corporatefinanceinstitute.com/resources/knowledge/other/corporate-governance/.

Harvard Business Review. (2019). A Guide to the Big Ideas and Debates in Corporate Governance. Retrieved from https://hbr.org/2019/10/a-guide-to-the-big-ideas-and-debates-in-corporate-governance.

Environmental, Social and Governance (ESG)

CFA Institute. (2015). Environmental, Social and Governance Issues in Investing — A Guide for Investment Professionals. Retrieved from https://www.cfainstitute.org/en/advocacy/policy-positions/environmental-social-and-governance-issues-in-investing-a-guide-for-investment-professionals.

McKinsey Quarterly. (2019). Five Ways that ESG Creates Value. Retrieved from https://www.mckinsey.com/business-functions/strategy-and-corporate-finance/our-insights/five-ways-that-esg-creates-value.

MSCI. (n.d.). ESG101: What is ESG? Retrieved from https://www.msci.com/what-is-esg.

Sustainability and Green Finance

Green Finance Platform. (n.d.). Explore Green Finance. Retrieved from https://www.greenfinanceplatform.org/page/explore-green-finance.

World Economic Forum (WEF). (2020). What is Green Finance and Why is it Important? Retrieved from https://www.weforum.org/agenda/2020/11/what-is-green-finance/.

2.5 Sample Questions

Question 1

The foundation and basis for trust in the work environment is best described by which of the following qualities in the professional:

(a) Compliance with laws and regulations
(b) Integrity
(c) Possession of the necessary knowledge and skills

Question 2

The professional who possesses privileged information concerning the client should:

(a) Use it for the benefit of the firm
(b) Respect the rights of the client and not abuse the advantage
(c) Balance the interests the employer with the interests of the client

Question 3
A good AI system possesses the following attributes:

(a) Transparent and low cost
(b) Low cost and explainable
(c) Transparent and explainable

Question 4
In designing a block chain system, the following are factors to consider except:

(a) Secrecy
(b) Accessibility
(c) Identifiability

Question 5
Which is true regarding data protection?

(a) No need to seek consent regarding use of data since user has waived rights
(b) Retention of data for seven years
(c) Consent before collection of data is allowed

Question 6
Anti-Money Laundering procedures:

(a) Are only required for financial institutions like banks
(b) Are not applicable to payment systems as no money is kept with the firm
(c) Require a KYC (Know Your Customer) process

Question 7
Corporate governance:

(a) Ensures that shareholders' returns are maximized
(b) Attempts to balance the interests various stakeholders in the firm
(c) Is based on a set of global industry standards

Question 8
The board of directors is responsible for the following except:

(a) Risk management of corporation
(b) Independence of auditors
(c) Implementation of strategy

Question 9
The ESG implementation approach that is most associated with excluding certain sectors or companies is:

(a) Negative screening
(b) Impact investing
(c) Integration

Question 10
Which of the following about ESG investing is correct?

(a) In investment analysis, environmental and social factors have been adopted more slowly than governance factors.
(b) ESG factors are not quantifiable.
(c) ESG terminology is fairly standardized.

Solutions

Question 1

Solution: Option **b** is correct.

Compliance with laws and regulation is a requirement for all professionals. Having the knowledge and skills is a prerequisite for doing a competent job. However, trust is based on the integrity of the professional.

Question 2

Solution: Option **b** is correct.

Putting the interest of the client first is the basis of good ethical behavior. The professional has an obligation not to abuse the advantage she has from possessing privileged information about the client.

Question 3

Solution: Option **c** is correct.

While cost is a consideration in any system, low cost should not be the goal. Transparency and explainability are the hallmarks of a good AI system.

Question 4

Solution: Option **a** is correct.

Secrecy is not a factor to consider as anonymity is a key feature of the Blockchain system. Who has access and what constitutes an identity are important factors to consider in designing the blockchain.

Question 5

Solution: Option **c** is correct.

Without consent any data collected cannot be used. Option (**a**) is not correct if waiving the right of consent is a condition for getting the service as this violates the principle of consent which should not be coercive. Option (**b**) is partially correct if there are legal obligations to retain data for a certain period. The principle is that data should not be retained if the original purpose for doing so is no longer valid.

Question 6

Solution: Option **c** is correct.

Options (**a**) and (**b**) are not correct as AML extends beyond financial institutions to firms involved in payment systems and deposit taking. To combat money laundering, the source of the money is important. This requires the KYC process.

Question 7

Solution: Option **b** is correct.

Options (**a**) is not correct as maximizing shareholders' returns have to be balanced with the interests of other shareholders. Option (**c**) is not correct as various principles of good governance have been proposed but there is no global industry standard by which the firm must conform.

Question 8

Solution: Option **c** is correct

The board of directors is not responsible for the implementation of strategy. That is the job of management over which the board has oversight.

Question 9

Solution: Option **a** is correct.

Option **b** is incorrect because it is more concerned with making a positive environmental and social impact, whereas Option **c** is incorrect because it is more concerned with using ESG factors to supplement conventional financial analysis. Neither Option **b** nor Option **c** necessarily requires exclusion of certain sectors or companies.

Question 10

Solution: Option **a** is correct.

Option **b** is incorrect because many ESG factors can be measured, even if it is challenging to translate the numbers to a dollar impact. Option **c** is incorrect because industry practitioners and ratings providers do not agree on the terminology.

Part B: Artificial Intelligence, Machine Learning, and Deep Learning in Finance

In recent years, the terms artificial intelligence (AI), machine learning (ML), and deep learning (DL) have appeared frequently in the media, news, and publications. The finance sector is one of the earliest to adopt and integrate AI technologies to serve their customers better. For example, the trading floor occupied by all the brokers and traders in the old days is now replaced with rooms full of algorithmic trading computers. Previously, it took customers weeks or months to get a loan application approved, with multiple physical visits to different branches/departments of the bank. In the era of AI, a loan can be verified and approved within minutes or hours. Most importantly, the whole process can be completed online.

The transformation will be unlike anything humankind has experienced before in its scope, scale, and depth. We are all standing at the turning point of a paradigm shift, participating, and witnessing the fourth industrial revolution. How this revolution will unfold is unknown, but one thing is for sure: no one will be excluded from this technological revolution. It will fundamentally transform the way everyone lives, studies, works, and connects. As the French poet and novelist Victor Hugo has said, "Nothing is more powerful than an idea whose time has come." The best way to face the future is to embrace the changes and keep up with the trends.

This module presents some advanced techniques, algorithms, and models to lift the magic veil of AI, ML, and DL. Chapter 3 presents various advanced supervised and unsupervised ML models and the underlying mechanism and rationale in model selection. This will equip you with the essential knowledge to develop, evaluate, and interpret an ML model. Chapter 4 presents a more in-depth discussion of various commonly used neural network architectures, including the artificial neural network (ANN), convolutional neural network (CNN), recurrent neural network (RNN), long short-term memory (LSTM), and generative adversarial networks (GANs). Chapter 5 presents another rising hot topic in AI, namely natural language processing (NLP). This chapter will have a detailed discussion of some core NLP techniques and NLP applications in finance.

Chapter 3

Machine Learning

3.1 Bias–Variance Tradeoffs

This chapter highlights the importance of machine learning (ML) design thinking, and one aspect of it is the tradeoffs in modeling. As Fintech professionals, we need to understand the model we are using, the tradeoffs of different models, and how the designs will affect the outcome. No statistical learning model will always dominate or outperform all other models across all types of data sets. A model that performs well in one aspect usually needs to forgo other desirable statistical properties or compromise on other aspects. In other words, there are some underlying tradeoffs behind different aspects of model performance. This is why model selection is essential in ML.

Learning Objectives
- Understand the bias–variance tradeoff.
- Distinguish between training MSE and testing MSE.
- Understand the concepts and relationships among flexibility, complexity, interpretability, generalization, and prediction precision.

Main Takeaways

Main Points
- There exists a tradeoff in terms of bias and variance in model performance.
- The model with higher flexibility tends to have lower bias but higher variance.

Main Terms

- **MSE:** Mean squared error.
- **Training MSE:** The MSE computed from the training set.
- **Testing MSE:** The MSE computed from the testing set.
- **Generalization:** Measures how well the model fitted from the observed data can be applied to instances that are not observed yet.

There are many models to select from in practice. How do we differentiate them, and how do we choose them? As one of the most critical objectives of ML is to predict, one can evaluate the model performance on how accurate the prediction is compared to the true value. This process is also called the quality of fit. It computes how closely the predicted output $\hat{f}(x_i)$ for an input x_i matches the actual value of y_i observed in the data set. If the prediction $\hat{f}(x_i)$ is close to y_i, the fitted model $\hat{f}$ has a high quality of fit. Otherwise, the fitted model is not satisfactory as a prediction model.

To quantify the quality of fit, we may use the mean squared error (MSE), expressed as

$$\text{MSE} = \frac{1}{n}\sum_{i=1}^{n}(y_i - \hat{f}(x_i))^2,$$

where n represents the size of the data set or the number of observations in the data set. The term $y_i - \hat{f}(x_i)$ is the prediction error.

Since the value of the prediction error can be positive or negative, we can either use its absolute or squared value. Here, we compute the sum of squares error to use it as a criterion to find the best fit. As the name suggests, MSE computes the average of the squared prediction errors for all observations. If a fitted model is accurate in estimating or matching the observations, the prediction errors will be small, and subsequently, the value of MSE will be small. MSE is commonly used to evaluate an ML model's quality of fit or prediction accuracy. The question is, should we always prefer the model with the highest prediction accuracy? The quick answer is, unfortunately, no.

Let us first have a sense of the answer through an example. Suppose you are trying to fit an ML model to predict the price of a stock. It is assumed that, based on your expertise, you believe that the price of this stock is somehow closely associated with the S&P 500 index. Your goal is to study their relationship, so that you can subsequently forecast the future stock price. The historical stock prices can be obtained easily from online platforms like Yahoo Finance. You download the data for the past three months and come up with some models. You are keen to know whether the fitted model will predict well using the MSE model developed above. The thing is, we can consistently achieve zero MSE, if we wish, by fitting a special model. This is not by luck or magic. This 100% accurate model can be easily constructed by storing all the three months' data into a table and using it as a database prediction. If we compare the predicted stock price with the historical observations, we can always identify a perfect match in the table, leading to zero prediction error.[1] Indeed, this is an extreme case, and it is not reasonable to fit a table model in practice. Nevertheless, as an example, it shows that intuition can go wrong if the prediction accuracy is not assessed carefully.

As you can see, this kind of table model memorized all the stock's historical prices. However, what the investor wants is not to predict the past but the future, that is, the response to a previously unobserved input value. The following sections cover the concepts and terminologies which explain why MSE does not work correctly in the above-contrived example.

3.1.1 *Generalization*

As mentioned above, we want the fitted model to summarize the existing observations and the general population from which the observed data set comes in order to predict future values. Generalization measures how well the fitted model using the observed data can be generalized to instances not yet observed. We want to test if the predictive power of the model calibrated from the existing observations is applicable to out-of-sample data. The observed and unobserved data terminology results from the convention in ML to divide the data set into a training set and testing set. As the name implies, the training set refers to the observed samples used to train the ML model.

In contrast, the testing set is reserved and excluded from the training process. The fitted ML model's prediction is used to test the quality of fit. Consequently, the MSE calculated based on the training set is called the

---

[1] Technically speaking, it might be possible that the S&P index coincides at different dates. For the sake of this example, it is assumed that the observed values of S&P 500 index are all unique so that we don't have to decide which value to choose for prediction.

training MSE, and the one computed from the testing set is called the testing MSE. As seen from its definition, training MSE measures the model's quality of fit using the training data. The testing MSE indicates how well the fitted model can be generalized to unobserved data samples such as those excluded data.

3.1.2 *Complexity (Flexibility)*

The complexity of a model generally refers to the number of predictor parameters included in the model and/or whether it is linear or nonlinear. The larger the number of predictors, the more complex the model is. A complex model tends to have higher flexibility in choosing its model form as it covers a broader range of possibilities. For instance, the K-nearest neighborhood (KNN) method is more complex than linear regression. The linear model is inflexible as its form is restricted (a straight line) compared to KNN, whose form can take any curly shape. A straightforward explanation is that KNN can join many local straight lines or points fitted by the nearest data. One can also adjust the penalty or weights of the penalty, which alters the slopes of those pieces of straight lines joining the points. The resulting fit may just be a curly shape. If one takes all the points as neighbors instead of limiting them to a local area, we have the same straight line as the linear regression using the same value of MSE.

As a general rule of thumb, an increase in model complexity decreases the training MSE, with the testing MSE first decreasing and then increasing due to the bias–variance tradeoff. For example, if one fits the points using a very high dimension instead of the two dimensions of a straight line above, we may end up with not enough points in the high dimension space. In other words, there may not be enough neighbors, and we cannot find any meaningful fit.

3.1.3 *Bias–Variance Tradeoff*

The expected training MSE, given a value x_0 can be expressed as

$$E[y_0 - \hat{f}(x_0)]^2 = \text{var}(\hat{f}(x_0)) + [\text{bias}(\hat{f}(x_0))]^2 + \text{var}(\varepsilon).$$

As can be seen, the expected training MSE consists of three parts: the variance of $\hat{f}$, the squared bias of $\hat{f}$, and the variance of the irreducible error ε.

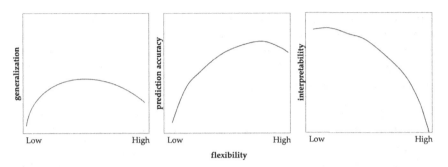

Figure 3.1: A summary of the relationships between model flexibility and generalization, prediction accuracy, and interpretability.

The model $\hat{f}$ is fitted based on the training data set. A different training data set will lead to a different $\hat{f}$. The variance refers to the extent to which the fitted model $\hat{f}$ will change if a different training data set is used. A high variance means that even a small difference in the training data could lead to a large variation in the form of $\hat{\ }$. The bias refers to the estimation error in predicting the real value of the response. Generally speaking, a less complex model will have a higher bias but a lower variance.

The change of testing MSE results from the relative rates of change of variance and bias. As the model's flexibility slowly increases, the bias decreases faster than the increase of variance initially. At a certain point, the rate of decrease in bias starts to slow down, whereas the speed of increase in variance starts to soar. Figure 3.1 summarizes the relationships between model flexibility and interpretability, generalization, and prediction accuracy.

In this section, we learn that we may achieve greater flexibility with more complexity. However, with more complexity, we may have a new set of problems. It is not always the case that more flexibility will lead to better results. It all depends on what we wish to get out from the chosen model or design, and a Fintech professional needs to understand what is the price we have to pay and the consequences when we get it wrong.

3.2 Subset Selection and Shrinkage Methods

This chapter further extends the variable selection techniques in fitting linear models, apart from the ordinary least square estimation. We introduce these methods because they may give us better prediction accuracy and interpretability for specific data sets. In particular, for high-dimensional data ($p \geq n$), the least square estimation often suffers from high variance and overfitting issues. The approaches introduced in this chapter can help overcome these issues.

Learning Objectives

- Design subset selection methods for a given data set using the three methods introduced.
- Discuss and compare the merits and drawbacks of different subset selection approaches.
- Identify the differences among various evaluation criteria.
- Appraise the advantages of shrinkage methods.
- Distinguish the difference between ridge and LASSO.
- Understand the pros and cons of ridge and LASSO.

Main Takeaways

Main Points

- A larger number of predictors may not always lead to better prediction accuracy.
- Variable selection identifies the predictors which are truly related to the response variable.
- Shrinkage methods have an advantage over the least square estimation regarding feature selection and prediction accuracy.
- All coefficients are shrunk toward zero in the ridge, but none is exactly set to zero.
- In LASSO, some of the coefficients can be constrained to equal to zero exactly.

Main Terms

- **Predictor:** The input variables which are believed to be related to the output variables. **Predictor variables** are used to fit the model to predict the output variable.
- **Response:** The output variable of the model, which is of main prediction interest in the problem.
- **SSE:** Sum of squared errors.
- **Shrinkage:** A penalty term that forces the coefficients to take small values.
- **Feature selection:** Also known as variable selection. It is defined as the process of selecting the appropriate features.

3.2.1 *Subset Selection*

Here we introduce three types of most commonly used subset selection approaches: the best subset selection, forward selection, and backward selection. These approaches are conducted in three steps. First, formulate a series of models, each of which includes only a subset of p predictor variables. The difference between the three approaches lies in how the subset of predictors is selected. Second, construct a fitting regression model for each subset model using the ordinary least square estimation. Third, based on a specific performance metric, pick the final model with the best performance.

In ML, we generally deal with p predictor variables, which we believe are associated with the response variable of interest. Take a case study of the credit card balance as an example. The first few rows of observations are listed in Table 3.1. Banks collect relevant information to predict the customer's credit card balance. The predictors collected include the credit card balance, income (in thousands of dollars), maximum credit debt limit, credit rating, number of credit cards owned, age, years of education, gender (male or female), whether the customer is a student or not, marital status, and ethnicity.

One possible approach is to fit an ordinary linear regression model:

$$y = \beta_0 + \beta_1 x_1 + \beta_2 x_2 + \cdots + \beta_p x_p + \varepsilon.$$

After estimation, we need to conduct an F-test and look at its F-statistic value to determine what variables should be included or excluded in the model. The null hypothesis of the F-test is stated as (H_0: all predictors are not significantly related to the response

Table 3.1: The Credit.csv data set.

	Income	Limit	Rating	Cards	Age	Education	Gender	Student	Married	Ethnicity	Balance
1	14.891	3606	283	2	34	11	Male	No	Yes	Caucasian	333
2	106.025	6645	483	3	82	15	Female	Yes	Yes	Asian	903
3	104.593	7075	514	4	71	11	Male	No	No	Asian	580
4	148.924	9504	681	3	36	11	Female	No	No	Asian	964
5	55.882	4897	357	2	68	16	Male	No	Yes	Caucasian	331
	...	...									...

Source: Gareth, J., Daniela, W., Trevor, H., & Robert, T. (2013). *An Introduction to Statistical Learning: With Applications in R.* Springer.

variable). If we reject the null hypothesis based on the F-statistic, we can conclude that not all predictors are useless in predicting y. This also means that at least some (though not necessarily all) predictors are truly associated with the response variable. However, the F-test leads to the binary decision of either excluding all the predictors or including all the predictors based on a level of statistical confidence. There is a limitation here. Some of the predictors may be more closely related to the response variable in practice, while the others may be very weakly or entirely unrelated to the response variable. These unrelated predictors are called noise variables. As a result, we need a variable selection mechanism to rank the importance of predictors. There is a misbelief that it is always good to include more predictors to give more information. However, as you have learned from the bias–variance tradeoff, including more predictors will lead to higher complexity of the model, which corresponds to worse performance in generalization, interpretability, and variance.

In summary, this chapter aims to teach you how to identify the combinations of predictors that are truly useful in predicting the response variable. The statistical terminologies used are variable selection, feature selection, and model selection.

3.2.2 The Best Subset Selection

The methodology of best subset selection is simple and straightforward. It simply enumerates all the possible combinations of predictors and fits a subset model for each combination based on the predictors selected. Suppose we have a total of p candidate predictors. For example,

- **0 predictor:** Suppose that all p predictors are not included. The model is $y = \beta_0 + \varepsilon$.
- **1 predictor:** Suppose out of the p predictors, only one predictor which is most closely related to the response variable can be chosen. There are p possibilities depending on which one of $x_1, \ldots, x_p$ is selected.
- **2 predictors:** Based on permutation, there are in total $\binom{p}{2} = \frac{p(p-1)}{2}$ possible combinations.
- **3 predictors:** There are $\binom{p}{3} = \frac{p(p-1)(p-2)}{3 \times 2}$ possibilities.
- … …
- p **predictors:** There is only one possible model.

Summing up all the possible combinations, there are in total $\sum_{k=0}^{p} \binom{p}{k} = 2^p$ possible combination of subset models. We will need to formulate a linear model using the least square estimation for each subset model in the best subset selection approach. As the name suggests, we will select the best model as the final model. The "best" model is evaluated based on specific performance measures introduced later in this chapter.

One of the apparent drawbacks of the best subset selection approach is that it can be computationally intensive. When p is large, the potential combinations of models to be computed will be exponential. As such, two alternative stepwise approaches (the forward selection and backward selection) are introduced next to reduce the number of subset models we need to consider.

(a) The Forward Selection

The forward selection is a stepwise subset selection approach. It starts with the null model (the model with no predictor). At each step, it adds in the one best predictor. This procedure repeats until all the predictors are included in the model. Here are the summarized steps:

- **Step 1:** Fit the null model: $M_0 : y = \beta_0$.
- **Step 2:** Add in one more predictor out of the p predictors and fit a linear model for each added predictor. Simply speaking, we need to try out $y = \beta_0 + \beta_1 x_1$, $y = \beta_0 + \beta_2 x_2, ..., y = \beta_0 + \beta_p x_p$, respectively. Depending on the evaluated performance, we select the best model as the final model for the class of one predictor. For instance, if x_2 is chosen, we have the model $M_1 : y = \beta_0 + \beta_2 x_2$, where M_1 denotes the best predictor model.
- **Step 3:** In forward selection, the next step is always conditioned on the previous decision. In this case, since the predictor x_2 is already selected in Step 2, we just need to add in one more predictor out of the remaining $(p - 1)$ predictors. Again, each of the two predictor models is evaluated and the best model is selected as the final model. Let's say, in this round, x_4 is chosen, and we now have the model $M_2 : y = \beta_0 + \beta_2 x_2 + \beta_4 x_4$.
- Repeat the same procedure ...
- **Step p:** All p predictors are included in the model as $M_p : y = \beta_0 + \beta_2 x_2 + \beta_5 x_5 + \cdots + \beta_p x_p$.
- By now, we should have obtained $(p + 1)$ models ($M_0, M_1, ..., M_p$), each of which represents the best k – predictor model, $k = 0,1, ..., p$. The last

step is to compare these models and select the model with the best performance. The selected best model will be our final model.

As can be seen from the number of subset models we need to compute, the forward selection approach is much less computationally intensive than the best subset selection. A potential drawback of the forward selection approach is that the model in the next step always builds upon the selected model in the previous step. As demonstrated in the case study above, the predictor x_2 chosen in Step 2 has to be included in all the subsequent models. Conceivably, the best 2-predictor model may be, let's say $y = \beta_0 + \beta_1 x_1 + \beta_3 x_3$, without x_2. Nevertheless, this 2-predictor model will be left out in the forward approach. Compared to the best subset selection approach, the forward selection approach is often unable to identify the optimal global solution in the space of subset models.

(b) The Backward Selection

Another alternative stepwise approach is called backward selection. As its name suggests, the approach is opposite to that of the forward selection approach. Instead of starting with the null model, the backward selection approach begins with the full model, where all p predictors are included. Instead of adding one predictor at each step in the forward selection approach, we now remove the least significant predictor. This procedure is repeated until no predictor is left in the model. Look at the following summarized steps:

- **Step 1:** Start with the full model as $M_p : y = \beta_0 + \beta_1 x_1 + \beta_2 x_2 + \cdots + \beta_p x_p$.
- **Step 2:** Remove one predictor from the model and fit it with the remaining $(p - 1)$ predictors. There are in total p possibilities on which predictor is to be excluded. Suppose x_2 is removed based on the performance comparison. We have the $(p - 1)$ − predictor model denoted as $M_{p-1} : y = \beta_0 + \beta_1 x_1 + \beta_3 x_3 + \cdots + \beta_p x_p$.
- **Step 3:** Conditional on M_{p-1}, one more predictor of the remaining $(p - 2)$ predictors (except for x_2) is removed from the model. The best model out of the $(p - 2)$ options are selected as M_{p-2}.
- Repeat the same procedure … …
- **Step** $p : M_0 : y = \beta_0$.
- With all the selected models $M_0, M_1, …, M_p$, at each step, the final model is identified as the one with the best performance based on the evaluation criterion.

The merit of the backward selection approach compared to the best subset selection approach is in terms of the lower computational complexity. One drawback of the backward selection approach is that it cannot be applied when the sample size n is smaller than the number of predictors p. With $n < p$, we cannot even fit the full model in the first step. In comparison, the forward selection can be applied even when $n < p$.

3.2.3 *The Evaluation Criteria*

As mentioned earlier, an evaluation criterion must be used to rank and select the model with the best performance. In statistics, SSE (sum of squared errors) and R-square have been used in ordinary linear regression to measure the quality of fit. Unfortunately, there is a limitation in using these criteria: they are only applicable for comparing models with the same number of predictors. The reason is rooted in the bias–variance tradeoff. A model with more predictors (a.k.a. higher complexity) inherently often returns smaller training SSE and larger R-square. Therefore, it is unfair to compare across models with different numbers of predictors using these criteria. The performance measure we use needs to be adjusted by the number of predictors for a fair comparison.

Here we introduce four commonly used evaluation criteria as listed in Table 3.2. It is assumed that the models are fitted using least square estimation with p predictors. The $\hat{\sigma}^2$ is the estimated variance of the residual ε.

These criteria adjust for the impact of the number of predictors, by adding a penalty term $\hat{\sigma}^2$. As for C_p, Akaike information criterion (AIC), Bayesian information criterion (BIC), the smaller the value, the better the model performance. In contrast, the larger the value of adjusted R^2, the better the model performance. The adjusted R-square computes the proportion of explained variation by the model. As such, the larger, the better.

3.2.4 *Shrinkage Methods*

All the subset selection approaches discussed so far require fitting the model using the least square estimation. This chapter looks at alternative methods that can replace the least square estimation. There are mainly two advantages of the alternative fitting processes over the least square estimation.

Table 3.2: Evaluation criteria for model selection.

Criterion	Formula	Remark
C_p	$\dfrac{\left(\text{SSE} + 2p\hat{\sigma}^2\right)}{n}$	The smaller the value of C_p, the lower the test error rate of the model.
AIC	$\dfrac{\left(\text{SSE} + 2p\hat{\sigma}^2\right)}{n\hat{\sigma}^2}$	The smaller the value of AIC, the smaller the test error rate of the model.
BIC	$\dfrac{\left(\text{SSE} + \log(n)p\hat{\sigma}^2\right)}{n}$	$\log(n) > 2$ when $n > 7$, as compared to AIC.
Adjusted R^2	$1 - \dfrac{\text{SSE}/(n-d-1)}{\text{TSS}/(n-1)}$	Conventional $R^2 = 1 - \dfrac{\text{SSE}}{\text{TSS}}$, $\text{TSS} = \sum_{i=1}^{n}(y_i - \bar{y})^2$.

(a) Feature Selection

As explained earlier, there exist noise variables among the predictors. To obtain a good model, we need to identify those predictors which are truly associated with the response variable. Unfortunately, it is highly unlikely for the least square estimation method to return a zero value for a coefficient. This means that all the corresponding predictors are eventually all included if we fit an ordinary linear regression model.

On the other hand, the subset selection approaches require us to repeatedly fit different models and test if the combination of coefficients returns a good model. This is extremely tedious. The shrinkage or regularization approaches to be introduced in this chapter can overcome these difficulties. Shrinkage methods will constrain and restrict a set of coefficients to be exactly zero while the model is fitted only once.

(b) Prediction Accuracy

The ordinary linear regression model is considered to be low in complexity. As a result, it often returns very commendable results in terms of low bias and low variance. Nevertheless, this is only true when the data set has a low dimension (i.e., the number of features is much smaller than the number of observations in the data set). On the contrary, if the number of observations n is close to or even smaller than the number of features p, the least square estimation will suffer from overfitting and high variance. Worse yet, if $p > n$, then there will be no unique solution to the least square estimation, and therefore the least square estimation has to be abandoned.

Some of the alternative fitting procedures to be introduced in this chapter achieve an overall improvement in prediction accuracy via reducing the variance without compromising on bias.

3.2.5 *Ridge Regression*

The least-square estimation tries to find the optimal set of coefficients $\hat{\beta}_0, \hat{\beta}_1, \ldots, \hat{\beta}_p$ which minimizes SSE:

$$\text{SSE} = \sum_{i=1}^{n} (y_i - \hat{y}_i)^2 = \sum_{i=1}^{n} \left(y_i - \beta_0 - \sum_{k=1}^{p} \beta_k x_{ik} \right)^2.$$

Ridge regression tries to add in a constraint on the coefficients as a penalty and tries to find the optimal set of coefficients that minimize

$$\text{SSE} + \lambda \sum_{k=1}^{p} \beta_k^2, \ \lambda \geq 0,$$

where the term $\lambda \sum_{k=1}^{p} \beta_k^2$ is called the regularization or shrinkage factor. λ is the tuning parameter that controls the magnitude of the penalty. The least-square estimation can be considered a special case of the ridge if we set $\lambda = 0$. As constrained by the shrinkage penalty, all the coefficients $\hat{\beta}_0, \hat{\beta}_1, \ldots, \hat{\beta}_p$ will be shrunk toward zero to some extent to minimize the objective function. A predictor variable x is considered less important in association with the response variable when its corresponding coefficient is close to zero. The inclusion of one predictor variable will lead to a decrease in SSE while increasing the shrinkage penalty. A predictor is considered the noise variable if the reduction in SSE is trivial compared to the increase in the shrinkage penalty. Since the objective is to minimize the sum of SSE and shrinkage penalty, this kind of noisy variable will be naturally removed in ridge regression.

The advantage of ridge regression compared to ordinary linear regression is rooted in the bias–variance tradeoff. When the number of predictors p is close to the number of observations n, the least square estimation will have a high variance. The flexibility of the ridge regression decreases with the increase of λ value. Consequently, the bias will increase, and the variance will decrease. In this case, ridge regression can significantly reduce variance via sacrificing a slight increase in bias.

3.2.6 *Least Absolute Shrinkage and Selection Operator*

Although ridge regression forces all coefficients to be shrunk toward zero, none of the coefficients assumes the value of zero eventually unless $\lambda = +\bowtie$. In such a situation, all predictors are still included in ridge regression despite some of them having coefficients close to zero. This leads to a model which is hard to interpret.

The Least Absolute Shrinkage and Selection Operator (LASSO) approach can address this issue via performing feature selection. Instead of constraining the coefficients by its square, LASSO penalizes the absolute value of the coefficients as

$$\text{SSE} + \lambda \sum_{k=1}^{p} |\beta_k|.$$

This kind of shrinkage penalty can force some coefficient to be exactly zero with certain tuning parameter λ. The proof is outside the scope of this chapter. From the perspective of optimization, using the constraint of absolute values, the optimal solution can be achieved at some sharp corner point where some coefficients are equal to zero exactly. When a specific estimate for the coefficient is equal to zero, the corresponding predictor variable will be removed from the fitted model. As such, this serves the purpose of feature selection.

Figure 3.2 displays the results of fitting a model using LASSO. As we can see, LASSO can perform feature selection effectively by setting coefficients of some predictors that are not closely associated with the response to exactly zero.

3.3 Principal Component Regression

This chapter introduces a dimension reduction technique called the principal component analysis (PCA). Based on the PCA technique, the principal component regression (PCR) method takes the principal components as the new predictors to fit a linear regression model using the least square estimation.

Learning Objectives
- Describe the steps in implementing PCA.
- Understand the merits and assumptions of PCA.
- Describe the formulation of PCR.

```
----------------------------------
----LASSO (alpha=1)--
-coefficients-
[-5.16647938e+00  9.34302514e-02  1.97985706e+00  4.50329130e-01
 -0.00000000e+00 -0.00000000e+00 -0.00000000e+00  3.48130154e+02
 -0.00000000e+00 -0.00000000e+00  0.00000000e+00  0.00000000e+00]
----------------------------------
----LASSO (alpha=3)--
-coefficients-
[-0.00000000e+00  2.99801700e-02  1.73290035e+00  0.00000000e+00
 -0.00000000e+00  0.00000000e+00  0.00000000e+00  1.99651224e+02
 -0.00000000e+00 -0.00000000e+00  0.00000000e+00  0.00000000e+00]
```

Figure 3.2: The model coefficients using LASSO with $\lambda = 1,3$ (in the Python package, λ is noted as alpha).

Main Takeaways

Main Points

- The idea of PCA is that a few key principal components or variables will be sufficient to explain the major portion of the variation in the data.
- There is always a misunderstanding that the quality of the fitted model will improve as more predictors are included. After studying this chapter, the reader should understand the importance of feature selection.

Main Terms

- **Principal component:** The direction of a line that summarizes the variation in the data.
- **Scree plot:** The percentage of variation explained by each principal component.

A data set is considered high dimensional when the number of features is larger than the number of observations. The classical approaches like the ordinary linear regression cannot be applied or may suffer from the issue of overfitting in this case. To illustrate this, we use a hypothetical case of $n = 12$ observations and use ordinary linear regression to get the best fit from 1 predictor to 12 predictors. We highlight that all these 12 predictors are simulated to be completely unrelated to the response variable. By right, the model should misbehave. But is this the case? Figure 3.3 shows the training MSE and testing MSE of the fitted models. It can be seen that the training MSE might eventually decrease to almost zero when we have 12 predictors in the model, even though the predictors are mentioned to be completely irrelevant to the response variable. Nevertheless, this does

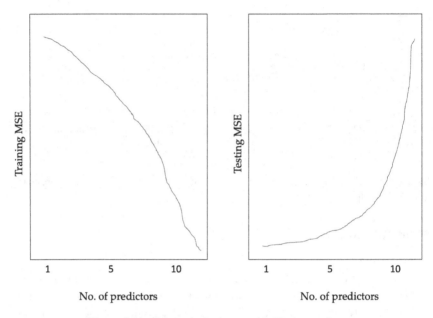

Figure 3.3: A hypothetical case with 12 observations.

not mean anything because the test MSE shown on the right plot can become extremely large as the number of predictors included gets closer to the number of observations we have. This gives an example that least square estimation can perform very poorly in the high dimensional case.

3.3.1 *Principal Component Analysis*

PCA is a technique used for dimension reduction. When dealing with a data set with many variables, PCA can identify the direction of a line along which the data is highly variable. These directions are the principal components that summarize the representative information of all variables.

Suppose we have a data set as shown in Table 3.3. It contains several financial information (like the market capital, number of employees, revenue, etc.) collected from different firms.

Suppose we are only interested in the market capital. It can be visualized using a 1D line, as shown in Figure 3.4. As seen from the clustering, companies 1–3 are close to each other and appear at the high-value end of the market capital line, while companies 4–6 are near each other and appear at the low-value end of market capital.

Table 3.3: A hypothetical data set.

Variables	Firm 1	Firm 2	Firm 3	Firm 4	...	Firm n
Market Cap. (in millions)	9	10.5	8.5	3.2	2.8	1.3
No. of employees (in thousands)	5.5	4.3	5.1	2.8	3.2	1
Revenue (in thousands)	10	6	7	2	1	3
... ...	... ...	... ...	... ...	... ...	... ...	... ...

Figure 3.4: 1D line of the market capital.

Similarly, we can visualize or identify relationships when we have two predictors or three predictors. The problem arises when we have more than four predictors. We are not able to plot in dimensions higher than three. The key idea of PCA is that we can summarize or represent the information from higher dimensions in a few (typically 2 or 3) key components. These summary components are called the principal components. They represent the major variation in the data. Consequently, instead of dealing with an enormous number of predictors, we only need to model a few representative components.

Here are the summarized steps on how PCA is implemented. We use two variables (name them as x_1, x_2) as an example for easy understanding. It can be extended to higher dimensions by analogy.

Step 1: Find the centroid point (the average of each direction of predictors), namely $\bar{x} = (\bar{x}_1, \bar{x}_2)$ based on the given observations.
Step 2: Make the centroid point the new origin (0,0). Or shift the coordinates of all observations until the centroid point coincides with the origin. This does not change the relative location of each observation. We are only changing the reference coordinate.
Step 3: Identify a straight line that goes through the origin that best fits the observations. The line is considered the best fitted because the sum of squared distances from all data points to the line is minimized. This best-fitted line is called the first principal component or, in short, PC 1.

Step 4: Going through the origin, identify another straight line perpendicular to the first principal component. This is called the second principal component or, in short, PC 2.

Step 5: We rotate the coordinates and the axes until PC 1 is horizontal. The obtained plot is called a 2D PCA plot.

Suppose PC 1 has a slope of 0.25. What it means is that to get PC 1, we need four units in the direction of x_1 and 1 unit of x_2. After normalizing the PC 1 vector to length 1, we obtain the corresponding proportion of x_1, x_2 as 0.97, 0.24. These values are called the loading scores. The resulting PC 1 vector of length 1 is called the singular vector or eigenvector of PC 1.

Another terminology to mention is the scree plot,[2] which measures the percentage of variation explained by different principal components. The variations are calculated as

$$\frac{\text{Sum of squared distance projected to PC1}}{n-1} = \text{Variation for PC1,}$$

$$\frac{\text{Sum of squared distance projected to PC2}}{n-1} = \text{Variation for PC2.}$$

Suppose the variation for PC 1 is computed as 16, and the variation for PC 2 is computed as 4. In this case, PC 1 accounts for $\frac{16}{16+4} = 80\%$ of the variation in the data, while PC 2 accounts for the remaining 20%. A scree plot is shown in Figure 3.5.

By following the same procedures mentioned above, we can obtain PC 1, PC 2, PC 3, ..., PC k generally for any number of variables. As said earlier, it is difficult to model 4D data. However, we can reduce its dimension to 2D. Suppose we have the scree plot of four variables as shown in Figure 3.6. PC 1 (75%) and PC 2 (15%) which together account for 90% of the variation of the data. Although not 100% complete, PC 1 and PC 2 will provide a reasonable summary of the variation in the original data. Nevertheless, if the variation is not concentrated on the first few principal components, the PCA approach may not work well.

---

[2]Scree Plot. (n.d.). Retrieved March 01, 2021, from https://en.wikipedia.org/wiki/Scree_plot.

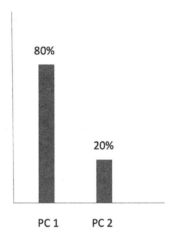

Figure 3.5: Scree plot of PC 1 and PC 2.

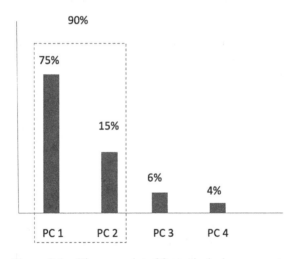

Figure 3.6: The scree plot of four principal components.

As a rule of thumb, it is best to use the least number of principal components to get a reasonably good understanding of the data. Depending on the application and data set, there is no single correct method to determine the number of principal components we should use. A general guideline is to review the first 1 to 3 principal components to see whether we can identify an interesting pattern in the data. If no interesting pattern can be spotted, it is improbable that including additional principal components will give an interesting pattern.

3.3.2 Principal Component Regression

In PCR, it is assumed that the directions that explain the most variation of the data correspond to the directions that are most closely associated with the response variable y. Although this is not a 100% accurate assumption, it often returns a reasonably good estimation. The PCR can mitigate overfitting for the ordinary linear regression in handling the high-dimensional data.

Mathematically, the fitted PCR model can be expressed as

$$y = \beta_0 + \beta_1(\text{PC1}) + \beta_2(\text{PC2}) + \cdots \beta_M(\text{PC M}) + \varepsilon.$$

3.4 Advanced ML Models in Classification

This chapter introduces some more advanced supervised learning models. In particular, we are going to introduce some commonly used classification approaches, including linear discriminant analysis (LDA) and quadratic discriminant analysis (QDA).

Learning Objectives
- Understand the confusion matrix and compute sensitivity, specificity, type I error, type II error, and precision.
- Describe the design of LDA and QDA.

Main Takeaways

Main Points
- The design of LDA and QDA is based on Bayes' theorem.
- LDA assumes all the predictors follow a Gaussian distribution with a common variance.
- QDA relaxes the assumption of common variance.

Main Terms
- **Posterior probability:** The conditional probability based on the observed value of predictors.
- **LDA:** Linear discriminant analysis.
- **QDA:** Quadratic discriminant analysis.

The classification problem occurs more frequently than the regression problem in practice. Here are some examples of classification problems in finance:

- **Bond-rating:** Classify corporate or government-issued bonds into different rating groups. Several well-known financial institutions, such as Moody's Standard & Poor's, and Fitch Investors Service, have been doing this in their bond ratings.
- **Stock classification:** Classify a stock into either a growth stock or a value stock based on its perceived return.
- **Fraud detection:** Classify whether an online transaction is fraudulent or not, based on the customer's IP address, transaction amount, etc.
- **Business prediction:** Predict whether a new start-up company will succeed or not.

3.4.1 *Linear Discriminant Analysis*

This chapter tries to solve a classification problem with $K \geq 2$ classes. The goal of the model is to place an observation into one of the K classes. Unlike modeling the conditional probability $\Pr(Y = k|X = x)$ directly using the logit function in logistic regression, this chapter introduces alternative methods (namely LDA and QDA) which are based on the Bayes' theorem.

If π_k denotes the prior probability that a random observation from the data set is actually from the kth class and $f_k(X) = \Pr(X = x|Y = k)$ is the conditional density function for the observation of the kth category of the response variable Y, then, according to Bayes' theorem, the posterior probability that an observation comes from the kth class is

$$(X = x) = \frac{\pi_k f_k(x)}{\sum_{l=1}^{K} \pi_l f_l(x)}.$$

This denotes the probability that we will classify a given observation $X = x$ into the kth category of response variable Y. As we are given K different classes, we can obtain K posterior probabilities, each of which is associated with one of the K classes. Solving the classification problem is then equivalent to finding $p_k(X)$, which corresponds to the class that returns the highest posterior probability.

The remaining question is how to estimate the posterior probabilities. It is not difficult to compute the prior probabilities π_k using an empirical distribution of an existing data sample (i.e., the proportion of observations belonging to different classes of Y). The challenging part is to estimate $f_k(X)$. LDA makes a simplifying assumption that the density function is normal or Gaussian.

(a) LDA for a Single Predictor

First, let's look at the case with only one predictor X. It is assumed that the density function $f_k(X)$ is Gaussian, which takes the form

$$f_k(X) = \frac{1}{\sqrt{2\pi}\sigma_k} e^{\left(-\frac{1}{2\sigma_k^2}(x-\mu_k)^2\right)},$$

where μ_k refers to the mean value of the responses in kth class, and σ_k stands for the standard error of the responses in the kth class. LDA further assumes a uniform variance across all classes, namely $\sigma_1 = \sigma_k = \cdots = \sigma_K = \sigma$. We can then plug $f_k(X)$ into the expression of $p_k(X)$ and obtain,

$$p_k(X) = \frac{\pi_k \frac{1}{\sqrt{2\pi}\sigma} e^{\left(-\frac{1}{2\sigma^2}(x-\mu_k)^2\right)}}{\sum_{l=1}^{K} \pi_l \frac{1}{\sqrt{2\pi}\sigma} e^{\left(-\frac{1}{2\sigma^2}(x-\mu_l)^2\right)}}.$$

To find the largest value of $p_k(X)$, we take the logarithm of the above expression, and it is easy to show that it is equivalent to finding

$$\mathrm{argmax}_k \left(x \cdot \frac{\mu_k}{\sigma^2} - \frac{\mu_k^2}{2\sigma^2} + \log(\pi_k) \right).$$

The term "linear" comes from the fact that the above discriminant function is linear with respect to x. The mean and variance can be estimated by a sample average and sample variance as

$$\hat{\mu}_k = \frac{1}{n_k} \sum_{i:\, y_i=k} x_i$$

$$\hat{\sigma}^2 = \frac{1}{n-K} \sum_{k=1}^{K} \sum_{i:\, y_i=k} (x_i - \hat{\mu}_k)^2,$$

where n is the sample size.

(b) LDA for Multiple Predictors

The LDA method can be extended to the case when we have multiple predictors $x_1,...,x_p$. Similarly, it is assumed the observations are drawn from a multivariate Gaussian distribution with a unique mean and a common variance across different classes.

The multivariate density function now takes the form

$$f_k(X) = \frac{1}{(2\pi)^{p/2} |\Sigma|^{1/2}} \exp\left(-\frac{1}{2}(x-\mu)^T \Sigma^{-1}(x-\mu)\right),$$

where Σ now represents the covariance matrix common to all K classes. By analogy, it can be shown that an observation should be assigned to the class for which

$$x^T \Sigma^{-1}\mu_k - \frac{1}{2}\mu_k^T \Sigma^{-1}\mu_k + \log(\pi_k)$$

is the largest.

3.4.2 *Quadratic Discriminant Analysis*

As assumed in the LDA, the K classes share a common variance. This can be a very unrealistic assumption in practice. As a result, the QDA tries to relax this assumption by assuming that each class of observations has its unique variance σ_k^2. In the multivariate case, the covariance matrix is now denoted as Σ_k for the kth class.

A natural question to ask is when to use LDA or QDA? The answer has to do with the bias–variance tradeoff. QDA needs to estimate a separate covariance matrix for different classes. This involves many more parameters than LDA. As such, QDA can be considered as a more flexible method than the LDA. Therefore, we can expect that QDA will have a relatively lower bias than the LDA model. This can lead to potential improvement in prediction accuracy.

However, as we know, the flexible method may suffer from high variance, especially if only a small number of observations are available. As a result, LDA is preferred when the training set is small and reducing the variance is crucial. QDA is chosen when the training set is large so that the variance is no longer a big concern or when the assumption of common variance is violated.

3.4.3 *Comparison of Different Classification Methods*

We have covered various classification methods, including logistic regression, KNN, LDA, QDA. We now compare and discuss when to use each method in different scenarios.

Both logistic regression and LDA produce the linear decision boundary (or linear classifier). The difference lies in how the coefficients of the linear classifier are estimated. The coefficients are estimated based on maximum likelihood in logistic regression, but are estimated based on the Bayes' theorem in LDA. You may expect these two methods to return similar and comparable results since their significant difference is in the fitting process. In addition, it is assumed that the observations follow a Gaussian distribution with uniform variance. If the given data set follows such a Gaussian distribution, LDA is expected to outperform logistic regression. However, if the Gaussian assumption is violated in the data set, logistic regression may return better results than LDA.

On the other extreme, KNN does not assume any distribution about the data as well as the form of the fitted model. As such, it is an entirely non-parametric method. KNN often results in a nonlinear decision boundary. If the data cannot be well separated using a linear decision boundary, KNN is preferred. The drawback of KNN compared to logistic regression and LDA is that its results are not easy to interpret. KNN does not give the magnitude of impact that each predictor has on the response variable since it does not estimate the coefficients like logistic regression and LDA. We cannot find out which predictor is more critical using KNN.

Lastly, QDA is considered a compromise between the two extremes. It is more flexible than LDA and can model a more comprehensive range of problems. Meanwhile, it is not as flexible as KNN, so it still maintains a good level of interpretability.

3.5 Cross-Validation

As discussed earlier, the training data set is used to fit the model, and the corresponding training MSE is a measure that indicates how well the model fits the training data. However, to understand the test error, which measures how well the fitted model can be generalized to an unseen data set, we need a testing data set. Recall that we divide the data set into two sets, with one subset used as the training set and the other subset used as the testing set. This approach will be discussed as the validation set approach in this chapter. In addition, this chapter will also introduce some alternative cross-validation approaches which may give better results. The key concept of cross-validation is that instead of using all the available data to fit the model, a subset of the data is held out to be used as the test set. This chapter will also introduce a few methodologies to determine the composition of the "holdout" subset.

Learning Objectives
- Understand the design of different cross-validation approaches.
- Appraise the pros and cons of different cross-validation approaches.

Main Takeaways

Main Points
- The key concept of cross-validation is that instead of using all the available data to fit the model, a subset of the data is held out to be used as the test set.
- The underlying assumption of conventional cross-validation is that all observations are independent and identically distributed (i.i.d.).

Main Terms
- **Training set:** The set of data used for calibrating the ML model.
- **Validation set:** The set of data reserved for testing the model performance in predicting the unseen observations.

3.5.1 *The Validation Set Approach*

In selecting a subset of data to "holdout", the most natural and straightforward way is to partition the data into two parts. One part is used for fitting the model, and the other part is held out for testing purposes. As suggested by its role, the subset used for training the fitted model is called the training set. The 'holdout' subset used for testing is named the validation set or testing set. Since the validation set is held out from the training process, the data points are considered "unseen" to the fitted model. As a result, the MSE computed from the validation set error rate serves as an estimate of the testing error rate or testing MSE.

As depicted in Figure 3.7, the validation set approach tries to partition the data set into two subsets in a random manner. The first subset with a sample size of K is used as the training set. The remaining $n - K$ is reserved as the validation set. As can be seen from the figure, the data that

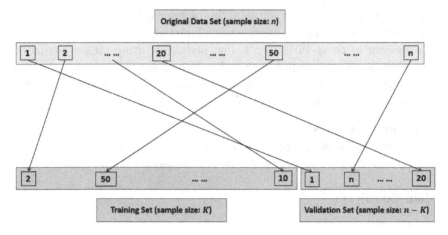

Figure 3.7:   Design of validation set approach.

is divided into the two subsets may not necessarily follow an ascending or descending order. This leads to the key feature of the validation set approach, which is that every time we split the data set into two parts, different training and validation sets are obtained.

Pros
- Easy to understand for users and simple to implement.
- Less computationally expensive as compared to the Leave-One-Out Cross-Validation (LOOCV) method.

Cons
- The resulting training and validation sets are always different every time they are generated. This means that the validation error computed will vary a lot in practice and makes it difficult to estimate or reproduce the testing MSE accurately.
- In the validation set approach, a subset of observations is held out for validation, which could have been previously used for training the model otherwise. This suggests that the validation error computed may appear to overestimate the actual test error if the model is fitted based on the entire data set.

3.5.2 *Leave-One-Out Cross-Validation*

Another alternative approach, namely the LOOCV, is introduced to overcome the two potential drawbacks of the validation set approach. Similar

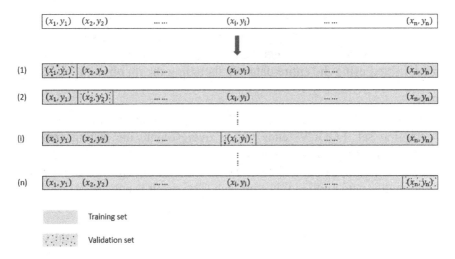

Figure 3.8: Design of LOOCV.

to the validation set approach, LOOCV also partitions the data set into two subsets. In contrast, the difference is that, instead of creating two data sets with comparable sizes, LOOCV holds out only one single observation as the validation set. In other words, the LOOCV can be considered as the validation set approach with the training set $K = n - 1$.

Figure 3.8 displays the design of the LOOCV. Suppose we have a data set $\{(x_1, y_1), (x_2, y_2), \ldots, (x_n, y_n)\}$. In LOOCV, each observation takes turns to be the validation set. For instance, we can reserve the first observation (x_1, y_1) as the validation set. The remaining $(n - 1)$ data points $\{(x_2, y_2), \ldots, (x_n, y_n)\}$ are used to fit the ML model. The performance of the fitted model is then tested based on the predicted $\hat{y}_1$ on the unused observation (x_1, y_1), which is denoted as $\text{MSE}_1 = (y_1 - \hat{y}_1)^2$. We can also hold out the second observation (x_2, y_2) as the validation set and use the remaining data $\{(x_1, y_1), (x_3, y_3), \ldots, (x_n, y_n)\}$ to fit the model. Consequently, the accuracy of this kind of testing MSE is very poor since it is solely based on only one observation.

To address this issue, we can repeat the same procedure for n iterations to average out the potential variation. In the LOOCV approach, the testing MSE is computed by the average of MSEs:

$$\text{LOOCV}_{(n)} = \frac{1}{n}\sum_{i=1}^{n}\text{MSE}_i = \frac{1}{n}\sum_{i=1}^{n}\left(y_{(i)} - \hat{y}_{(i)}\right)^2.$$

Remark: $\hat{y}_{(i)}$ is denoted with a bracket subscript to emphasize that it is the prediction from the ith partition of training and testing set. This is to distinguish with $\hat{y}_i$, which generally means the prediction made from a model fitted using the entire data set, including the ith observation itself.

Pros

- Since most of the data or $(n-1)$ of the observations are used in the training set, LOOCV tends not to overestimate the testing error as much as the validation set approach.
- LOOCV always returns the same estimated testing error when repeated no matter who applied this approach. The result is consistent.

Cons

- LOOCV can be computationally intensive. The computational complexity comes from two aspects. In LOOCV, we need to fit a model using each of the training-testing partitions. First, it is affected by the complexity of the model we choose to fit the data. For instance, if the model selected is linear, it can be very fast to fit. However, if the model is nonlinear, it takes longer to solve. Second, no matter how much time it takes to fit one model, it has to be performed for n times. If n happens to be large, the computational complexity will increase.

3.5.3 *K-Fold Cross-Validation*

As can be seen, both the validation set approach and the LOOCV are a bit extreme, as shown by their respective pros and cons. Now let's look at a more balanced approach known as the k-fold cross-validation.

Figure 3.9 presents the design of the typical k-fold cross-validation. First, the original data set is divided into k subsets of comparable size or, in statistics, we call them k folds. Second, one of the k folds is randomly selected as the validation set, and the remaining $(k-1)$ folds are used as the training set. The respective test error is then estimated based on the performance of prediction in the validation set. Last, repeat the exact procedure k times by using each fold as the validation set. The testing MSEs estimated using different validation sets are denoted as MSE_1, MSE_2,..., MSE_n. The k-fold cross-validation estimates the testing MSE by calculating the average of the sum of the testing MSEs:

$$CV_{(k)} = \frac{1}{k}\sum_{i=1}^{k} MSE_i.$$

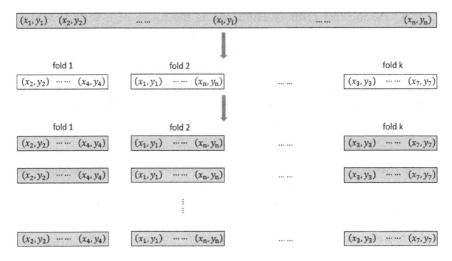

Figure 3.9: The design of k-fold cross-validation.

Both the validation set approach and LOOCV can be considered a particular case of the k-fold cross-validation approach. LOOCV is n-fold cross-validation (i.e., $k = n$). The validation set approach is a two-fold cross-validation (i.e., $k = 2$).

Pros

- Compared to LOOCV, which can become computationally intensive when n is large, k-fold cross-validation is computationally feasible as it only needs to fit the model for k times.

- Regarding the bias–variance tradeoff, k-fold cross validation possesses a much smaller bias than the validation set approach. As mentioned earlier, the validation set approach tends to overestimate the actual test error rate, as only a small subset of data is used for fitting the model. In comparison, $(k - 1)$ folds of data (that is $\frac{n(k-1)}{k}$ observations) are used as the training data in the k-fold cross-validation. Although k-fold cross validation may still overestimate the actual test error, it is much less biased than the validation set approach. In fact, in terms of bias reduction, the performance ranking is LOOCV > k-fold cross validation > validation set approach. LOOCV returns a nearly unbiased estimate since it uses almost all data points ($n - 1$ observations) to fit the model.

- k-fold cross validation possesses a much smaller variance as compared to LOOCV. As can be proved in statistics, the mean of highly correlated variables has a higher variance than those not highly correlated. In

LOOCV, the test error is estimated as the mean of n testing MSEs. Since the training data used for fitting the n different models differ by only one observation, their results will be highly correlated. The estimate of test error rate from LOOCV will have higher variance since it is calculated as the mean of n highly correlated MSEs. In terms of variance reduction, the performance ranking is validation set approach > k-fold cross validation > LOOCV.

Cons
- The user needs to choose the parameter k. Nevertheless, the good news is that researchers have already identified the recommended choice of k values based on multiple empirical experiments. As a rule of thumb, $k = 5$ or $k = 10$ often gives quite balanced performance: not excessively high bias, nor excessively high variance.

Remark: All the three cross-validation approaches discussed so far are constrained by an underlying assumption: the data points (to be resampled) come from an *i.i.d.* (independent and identical distribution) process. Unfortunately, this assumption is often violated in practice, especially in the financial industry. Taking the stock price as an example, the data consists of a time series. The stock price tomorrow is very likely correlated with the price today. The assumption of prices being independent does not hold in this situation. Examples that show the impact of non-compliance with the i.i.d. assumption on the cross-validation results can be found in Ogrisel (2013).[3] Two alternative cross-validation approaches are needed to handle cases when the data points are not *i.i.d.*

References/Further Readings

Bacallado, S. & Taylor J. (2020). Shrinkage methods. Retrieved April 30, 2021, from https://web.stanford.edu/class/stats202/notes/Model-selection/Shrinkage.html.

Friedman, J., Hastie, T., & Tibshirani, R. (2001). *The Elements of Statistical Learning: Data Mining, Inference, and Prediction.* (Vol. 1, No. 10). New York: Springer series in statistics.

James, G., Witten, D., Hastie, T., & Tibshirani, R. (2013). *An Introduction to Statistical Learning: With Applications* in R. (Vol. 112, p. 18). New York: Springer.

---

[3] Ogrisel. (August 20, 2013). Impact of the dependency between samples on cross-validation test score estimate. Retrieved from https://github.com/ogrisel/notebooks/blob/master/Non%20IID%20cross-validation.ipynb.

Jason, B. (March 18, 2016). Gentle introduction to the bias−variance tradeoff in machine learning. Retrieved April 20, 2021, from https://machinelearning mastery.com/gentle-introduction-to-the-bias-variance-trade-off-in-machine-learning/.

Jason, B. (May 23, 2018). A gentle introduction to *k*-fold cross-validation. Retrieved from https://machinelearningmastery.com/k-fold-cross-validation/ #:~:text=Cross%2Dvalidation%20is%20a%20resampling,k%2Dfold%20 cross%2Dvalidation.

Matt, B. (April 18, 2017). A one-stop shop for principal component analysis. Retrieved from https://towardsdatascience.com/a-one-stop-shop-for-principal-component-analysis-5582fb7e0a9c.

Matthias. D. (November 30, 2018). Linear, quadratic, and regularized discriminant analysis. Retrieved from https://www.datascienceblog.net/post/machine-learning/linear-discriminant-analysis/.

Michal, O. (April 06, 2019). A comparison of shrinkage and selection methods for linear regression. Retrieved from https://towardsdatascience.com/a-comparison-of-shrinkage-and-selection-methods-for-linear-regression-ee4dd3a71f16.

Park, J. (September 25, 2020). ML: Subset selection & shrinkage methods. Retrieved from https://jeheonpark93.medium.com/ml-subset-selection-shrinkage-methods-74d6e99ecaaf.

Seema, S. (May 21, 2018). Understanding the bias−variance tradeoff. Retrieved April 30, 2021, from https://towardsdatascience.com/understanding-the-bias-variance-tradeoff-165e6942b229.

3.6 Sample Questions

Question 1
Which of the following is wrong about MSE (mean squared error)?

(a) MSE measures how well a model fits a data set
(b) A model usually returns smaller training MSE than testing MSE
(c) The value of MSE is the same regardless of which data set you use

Question 2
With the increase of model flexibility, the training MSE will

(a) Increase
(b) Decrease
(c) It depends

Question 3
With the increase of model flexibility, the testing MSE will

(a) Increase
(b) Decrease
(c) It depends

Question 4
Which one of the following is true for a model with low complexity?

(a) High bias, low variance
(b) High bias, high variance
(c) Low bias, high variance

Question 5
Which of the following is true?

(a) Compared to the least square estimation, LASSO is more flexible and hence will return better prediction accuracy.
(b) Compared to the least square estimation, LASSO is more flexible and hence will return worse prediction accuracy.
(c) Compared to the least square estimation, LASSO is less flexible and hence will return better prediction accuracy.

Question 6
Which one of the following approaches may return model coefficients of exactly value zero?

(a) Linear regression
(b) Ridge regression
(c) LASSO

Question 7
Which one of the following statements is wrong?

(a) LASSO consistently outperforms Ridge regression
(b) Ridge regression and linear regression may return the same fitted model
(c) LASSO can perform variable selection

Question 8

If the predictors in a k-variable model ($k < p$) are selected by the forward selection approach then:

(a) The ($k + 1$)-variable model is identified by the forward selection approach.
(b) The ($k + 1$)-variable model is identified by the backward selection approach.
(c) The ($k + 1$)-variable model is identified by the best subset selection approach.

Question 9

Which one of the following approaches may return model coefficients of exactly value zero?

(a) Linear regression
(b) Ridge regression
(c) LASSO

Question 10

Which one of the following statements is wrong?

(a) LASSO consistently outperforms Ridge regression.
(b) Ridge regression and linear regression may return the same fitted model.
(c) LASSO can perform variable selection.

Question 11

Which one of the following statements is wrong in PCR?

(a) The first principal component has the largest percentage of variation explained.
(b) There is no strict rule on how many principal components we should choose.
(c) PCR consistently outperforms linear regression as it overcomes the overfitting issue.

Question 12
What kind of information can we obtain from a scree plot?

(a) The percentage of variation explained by each principal component.
(b) The total number of principal components.
(c) Both a and b.

Question 13
Which one of the following statements is correct?

(a) The decision boundary of LDA can be either linear or nonlinear.
(b) LDA is expected to outperform logistic regression.
(c) LDA can be used to classify multiple predictors.

Question 14
Which one of the following statements is not correct?

(a) If the data follows approximately a normal distribution, LDA will outperform logistic regression.
(b) In terms of flexibility, LDA < QDA < KNN.
(c) QDA is always preferred to LDA.

Question 15
What is not true about the validation set approach?

(a) It is simple to implement
(b) It is easy to understand
(c) It always gives the same result when the procedure is repeated

Question 16
Which of the following best describes the LOOCV approach?

(a) It repeats for $n-1$ iterations
(b) It returns the same results no matter how many times it is repeated
(c) It is fast in computation

Question 17

Which one of the following approaches is the worst in overestimating the actual test error?

(a) Validation set approach
(b) K-fold cross-validation
(c) LOOCV

Question 18

Which one of the following is correct?

(a) For k-fold cross-validation, a larger k value usually means a larger variance.
(b) LOOCV approach can be considered as 1-fold cross-validation.
(c) K-fold cross-validation may still return a good estimate of the test error rate for time series data.

Solutions

Question 1

Solution: Option **c** is correct.

The MSE is different when it is computed using a different data set.

Question 2

Solution: Option **b** is correct.

Question 3

Solution: Option **c** is correct.

With the increase in flexibility, the testing MSE will first decrease and then increase.

Question 4

Solution: Option **a** is correct.

Question 5

Solution: Option **c** is correct.

Question 6

Solution: Option **c** is correct.

Question 7

Solution: Option **a** is correct.

Question 8

Solution: Option **a** is correct.

In forward selection, the predictors selected in the previous iteration are always kept for the next iteration.

Question 9

Solution: Option **c** is correct.

Only LASSO can constrain the coefficients to exactly zero.

Question 10

Solution: Option **a** is correct.

No model is consistently better than another in all data sets.

Question 11

Solution: Option **c** is correct.

When the dimension is low, linear regression may perform better.

Question 12

Solution: Option **c** is correct.

Question 13

Solution: Option **c** is correct.

Question 14

Solution: Option c is correct.

Question 15

Solution: Option **c** is correct.

The training and testing are different every time. As such, the result is different.

Question 16

Solution: Option **b** is correct.

It repeats for n iterations and it is usually slow in computation.

Question 17

Solution: Option **a** is correct.

It has the highest bias usually.

Question 18

Solution: Option **a** is correct.

When the k value is large, the data are divided into more folds and each fold has less amount of data. The results tend to have larger variations across the fold. LOOCV approach is an n-fold cross-validation approach.

Chapter 4

Deep Learning

4.1 Artificial Neural Networks (ANN)/ Multilayer Perceptron (MLP)

In this chapter, you will learn what deep learning is. We will explore specifically the artificial neural networks (ANN), which is also known as the multilayer perceptron (MLP).

Learning Objectives
- Understand the architecture of ANN.
- Understand the forward feed and backpropagation algorithms.
- Understand different types of activation functions.
- Understand how loss function and stochastic gradient descent optimize the learning process.
- Distinguish between batch and epoch.

Main Takeaways

Main Points
- ANN is the fundamental archetype of neural networks. It is the basic building block of many other more complex neural network archetypes.
- Optimization is the core of fitting the neural network models.

Main Terms
- **Neural network:** An algorithm represented by nodes and connectors that predict the output value from input values.

- **Activation function:** Nonlinear function that will further refine the change of the output value.
- **Backpropagation:** The process of revising and optimizing the weighting factors.
- **Loss function:** The function to evaluate the quality of fit of the model.
- **Batch:** The number of observations used for backpropagation in one iteration.
- **Epoch:** The number of times that all observations run through all the iterations.

4.1.1 *What is Deep Learning?*

As a subfield of machine learning, deep learning tries to learn from successive layers of increasingly meaningful data representation. The term "deep" means repeated simple manipulation or representation for many layers. The manipulation of data in each layer can be simple. However, when the layer gets deeper, the power of deep learning will be revealed.

(a) Why Deep Learning?

For those familiar with the history of deep learning, the concept of neural networks is not something new. It has existed since the 1980s. In addition, the majority of the underlying theories which govern the deep learning models have barely progressed in the past decades. In other words, the basic theories we use today are the same as what has developed a few decades ago. So what is the reason that deep learning has become so popular lately?

The following are a few driving forces that push the widespread use of deep learning.

(1) **Big data:** The number of users of mobile devices has increased several times in the past decade. With the advancement of the Internet and sensors, the cost of collecting data has decreased substantially. As a result, hundreds or even thousands of data can be generated and collected every second. Therefore, deep learning algorithms can train good models with much data.

(2) **Computational power:** The empirical instead of the theoretical guides the development of this area. The training of deep learning models requires much computational power. This was a significant limitation in the 1990s. With the fast progress in CPU, and GPU, we can now run operations a few hundred times faster than before.

(3) **Development of deep learning platforms and tools:** Only computer experts could work on deep learning projects in the old days when neural networks were coded from scratch. Today, various excellent neural network modeling platforms like tensorflow, Keras, allow the development of a deep learning model with few codes.

(b) Neural Networks Zoo

Since neural networks are the building blocks of deep learning, the terms neural networks (NN) and deep learning (DL) are often used interchangeably. Although the biological neurons inspire the term neural network, there is no evidence showing that our brain works the same way as NN. As such, you do not need any knowledge of neuroscience to understand DL. We often call it an artificial neural network (ANN) to distinguish from the biological neural network.

With the development of DL, there are quite a number of NN architectures popping up now and then. Fjodor van Veen[1] from Asimov institute compiled a neural network zoo as displayed in Figure 4.1. You probably have seen it from somewhere if you are not entirely new to DL. Since each type of NN architecture may be suitable for a different kind of problem, it is impossible to cover all of them in-depth. In this chapter, we will only cover five of the most commonly used and foundational types of NN, namely *artificial neural networks* (ANN), which is also known as the multiple layer perceptron (MLP), *convolutional neural networks* (CNN), *recurrent neural networks* (RNN), long short-term memory (LSTM), and generative adversarial network (GAN).

ANN or MLP is the fundamental archetype of NNs. It is made up of a few layers of neurons or nodes. It is the building block of other NN archetypes like CNN or RNN. A simple structure of ANN or MLP is shown in Figure 4.2.

The neural network is represented using circles and directed arrows. The circles are called *nodes* or *neurons*. The links connecting all the nodes are called *connectors*. On the left side, it starts with a series of nodes called the *input layer*. This takes in the values of input variables. For instance, if we are to use this NN to predict a handwritten number (0 to 9), the input layer will be the pixels of the image. If the image of a

---

[1]Van Veen, F. & Leijnen, S. (2019). The Neural Network Zoo. Retrieved from https://www.asimovinstitute.org/neural-network-zoo.

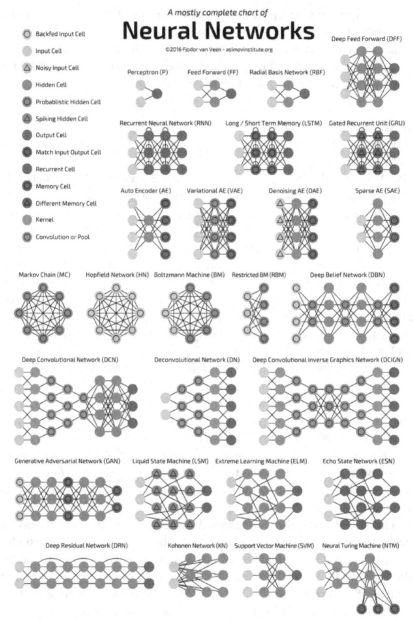

Figure 4.1: The neural network zoo.

Source: Van Veen, F. & Leijnen, S. (2019). The Neural Network Zoo. Retrieved from https://www.asimovinstitute.org/neural-network-zoo.

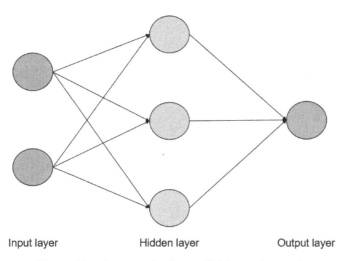

Input layer   Hidden layer   Output layer

Figure 4.2: An example of an artificial neural network.

handwritten letter contains 28 × 28 pixels, the input layer will consist of 784 nodes. Each node includes a value in the range [0,1], representing the blackness scale for each pixel. For example, 0 represents white, 1 represents black, and other numbers in-between stand for a different level of grey.

The output layer is on the right-hand side. This represents the output variables we want to predict from this NN model.

The nodes in the middle are called the *hidden layer*. In contrast to the input and output layer, which are meaningful variables with tangible values, the nodes in the middle are called the hidden layers because their meanings are hidden. In terms of modeling, the core is used to determine the structure of the hidden layers which infer the output based on the input information.

(c) Forward Feed Algorithm
To learn about the underlying mechanism of an ANN model, let's work through a simple example.

Figure 4.3 is a two-layer (excluding the input layer) ANN with 2 input nodes x_1, x_2, 3 hidden nodes h_1, h_2, h_3 and 1 output node y. The weighting factors of each connector are represented as w_{ij} where i, j are the index of

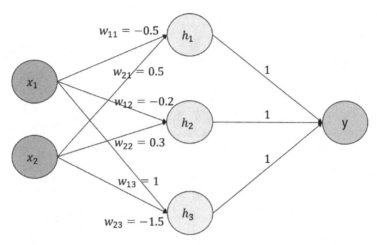

Figure 4.3:   An example of 2-layer ANN.

nodes linked by the connector. What the ANN does is compute the weighted sum.

For instance, we are given an observation $(x_1, x_2, y) = (1,2,1)$

$$h_1 = x_1w_{11} + x_2w_{21} = 1 * (-0.5) + 2 * (0.5) = 0.5;$$

$$h_2 = x_1w_{12} + x_2w_{22} = 1 * (-0.2) + 2 * (0.3) = 0.4;$$

$$h_3 = x_1w_{13} + x_2w_{23} = 1 * (1) + 2 * (-1.5) = -2.$$

So far, all relationships are linear. To introduce nonlinearity, we will apply an activation function to the signal received in the hidden node and output node.

(d) Activation Functions
Activation functions are nonlinear functions that will further manipulate the small change of the value. Here are a few commonly used activation functions:

(i) **Rectified linear unit activation function (ReLU):** In mathematics, $\text{ReLU}(x) = \max(0, x)$. Its shape is shown in Figure 4.4.

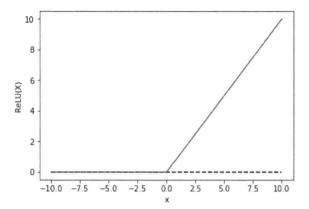

Figure 4.4: ReLU function.

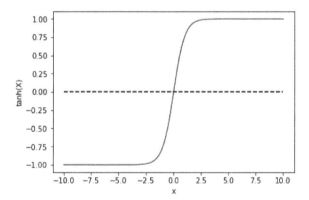

Figure 4.5: Tanh(x) function.

(ii) **Tanh(x):** It ranges from $[-1,1]$. The advantage is that the negative inputs will be mapped strongly negative, and the zero inputs will be mapped near zero in the tanh graph. The function is differentiable and monotonic. It is also a sigmoid (s-shaped curve), as seen in Figure 4.5.

(iii) **Sigmoid function:** It is called a sigmoid as it has an S-shape curve. The good thing about sigmoid is its value exists between $[0,1]$. It is helpful if the problem predicts a probability or predicts the classification. A typical sigmoid curve is plotted in Figure 4.6.

(iv) **Leaky ReLU:** As compared to conventional ReLU, the curve of leaky ReLU has a slight leak which provides a larger range of values to the function. For instance, in Figure 4.7, the value for the slope a can be 0.01. If $a \neq 0.01$, it is called randomized ReLU.

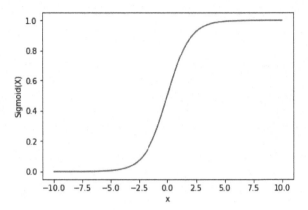

Figure 4.6:   Sigmoid function.

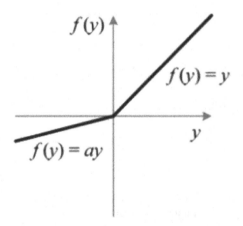

Figure 4.7:   Leaky ReLU function.

Now let us get back to the forward feed algorithm. After we computed the signal values for h_1, h_2, h_3 as 0.5, 0.4, −2 suppose a ReLU activation is applied.

The hidden node values after activation will be:

$$h_1 = \text{ReLU}(0.5) = 0.5;$$

$$h_2 = \text{ReLU}(0.4) = 0.4;$$

$$h_3 = \text{ReLU}(-2) = 0.$$

The hidden node values are then passed to the output layer. Suppose we apply the sigmoid activation function to the output node, then the final output value will be

$$y = \text{ReLU}(0.5 * 1 + 0.4 * 1 + 0 * 1) = 0.9.$$

Based on the input and the current weighting factors, the predicted output value is 0.9. But the actual observation of output is 1. There is an error of 0.1 in the sense of mean absolute error (MAE) or 0.01 in mean squared error (MSE).

Next is the loss function concept, which defines the penalty for the error.

(e) Loss Function
For the regression problem, we can use the following loss functions:

- mean absolute error (MAE)
- mean squared error (MSE)
- mean absolute percentage error (MAPE)

For a classification problem, we can use the following loss functions:

$$H_p(q) = -\frac{1}{N}\sum_{i=1}^{N} y_i \cdot \log(p(y_i)) + (1 - y_i) \cdot \log(1 - p(y_i))$$

Binary cross entropy error computes the distance between two probability vectors, namely the prob (output label = class 1) and prob (output label = class 0).

(1) Optimization (learning process)
The rule of thumb is to minimize the loss function value as much as we can. Finding a smaller loss or the optimal loss is called the learning process or the optimization process. The idea is simple.

First, starting with a randomized assignment of weighting factors compute the predicted output using the forward feed algorithm.

Next, evaluate the error using the chosen loss function.

Repeat the first two steps via revising the weighting factors and re-evaluating the error. The revision should be done so that the updated error becomes at least no worse than the previous iteration.

(2) Backpropagation algorithm[2] and stochastic gradient descent
Revising and optimizing the weighting factors is known as the backpropagation algorithm. It is called backpropagation (short for "backward propagation of errors") because we are revising the weighting backwards from the error of output to input.

Since the signal values are computed as the activated value on top of the dot products of node values and weighting factors, we can theoretically identify the explicit expression of $L_e(w)$. L_e denotes the loss function or prediction error of the model, and it is a function of the weighting factors w.

If the activation functions are all convex (for example, the linear activation function), the optimal global solution can be computed.

If the activation is nonconvex, we can use the heuristic method like the stochastic gradient descent (SGD) algorithm to find the Pareto optimal solution.

Training the NN with gradient descent requires calculating the gradient of the error function $E(X, \theta)$ with respect to the weightage w and bias b. Depending on the learning rate α in the gradient descent algorithm, each iteration updates the weightage and bias parameters as

$$\theta^{t+1} = \theta^{t} - \alpha \frac{\partial E(X,\theta^{t})}{\partial \theta},$$

where the superscript of θ represents the parameter value at the corresponding iteration.

(3) Batch and epoch
To run the backpropagation algorithm, you need to specify the batch size and the number of epochs. On the one hand, you can input one data observation to apply the SGD for each iteration. However, this is not very efficient. On the other hand, you can also input all data available at one go. But the amount of data may be too large for the machine to handle. As such, we pass small batches of data into the machine each time.

---

[2]Backpropagation. Brilliant.org. Retrieved May 12, 2021, from https://brilliant.org/wiki/backpropagation/#:~:text=Backpropagation%2C%20short%20for%20%22backward%20propagation,to%20the%20neural%20network's%20weights.

The batch size is the number of observations that we input to the SGD for one iteration.

One epoch is when the entire data set is passed forward and backward through the NN once. We need to pass the entire data set through the NN multiple times to use the limited data fully.

The number of epochs can be set to an integer value between one and infinity. That is to say, you can run the algorithm for any number of iterations as you deem appropriate. Apart from specifying a fixed number of epochs, you may also set a stopping criterion. For instance, one possible criterion is that when the value of error in the loss function is smaller than a threshold value or there is no more significant improvement in the error rate, the algorithm can stop. In this case, the user does not need to physically fix the value for the epoch and the algorithm itself will determine internally what is the best number of epochs.

4.2 Convolutional Neural Network (CNN)

Another commonly used NN is the convolutional neural network (CNN). CNN is best used for the data in which the sequence matters. For instance, if we try to analyze voice data, the intensity in each voice frequency band across different time stamps matters. If we switch the order of the voice data in a speech, its meaning will be changed completely. Similarly, for an image, the pattern is based on the sequence of pixels. If we reorganize the pixel column, it will not look like the same picture. The underlying guideline for CNN is that the closer the data columns are, the more closely related they are.

Learning Objectives
- Understand the architecture of CNN.
- Understand the working mechanism of CNN.

Main Takeaways

Main Points
- The working mechanism of CNN can be summarized as a sequence: [Input — Conv — Pool — Activation — FC].

Main Terms
- **Feature (Filter) Matrix:** The composing features or patterns (like vertical lines, horizontal lines, edges, bends) that constitute the image.

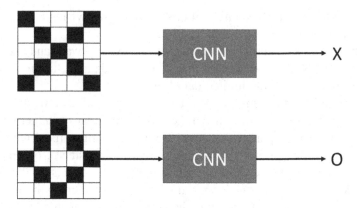

Figure 4.8: Input image and output predicted letter.

- **Conv:** Computes the dot product between the input and feature matrices across all local regions.
- **Pool:** This layer is based on the rationale that the pooled outputs should not change when the input is varied by a small amount.

4.2.1 *What CNN Can Do?*

A CNN is a DL algorithm which takes in an input image, examines the features of various aspects/objects in the image (via assigning different weights and biases to the neural network), and eventually produces the predicted output or differentiates the image from others, or classifies it.

For instance, in Figure 4.8, given an input letter, the CNN is able to differentiate which is letter "X" and which is letter "O".

However, in practice, the handwritten letter will not be as regular as what is shown in Figure 4.8, otherwise there is no difficulty in recognizing what letter it is at all. The letter can be written very differently depending on each person's writing style. Figure 4.9 shows four possible cases of a handwritten letter. Translation: the letter is not written in the middle of the square. Scaling: the letter is not filling up the square. It is either larger or smaller than expected. Rotation: the letter is tilted or twisted. Weight: the letter is thicker or thinner than expected. CNN is trying to capture the key pattern by analyzing the spatial or temporal dependency.

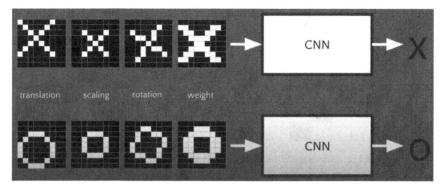

Figure 4.9: Variations of the handwritten letters.
Source: https://www.youtube.com/watch?v=JB8T_zN7ZC0.

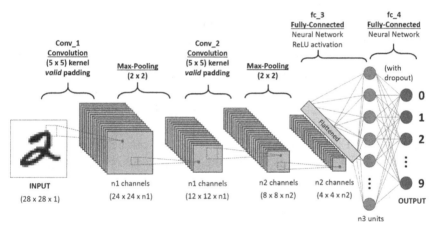

Figure 4.10: Example of convolutional neural networks.
Source: https://towardsdatascience.com/a-comprehensive-guide-to-convolutional-neural-networks-the-eli5-way-3bd2b1164a53.

4.2.2 The Working Mechanism of CNN

Figure 4.10 shows an example of the flow for CNN. The working mechanism of CNN can be summarized as a sequence:

[Input — Conv — Pool — Activation — FC].

Some of the procedures can be repeated for easy processing or better results. For instance, in Figure 4.10, pooling is done twice. Taking some simple patterns as an example, we explain how CNN works in a highly simplified setting where each procedure is done only once.

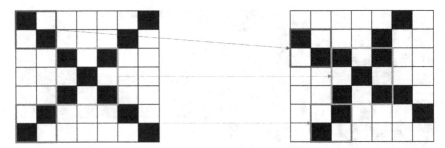

Figure 4.11:   An image is made up from various composing building blocks.

Input: The raw pixel data of the image. If the pixel is in black, it has a value of 1. If the pixel is in white, it has a value of -1. The input can be represented as a matrix of pixel values. For instance, the image is represented by a 28×28 matrix of pixel values.

Conv: Computes the dot product between the input and feature matrices across all local regions.

Feature (filter) matrix: These are like the small Lego bricks which are used to build up the house. CNN identifies the composing features or patterns (like vertical lines, horizontal lines, edges, bends) that make up the image. The pixel values denote the feature matrix associated with different pixels. Like in Figure 4.11, the letter "X" can be decomposed into building blocks. As long as these composing patterns can be mapped, the CNN is able to differentiate the letter from the others.

Suppose the dimension of the feature matrix is 3×3. In that case, you can imagine that we overlay the 3×3 matrix on top of the 28×28 input matrix and shift it over all possible overlapping regions without repetition as depicted in Figure 4.12. This will lead to a feature map of dimension 26×26, whose entry values are computed as the dot product between the input and feature matrices.

Pool: This layer is based on the rationale that the pooled outputs should not change when the input is varied by a small amount. The commonly used pooling methods include the max pooling, min pooling and average pooling. As the names suggest, max, min, and average pooling return the max, min, and average values of all entries in a window. For pooling, we need to decide the *pooling window size* (for example, 2×2) and the *pooling stride* (usually 2). The pooling stride defines how many

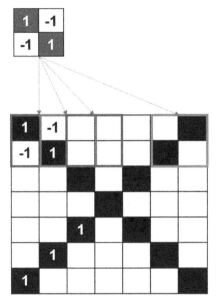

Figure 4.12: Overlay the feature matrix on the input image without repetition.

steps to shift the pooling matrix every iteration. This will result in an updated matrix of dimension 13×13. Similarly, it will overlay the pooling matrix onto the output from the "Conv" procedure.

Activation: The most popular activation function is the rectified linear function (ReLU). This introduces nonlinearity to the system. The following is a ReLU function. if the number is negative, ReLU function returns 0. If the number is positive, its value remains the same.

Depending on the requirements of the problem, we can have multiple combinations of Conv, pool, and activation before we go to the FC stage.

FC: Fully connected layer. The matrix obtained from the pooling layer is re-written as a string of nodes. This manipulation is also called *flattening*. The value of each node is considered as a vote on the final output. For instance, in Figure 4.13, suppose the final output is a 2×2 matrix. Flattening re-writes the matrix as a list of numbers. Then we can fit a conventional neural network. It is called a fully connected layer as each cell is connected with all possible cells. Based on the training, the

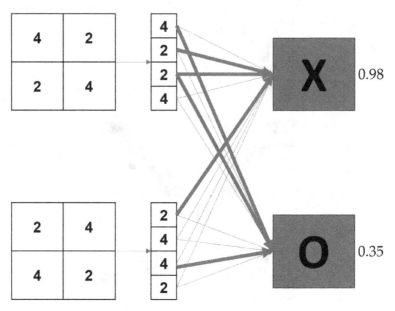

Figure 4.13: Flattening and fully connected layer.

chance of having the letter as "X" has a probability of 0.98[3] while there is a probability of 0.35[4] it is the letter "O". Consequently, the CNN will conclude that the input image is the letter "X".

4.3 Recurrent Neural Network (RNN) and Long Short-Term Memory (LSTM)

This chapter will explain another two types of NNs, namely recurrent neural network (RNN) and long short-term memory (LSTM).

Learning Objectives
- Understand the architecture of RNN.
- Understand the architecture of LSTM.

---

[3]This is just an artificial value I created for the purpose of demonstration. The actual value depends on the training data available.
[4]*Ibid.*

Main Takeaways

Main Points
- RNN is an ANN that works best on sequential data.
- Long short-term memory networks are a special kind of RNN, capable of learning long-term dependencies.

Main Terms
- **RNN:** Recurrent neural networks.
- **LSTM:** Long short-term memory.

4.3.1 *Recurrent Neural Network (RNN)*

RNN is an ANN that works the best on sequential data like stock price, interest rate (ordered by time stamp), and the sentence (the order of words determines the meaning).

Suppose you are only given a ball on the left-hand side of Figure 4.14. It will be very difficult to predict the direction that the ball is moving towards. It can be left, right, up, or down. Your prediction will be as good as random guesses with this limited information. However, if we are given the snapshots of the ball at different time stamps (right-hand side of Figure 4.14), it is much easier to predict the ball's movement direction. This is a sequence, in which data has a particular order.

For instance, if we want to ask ANN to remember the past information when predicting the future value, what we can do is shown in Figure 4.15. The output will re-enter the model as input to predict the next value.

Text is one type of sequential data. For example, the two sentences "he is George" and "is he George" are both made of the same data components {"he", "is", "George"}. However, due to the sequence of the data, the two sentences have different meanings.

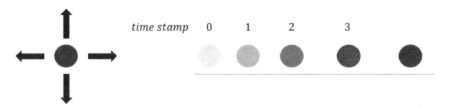

Figure 4.14:   Predict the direction of ball movement.

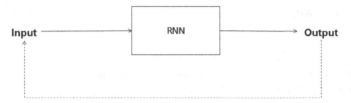

Figure 4.15: RNN architecture.

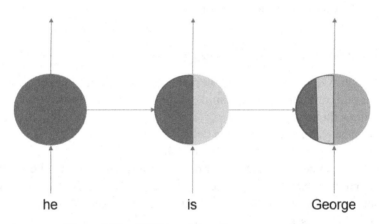

he   is   George

Figure 4.16: RNN remembers the sequence of data.

Figure 4.16 shows how to fit the sentence "he is George". While processing, it passes the previous hidden state to the next step of the sequence. The encoded output of a cell or layers of cells is called the hidden state. The hidden state acts as the NN's memory. It holds information regarding prior data the network has encountered. For instance, the first step is to input the word "he" and RNN encodes "he" and produces an output. For the next step, we input the word "is" and the hidden state from previous step. The hidden state is the output from the cell after encoding the word "he". The RNN will now have information on both words "he" and "is". As will be further explained later in long short-term memory, the LSTM retains an internal state which is called the cell state which is not an output. Cell state is a memory of the LSTM cell and hidden state is the output of the cell.

(a) Exploding/Vanishing Gradient Problem
In theory, RNNs are capable of handling long-term dependency. However, you may have noticed the odd distribution of shades in the hidden states.

This illustrates an issue with RNNs known as short-term memory. Short-term memory is caused by the infamous exploding/vanishing gradient problem.

As the RNN processes more steps, it has trouble retaining information from previous steps. As you can see, the information from the word "he" is almost non-existent at the final time step. Short-Term memory and the vanishing gradient are due to the nature of back-propagation. The problem was explored in depth by Hochreiter (1991)[5] and Bengio *et al.* (1994),[6] who found some pretty fundamental reasons why it might be difficult.

RNN is not something completely different from a normal NN. It can be considered multiple copies of the same normal NN if we unroll it, each passing a feedback message to its successor. According to the chain rule, the gradient is represented as the product of a series of derivatives when doing backpropagation. On the one hand, the product of many large values will explode. This will lead to what we called the **exploding gradient problem**. On the other hand, the product of many small values will shrink to zero. This corresponds to what we call the **vanishing gradient problem**.

If the gradient explodes, changes in the weights will cause a dramatic fluctuation in the final output. It will lead to NaN[7] weight parameters that can no longer be updated at the extreme. This will result in a very unstable network. If the gradient is vanishing, even a large change in the weights and biases of the initial layer, which should represent the core features of the NN, may not affect the output effectively. In the extreme case, the gradient may approach zero and stop the network from learning at all.

Due to the exploding/vanishing gradient problem, the traditional RNN model may not learn effectively. This can be resolved by introducing LSTM, which can choose to forget or remember certain information in the earlier states.

(b) Long Short-Term Memory (LSTM)

LSTM networks are a special kind of RNN, capable of learning long-term dependencies. They were introduced by Hochreiter & Schmidhuber

---

[5] https://people.idsia.ch//~juergen/SeppHochreiter1991ThesisAdvisorSchmidhuber.pdf.

[6] Bengio, Y., Simard, P., & Frasconi, P. (1994). Learning long-term dependencies with gradient descent is difficult. *IEEE Transactions on Neural Networks*, 5(2), 157–166.

[7] "In computing, NaN, stands for Not a Number. It is a member of a numeric data type that can be interpreted as a value that is undefined or unrepresentable, especially in floating-point arithmetic". For example NaN can be caused by infinity or division of zero.

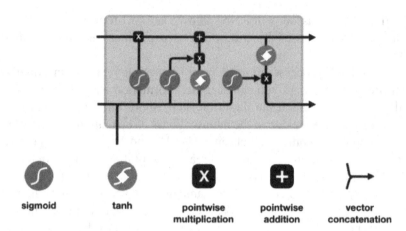

Figure 4.17:   Architecture of LSTM.

Source: https://towardsdatascience.com/illustrated-guide-to-lstms-and-gru-s-a-step-by-step-explanation-44e9eb85bf21.

(1997). An LSTM has a similar control flow as a RNN. It processes the current data, meanwhile taking the historical information passed down from previous steps into consideration, as it propagates forward. The differences are the operations within the LSTM's cells.

The fundamental components of LSTM architecture are the cell states and various gates is shown in Figure 4.17. The cell state serves as a database which memorizes the state information at the different time stamps. In theory, the cell state can go through all stages of the network sequence, carrying all the information from early history. This is to overcome the obstacle of short-term memory.

The job of the gate is to control whether certain information should be added to or removed from the cell state at a time stamp. The gates are also different types of NNs that control the cell state's information flow via manipulations of the values. Not all historical information from time 0 is useful in determining the next output. The gates will help the network decide how long should the past memory should be. This is also why the network is called LSTM. Essentially, some data are kept in the long term memory, while others are remembered only for the short term.

In LSTM, we make frequent use of the sigmoid activation function. Whatever values go into the sigmoid activation function, it will be scaled between 0 and 1. How will this help decide whether memory should be removed or kept? The NN will compute the dot product between the cell state values and the sigmoid function. No matter what value is multiplied by 0, the result is 0. This means that the network learns that this value is unimportant and should be forgotten. On the contrary, whatever value you have in the cell, after being multiplied by 1, will return the same value itself. In this sense, the information is well-retained and remembered.

Let us dig a little deeper into what the various gates are doing. We have three different gates that regulate information flow in an LSTM cell: a forget gate, an input gate, and an output gate.

(1) Forget gate

As its name suggests, this gate decides what information should or should not be forgotten. The input to the forget gate includes the cell information from the previous hidden state and input information from the current state. The forget gate contains a sigmoid function as the activation function. It determines what information from the past should be kept or removed based on the current state. The output of the forget gate is a value in the range [0,1], which can be thought of as the probability of keeping the memory. The closer to 0 means to forget and the closer to 1 means to keep.

(2) Input gate

The input gate is used to update the cell state. Again, the previous cell state values and the current input features are passed to the input gate. These inputs are passed to a sigmoid function that will decide what values will be updated by transforming the values to be between 0 and 1. A value close to 0 means not important and 1 means important. You also pass the hidden state and current input into the tanh function to squish values between −1 and 1 to help regulate the network. Then you multiply the tanh output with the sigmoid output. The sigmoid output will decide which information is important to keep from the tanh output.

(3) Cell state

The cell state gets pointwise multiplied by the output from the forget gate. If the values from the forget gate are close to 0, it will drop the memory from an earlier state. Then we take the output from the input gate and do a pointwise addition which updates the cell state to new values that the NN finds relevant. That gives us our new cell state.

(4) Output gate
The output gate decides what the next cell state should be. Remember that the cell state contains information on previous inputs. The hidden state is also used for predictions. First, we pass the previous hidden state and the current input into a sigmoid function. Then we pass the newly modified cell state to the tanh function. We multiply the tanh output with the sigmoid output to decide what information the hidden state should carry. The output is the hidden state. The new cell state and the new hidden state are then carried over to the next time step.

4.4 Generative Adversarial Networks (GAN)[8]

GANs were introduced in 2014 by Ian J. Goodfellow and co-authors. It belongs to the set of generative models. It means that they can produce/generate (we'll see how) new content. Yann LeCun described it as "the most interesting idea in the last ten years in Machine Learning".

Learning Objectives
- Understand the architecture of GAN.
- Understand the applications of GAN.

Main Takeaways

Main Points
- GANs is a generative model which can produce/generate new content.

Main Terms
- **GAN:** Generative adversarial networks.

Before we explain the GAN model, let us first look at a generative model. As its name suggests, it is used to generate data that has never been seen before yet still follows some specific pattern of distribution. The distribution comes from the pattern of existing data available.

Figure 4.18 shows the GAN structure have two components to their network: a generator (G) and a discriminator (D). These two components come together in the network and work as adversaries, pushing the performance of one another.

---

[8]Goodfellow, I. J., Pouget-Abadie, J., Mirza, M., Xu, B., Warde-Farley, D., Ozair, S., ... & Bengio, Y. (2014). Generative adversarial networks. arXiv preprint arXiv:1406.2661.

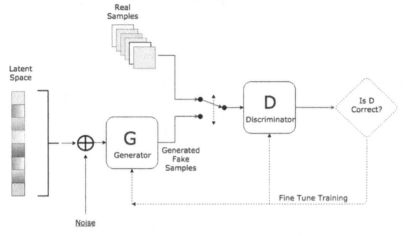

Figure 4.18: An overview of GAN structure.

Source: http://hunterheidenreich.com/blog/what-is-a-gan/.

4.4.1 *The Generator*

The generator is responsible for generating new examples of data. It inputs some latent variable (which we will refer to as z) and outputs data of the same form as data in the original data set. Compared to the existing data we observed, these samples are considered fake.

Latent variables are hidden variables. When discussing GANs, we have this notion of a "latent space" that we can sample from. We can continuously slide through this latent space that will have substantial (and often somewhat understandable effects) on the output when you have a well-trained GAN. We can think of the network generator as learning a function that maps from z (the latent space) to × (the target variable or, ideally, the real data distribution).

The goal of the generator is to produce fake samples of data that look like the real ones as much as possible.

4.4.2 *The Discriminator*

We can think of the discriminator as a policeman or detective. While the generator is trying to produce some fake data which looks real, the discriminator's role is to monitor or discriminate if the sample of data is real or fake. It is responsible for predicting if a given sample is real or fake. The output of the discriminator is a probability that reveals how real it thinks the sample data is. Of course, the higher the probability, the more closely the generator mimics the real distribution.

(a) Adversarial Competition

It is called "adversarial" because these two components are battling with each other. The generator and discriminator have opposite and conflicting goals: The generator wants to confuse the discriminator by creating samples that look more and more real. The discriminator wishes to always correctly identify whether a sample of data is real or fake.

(b) The Underlying Maths

Briefly speaking, the key goal of GANs is to find an equilibrium between the two halves of their network by solving the following minimax equation:

$$\min_{G} \max_{D} V(D,G) = \mathbb{E}_{x \sim p_{data}(x)}[\log D(x)] + \mathbb{E}_{z \sim p_z(z)}[\log(1 - D(G(z)))]$$

This is a minimax optimization problem. In this problem, we are trying to identify the optimal networks G (generator) and D (discriminator), specified by the weighting parameters. The failure of G is minimized while the chance of confusing D is maximized. In the first expectation, the data comes from the real sample. In this case, we want the discriminator to recognize it as real correctly. That's why we have the maximization of $logD(x)$ since the natural logarithm function is monotonically increasing. On the other hand, when the data is generated from the fake samples, we want it to look as real as possible. In other words, we want the chance of being identified as fake by the discriminator to be as small as possible.

At first glance, this may seem to be contradictory. From the perspective of D, it tries to maximize the objective function. When a real data sample comes, it maximizes the output and when a fake data sample comes, it minimizes the output (or maximizes its negation).

From the perspective of G, it tries to confuse D into thinking the fake data is the real one. G wishes to trick D into maximizing its output when handed a fake sample. That's why D is trying to maximize while G is trying to minimize.

Assuming that G and D are well parametrized and thus have enough capacity to learn, this minimax equation can help us reach the Nash equilibrium between the two.

4.5 Deep Learning Applications in Finance

There are several important areas where DL can be applied in the financial world. This chapter will introduce some of the representative applications.

Learning Objectives
- Identify and appraise the applications of DL in finance.
- Project the future potential of DL in finance.

Main Takeaways

Main Points
- DL has wide applications in finance, including stock market prediction, process automation, algorithmic trading, security, robot advisory, loan evaluation, underwriting, and credit scoring.
  Figure 4.19 lists some important areas of applications for DL.
- Prediction of stock market

In particular, the NNs, in particular RNN and LSTM, can be used to predict the future value of sequential data like the stock price. Another good thing about the stock market is that it generates an enormous amount of data every day. More hidden layers can be added to the DL models, gradually improving prediction accuracy. So far, the NN models are considered as one of the best models in terms of stock market prediction accuracy.

- Process automation
The automation of various processes which were labor-intensive is one of the most important applications of DL in finance. For instance, automating call service center, paperwork, report generating, staff training, manpower recruitment, and much more. It enables the company to lower costs while increasing productivity. Also, humans may make careless mistakes, especially for repetitive tasks. Machines are more reliable in this case.

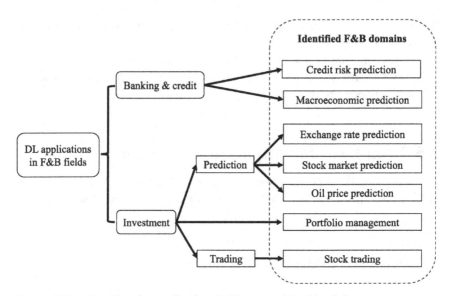

Figure 4.19:   Deep learning applications in Finance and Banking industry.

Note: Huang, J., Chai, J., & Cho, S. (2020). Deep learning in finance and banking: A literature review and classification. *Frontiers of Business Research in China*, 14, 1–24.

Below are some examples of process automation in banking[9]:

"JPMorgan Chase launched a Contract Intelligence (COiN) platform that leverages Natural Language Processing, one of the machine learning techniques. The solution processes legal documents and extracts essential data from them. Manual review of 12,000 annual commercial credit agreements would typically take up around 360,000 labor hours, whereas, machine learning allows us to review the same number of contracts in just a few hours".

"BNY Mello integrated process automation into their banking ecosystem. This innovation is responsible for $300,000 in annual savings and has brought about a wide range of operational improvements".

• Algorithmic trading

Since DL can deal with a large amount of data with hundreds or thousands of features, it can analyze information from a wide range of data sources much

---

[9]Konstantin, D. (July 11, 2018). Machine Learning in Finance: Why, What & How. Retrieved from https://towardsdatascience.com/machine-learning-in-finance-why-what-how-d524a2357b56.

faster than human beings. As we all know, the financial market is affected by many factors, and the decision to act has to be made within a short time. In algorithmic trading, the DL model can monitor and abstract information from various sources, including news, reports, databases. In addition, with the aid of high-performance computing and quantum computing, the model can be solved very quickly. This can provide the traders real-time decision support, which enables human traders to squeeze a slim advantage over the market average. Given the high frequency and large volume of trading operations, such small advantages could lead to significant profits.

- Security

With the growth and widespread adoption of digital banking, online transactions have increased dramatically. Fraud threats have become one of the significant risks in finance. DL is useful in detecting fraud activities which is essentially a classification problem.

Banks can use DL technologies to monitor thousands of transaction parameters for every account in real-time. The model can pick up the pattern of suspicious transaction behaviors. If a transaction is identified as a suspicious fraud behavior, the system can request additional identification from the user to validate the transaction or freeze it to protect the bank from loss. This verification and validation process takes just a few seconds, and the accuracy rate can be as high as 95%.

Other applications of financial security include the monitoring of money laundering, cybersecurity, and so on.

- Robo advisory

Robo advisory can be considered as some sort of automatic financial assistant. It is pretty common nowadays in the financial industry. It is usually deployed in two applications.

First, it can be seen in portfolio management. There are well-structured online wealth management platforms for most banks today. These platforms use algorithms and statistics to automatically optimize the portfolio allocation based on the customer's objective. For example, the customer can enter his or her present saving and investment goals (like the expected return rate). The robot assistant will automatically recommend the appropriate combination of assets across various investment opportunities.

Second, it can recommend personalized insurance plans or retirement plans. The customers may prefer the Robo advisory due to lower fees and personalized and calibrated recommendations.

- Loan application evaluation

Based on the applicants' profile and historical pattern of approving/rejecting loan applications, DL models can help loan issuers decide whether to approve a loan application, depending on the default probability.

- Underwriting and credit scoring

Underwriting tasks are widespread in the finance and insurance industry. Based on thousands of customer information, the machine can automatically learn how to assess risks and evaluate the credit score of a new customer. Banks and insurance companies have a large number of historical consumer data to use to train models.

References/Further Readings

Brandon, R. (August 19, 2016). How Convolutional Neural Networks Work? Available at https://www.youtube.com/watch?v=FmpDIaiMIeA.

Colah's blog. (August 27, 2015). Understanding LSTM Networks. Retrieved from https://colah.github.io/posts/2015-08-Understanding-LSTMs/.

Chollet, F. (2018). Deep Learning with Python (Vol. 361). New York: Manning.

Greff, K., Srivastava, R. K., Koutník, J., Steunebrink, B. R., & Schmidhuber, J. (2016). LSTM: A search space odyssey. *IEEE Transactions on Neural Networks and Learning Systems*, 28(10), 2222–2232.

Huang, J., Chai, J., & Cho, S. (2020). Deep learning in finance and banking: A literature review and classification. *Frontiers of Business Research in China*, 14, 1–24.

Hunter, H. (August 18, 2018). What is a Generative Adversarial Network? Retrieved from http://hunterheidenreich.com/blog/what-is-a-gan/.

Joseph, R. (January 08, 2019). Understanding Generative Adversarial Networks (GANs). Retrieved from https://towardsdatascience.com/understanding-generative-adversarial-networks-gans-cd6e4651a29.

Jozefowicz, R., Zaremba, W., & Sutskever, I. (June, 2015). An empirical exploration of recurrent network architectures. In *International Conference on Machine Learning* (pp. 2342–2350). PMLR.

Michael, P. (September 25, 2018). Illustrated Guide to LSTM's and GRU's: A Step by Step Explanation. Retrieved from https://towardsdatascience.com/illustrated-guide-to-lstms-and-gru-s-a-step-by-step-explanation-44e9eb85bf21.

Murat Ozbayoglu, A., Ugur Gudelek, M., & Berat Sezer, O. (2020). Deep Learning for Financial Applications: A Survey. arXiv e-prints, arXiv-2002.

Nielsen, M. A. (2015). *Neural Networks and Deep Learning* (Vol. 25). San Francisco, CA: Determination press.

Nushaine, F. (January 19, 2020). A Simple Guide to Convolutional Neural Networks. Retrieved from https://towardsdatascience.com/a-simple-guide-to-convolutional-neural-networks-751789e7bd88.

Sumit, S. (December 16, 2018). A Comprehensive Guide to Convolutional Neural Networks — The ELI5 way. Retrieved from https://towardsdatascience.com/a-comprehensive-guide-to-convolutional-neural-networks-the-eli5-way-3bd2b1164a53.

4.6 Sample Questions

Question 1
Which of the following layers is not found in ANN?

(a) Hidden layer
(b) Convolutional layer
(c) Input layer

Question 2
What is the output range of the sigmoid function?

(a) $[-1,1]$
(b) $[0,1]$
(c) $[0,+\infty]$

Question 3
Which of the following is not true about the batch size?

(a) The minimum batch size is 1
(b) The maximum batch size is the sample size
(c) The batch equals the number of iterations that the optimization algorithm runs

Question 4
Which of the following is not a mechanism in fitting the CNN model?

(a) Conv
(b) Output
(c) Pool

Question 5
Which of the following data types is not suitable for CNN?

(a) Images of cars
(b) Audio of speech
(c) Grades of different students

Question 6
Which of the following is not true?

(a) Pooling is a dimension reduction technique
(b) Only the choice of pooling window size will affect the result of pooling
(c) A feature matrix is usually a small square matrix

Question 7
Which one of the following is correct?

(a) The output range of the sigmoid function is $[-1,1]$.
(b) The sigmoid function determines whether the information should be kept or forgotten.
(c) The tanh and sigmoid functions can be used interchangeably in LSTM.

Question 8
How many types of gates are there in a conventional LSTM?

(a) 1
(b) 2
(c) 3

Question 9
Which of the following is true?

(a) If the output of the input gate is close to 0, it means that the network should forget the memory.
(b) If the output of forget gate is close to 1, it means that the network should keep the memory.
(c) If the output of the input gate is close to 1, it means the information is important, and it will update the cell state.

Question 10
Which one of the following is correct?

(a) GANs are used to generate fake data that looks real.
(b) GANs are used to generate real data based on existing data patterns.
(c) GANs are used to manipulate the existing data.

Question 11
The goals of generator and discriminator are the opposite?

(a) True.
(b) False.
(c) It cannot be determined.

Question 12
Which one of the following is the least likely application of GANs?

(a) Generate new human faces.
(b) Predict stock price.
(c) Image translation.

Question 13
Which of the following is not an application of deep learning in finance?

(a) Security
(b) Algorithmic trading
(c) Self-driving car

Question 14
What is the likely deep learning techniques used in auto approval of loan application?

(a) Face recognition
(b) Credit rating
(c) Both (a) and (b)

Question 15

Deep learning can be applied in portfolio management.

(a) True.
(b) False.
(c) Not sure.

Solutions

Question 1

Solution: Option **b** is correct.

The convolutional layer is in CNN.

Question 2

Solution: Option **b** is correct.

Refer to Figure 4.6.

Question 3

Solution: Option **c** is correct.

The batch size is equal to the number of observations we used for one iteration of optimization.

Question 4

Solution: Option **b** is correct.

Output is not used to fit the model. It is the result of the fitting.

Question 5

Solution: Option **c** is correct.

CNN is particularly useful for sequential data. Image and audio are all sequential data as the order of the data will make a difference. The student grades are cross sectional data which can be essentially considered as independent observations.

Question 6

Solution: Option **b** is correct.

The pooling stride will affect the result as well.

Question 7

Solution: Option **b** is correct.

The range of sigmoid function is [0,1].

Both sigmoid and tanh function are used in LSTM. However, their roles are not interchangeable. Please refer to Figure 4.17.

Question 8

Solution: Option **c** is correct.

They are input gate, output gate, and forget gate.

Question 9

Solution: Option **c** is correct.

Option a: If the value of input gate is 0, it means the weightage of the new input is 0. As such, we will not update the cell state based on the new input. Option b: As the forget gate will be multiplied with the cell state, it means "forget" if its value is close to 0 and "memorizing" if its value is close to 1.

Question 10

Solution: Option **a** is correct.

Option b: The data generated by GANs, no matter how real it looks like, is still fake.
Option c: GANs are used to generate new data, instead of manipulating the existing data.

Question 11

Solution: Option **a** is correct.

The role of generator and discriminator are against each other.

Question 12

Solution: Option **b** is correct.

Question 13

Solution: Option **c** is correct.

Self-driving car is an application of deep learning. However, it is not an application in finance.

Question 14

Solution: Option **c** is correct.

Face recognition is used for identity verification and credit rating is to evaluate the loan default rate. Both are used in loan application.

Question 15

Solution: Option **a** is correct.

Chapter 5

Natural Language Processing (NLP)

5.1 Natural Language Processing (NLP)

Natural language processing (NLP) is a subfield of linguistics, computer science, information engineering, and artificial intelligence concerned with the interactions between computers and human (natural) languages, particularly how to program computers to process and analyze large amounts of natural language data.

Learning Objectives
- Understand the concept of NLP, NLU, and NLG.
- Identify and appraise the NLP applications in the real world.
- Understand various discussed NLP techniques.

Main Takeaways

Main Points
- NLP is a useful AI technique with extensive applications in many areas.
- Despite its usefulness, NLP still has some challenges and limitations.

Main Terms
- **NLP:** Natural language processing.
- **NLG:** Natural language generation.
- **NLU:** Natural language understanding.

5.1.1 *What is NLP?*

The process of deriving meaningful information from natural language text:

- structuring the input text;
- deriving patterns within the structured data;
- evaluating and interpreting the output.

Natural language understanding (NLU) or natural language interpretation (NLI) is a subfield of NLP that deals with machine reading comprehension. NLU is about understanding the context, intent, syntax, and sentiment of the text.

Natural language generation (NLG) responds to the input text and generates human language text. An example is the chatbot.

NLP can be considered as the combination of NLU and NLG. The differences among NLP, NLU, and NLG are summarized in Figure 5.1.

5.1.2 NLP Applications

Sentiment analysis: This is related to the sentimental context of a document. In NLP, the sentiment is normally classified into positive, neural, and

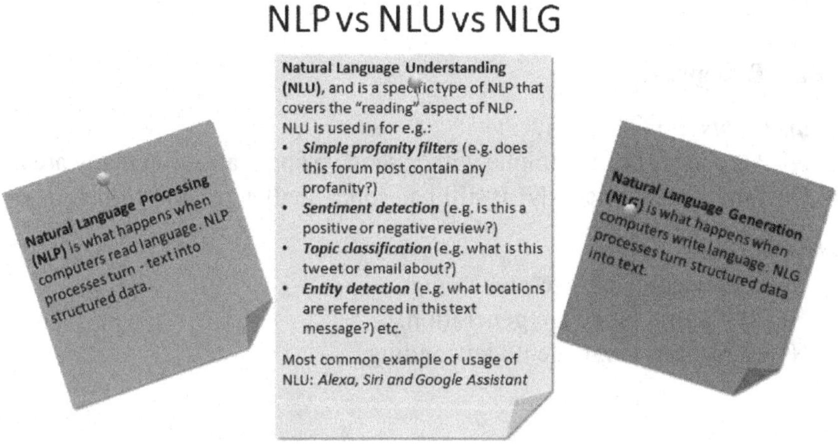

NLP vs NLU vs NLG

Figure 5.1: NLP vs. NLU vs. NLG.

Source: http://www.cellstrat.com/2017/10/27/nlp-vs-nlu-vs-nlg/.

negative. For instance, it can be used to analyze customer service reviews based on the percentage of positive and negative feedback received.

Spelling check: Based on word association (i.e., what kind of words often come together), it can help improve the writing or check the sentence structure. One of the more popular applications is "Grammarly".

Text-to-speech: As the name suggests, it translates text into audio. It involves two steps. The first is that the machine needs to read and understand the text. The second is to convert the text into speech. This is to help those who have a reading disability or are visually impaired to understand the written text.

Speech recognition: In contrast to the text-to-speech function, NLP can also do the reverse. It can convert speech to written text. Chatbots and smart speakers (Siri) are important applications of this functionality.

Topic modeling: This classifies the input text into different categories based on its theme. If you have used the chatbot on an E-commerce platform, and you asked a question like "The delivery of my purchase is delayed. Can I return it?", it will place the topic under the theme "cancellation/refund".

There are many other applications in healthcare (disease recognition), human resource management (talent recruitment), and so on.

5.1.3 *NLP Techniques*

(a) Sentence Tokenization (Segmentation)
It tries to break down a string of text or a document into its component sentences.

For example, if we are given a document as shown below:

"Natural language processing (NLP) is a subfield of linguistics, computer science, and artificial intelligence concerned with the interactions between computers and human language. The result is a computer capable of understanding the contents of documents. The technology can then accurately extract information and insights contained in the documents as well as categorize and organize the documents themselves".

The technique of sentence tokenization will return the following:

"Natural language processing (NLP) is a subfield of linguistics, computer science, and artificial intelligence concerned with the interactions between computers and human language".

"The result is a computer capable of understanding the contents of documents".

"The technology can then accurately extract information and insights contained in the documents as well as categorize and organize the documents themselves."

In many languages, including English, it is common to separate sentences by a period or punctuation. This may look trivial as we just need to tell the machine to cut the sentence whenever it encounters a period. However, this may incur an issue when it comes across the abbreviations that contain periods (e.g., U.S.) or numbers that have a comma (for example, 10,000) in the middle of a sentence. In NLP, it is resolved by defining a library of abbreviations or numbers.

(b) Word Tokenization (or Word Segmentation)

After chopping a long text into its short component sentences, the next step is to divide the sentence into its component words further. In English, a blank space is a natural separator for words.

For example, input the following sentence,

"His name is George".
Output:
{"His", "name", "is", "George", "."}

All the components, including punctuations, are separated. The tricky part is that compound nouns are literally one single word but separated by a space. For example, "New York", "bus stop". In this case, we do not want to separate them into "New" and "York", as their meaning will be distorted.

(c) Text Lemmatization and Stemming

Lemmatization and stemming are used to remove the inflectional and derivational forms in the text data for easier processing. For instance, in English, we have the words "meeting", "meet", "met", "meetings". They are an inflectional or derivational form of the root word "meet". In terms of understanding the meaning, these forms of variation can be removed to reduce the complexity.

What stemming does is simply chop off the derivational affixes at the end of the word without understanding the context. For example, "meeting" to "meet", "works" to "work". In contrast, lemmatization tries to conduct a morphological analysis of the word to identify the removable inflectional forms of a word. For example, "am", "are", "is", to "be".

There are pros and cons to these two techniques. Stemming is easy and fast to implement. However, stemming does not analyze the context of the text, and therefore, it cannot distinguish words that have different meanings in a distinct context. For example, the word "working" can be reduced to a base form of either a noun or verb ("to work"). Lemmatization can provide better accuracy while it is relatively harder to understand and implement.

(d) Part of Speech (POS)

Part of speech (POS) identifies the functionality of a word in terms of how it is used in a sentence. There are eight main parts of speech:

Nouns: Examples of nouns include names, places, things, ideas, e.g., George, Singapore, mountain, book, car, happiness.

Pronouns: They substitute for nouns and act as nouns. For example, {you, I, he, she, they, this, that, which, who, everybody}.

Verbs: This often explains the intention, the actions, occurrences, or states of being, like {be, watch, like, eat, work}.

Adjectives: These are words that provide description or modification of nouns or pronouns, like {friendly, beautiful, gentle, big}.

Adverbs: They describe or modify verbs, adjectives, or other adverbs. Examples of adverbs include {nicely, quietly, almost, someday}.

Prepositions: Serves as the connector between nouns or pronouns and other words in a sentence, like {at, on, for, about, with}.

Conjunctions: They are used to link words, clauses, and phrases.

"I like cooking **and** eating, **but** I don't like washing dishes afterward. Sophie is clearly exhausted, **yet** she insists on dancing till dawn".

- Coordinating conjunctions: link words, clauses, or phrases of equal importance. Examples: {for, and, nor, but, or, yet, so}.
- Correlative conjunctions: pairs of conjunctions that work together. Examples: {both/and, either/or, neither/nor, not only/but, whether/or}.

- Subordinating conjunctions: that introduce subordinate clauses and link them to main clauses. Examples: {after, although, as, as if, as long as, as much as, as soon as, as though, because, before, by the time, even if, even though, if, in order that, in case, in the event that, lest , now that, once, only, only if, provided that, since, so, supposing, that, than, though, till, unless, until, when, whenever, where, whereas, wherever, whether or not, while}.

Interjections: They are used to express feelings or command attention. Examples: {hey, oh, wow}.

Identifying the role of each word in a sentence can help us figure out the meaning of the sentence. This is done by fitting each word into a pre-trained POS classification model.

(e) Bag of Words

A computer is only able to work with numbers, not texts. We need to convert the raw text to numbers for the machine to understand it. Bag of words is a feature extraction technique that tries to break down a given text document into a list of distinct words. The same words are grouped together, and the frequency each word appears is counted. The given document is then represented as a list of frequency numbers, each of which is associated with a unique word.

(f) Sentiment Analysis

The key in sentiment analysis is to analyze the subjective emotion expressed by a text. In NLP, the sentiment is scored with a positive or negative value named *polarity*. Depending on the sign of the polarity score, the sentiment of a sentence can be categorized as positive, negative, or neutral.

A naive sentiment analysis method is called the rule-based method. It defines a sentiment dictionary. Words such as "Like", "nice", "good" are listed as positive; "bad", "terrible" are categorized as negative; "fine", "ok" are defined as neutral. The dictionary is then used to compare against the text and compute the polarity score. Depending on the sign of the polarity score, we can decide the overall sentiment of the sentence.

5.1.4 *Major Challenges of NLP*

(a) Homonyms

The same word or phrase sometimes may have distinct meanings depending on the context of the sentence. For example,

"I **ran** to the market because we **ran** out of sugar".

The word "ran" has the same spelling in the sentence, while their meanings are quite different. It is also very common in English that some words may have very similar pronunciation while completely different meanings. For examples,

"to" Vs "too" Vs "two".
"their" Vs "there".

Homonyms: Two or more words that are pronounced or spelled the same but have different meanings. This can be further divided into two scenarios, homograph and homophone.

- Homograph: Two or more words have the same spelling but have different pronunciation and/or meaning.
  lead (to go in front of)/lead (a kind of metal)"
- Homophone: Two or more words have the same pronunciation but have different spelling and/or meaning.
  "pray/prey".

Humans are good at reading the context of the sentence and understanding all of the different definitions. However, NLP language models may need to learn all of the definitions and be trained to differentiate them in context.

(b) Synonyms

Synonyms can lead to issues similar to contextual understanding because we use many different words to express the same idea. Although synonyms are considered as alternative words with the same meaning, there might still be slight differences in the level of complexity. For example, small/little/tiny. This also depends on different people's understanding of these synonyms. While training the NLP model, it is essential to define all synonyms and their meanings. With more and more training data available, the model is able to understand synonyms better.

(c) Irony and Sarcasm

Humans can understand irony and sarcasm easily. Nevertheless, this may impose difficulty for the machine. A sentence generally appears as, strictly by definition, positive or negative, but actually, could connote the opposite because of irony or sarcasm. The NLP model needs to be trained with commonly seen ironic or sarcastic phrases to address this issue. We hope the NLP model can identify the pattern when seeing it next time with more data. Nevertheless, this is still a challenging task.

(d) Ambiguity

Being ambiguous means that the sentence appears to have more than one possible interpretation. For example:

"I saw the boy on the beach with my binoculars".

This could mean that I saw a boy through my binoculars or the boy had my binoculars with him. What the intended meaning is difficult for humans to discern, let alone machines.

(e) Colloquialisms and Slang

One of the biggest challenges in NLP is how to handle the informal phrases, expressions, idioms, and culture-specific lingo. Colloquialisms often have no official "dictionary definition", and these expressions may even be used differently or have different meanings in distinct geographic areas. Worse still, cultural slang is constantly morphing and expanding, and there are many new words created every day. All these will create big challenges to NLP.

As a result, training and regularly updating models and libraries can be helpful, although it frequently requires quite a lot of data.

(f) Domain-Specific Language

Different businesses and industries have their own domain-specific jargon. The NLP model trained in the healthcare industry may not apply to the financial industry. As a result, the NLP models trained are also classified based on their fields. Those extremely niche fields may need to adopt a very specially trained NLP model.

(g) Low-Resource Languages

Theoretically, NLP can be applied to any language. Nevertheless, the current NLP libraries and models are mostly built for the most common and widely used languages only. However, there are thousands of languages in the world. Most of the existing languages are overlooked and under-processed. This is simply because those languages are spoken only by a small population or by those with less access to modern technology. As such, there is not enough data of these languages. It is challenging to build up the NLP library and model without enough data. There are new techniques, like multilingual transformers (using Google's BERT "Bidirectional Encoder Representations from Transformers") and multilingual sentence embeddings aimed at identifying and leveraging universal similarities that exist between languages.

References/Further Readings

Bird, S., Klein, E., & Loper, E. (2009). *Natural Language Processing with Python: Analyzing Text with the Natural Language Toolkit.* "O'Reilly Media, Inc.".

Chethan, K. (September 25, 2018). NLP vs NLU vs NLG (Know what you are trying to achieve) NLP engine (Part-1). Retrieved from https://towardsdatascience.com/nlp-vs-nlu-vs-nlg-know-what-you-are-trying-to-achieve-nlp-engine-part-1-1487a2c8b696.

Collobert, R., Weston, J., Bottou, L., Karlen, M., Kavukcuoglu, K., & Kuksa, P. (2011). Natural language processing (almost) from scratch. *Journal of Machine Learning Research*, 12(ARTICLE), 2493–2537.

Indurkhya, N., & Damerau, F. J. (Eds.). (2010). *Handbook of Natural Language Processing* (Vol. 2). CRC Press.

Ines, R. (December 22, 2020). Major Challenges of Natural Language Processing (NLP) for AI.MonkeyLearn. Retrieved from https://monkeylearn.com/blog/natural-language-processing-challenges/.

5.2 Sample Questions

Question 1
Which of the following is not an application of NLP?

(a) Speech recognition
(b) Chatbot
(c) Image recognition

Question 2
If the input text is "he is meeting the client", what will be the output if we apply lemmatization and stemming to "is" and "meeting"?

(a) "is", "to meet", "be", "to meet"
(b) "be", "meet", "be", "meet"
(c) "be", "to meet", "is", "meet"

Question 3
Which of the following is not true?

(a) Topic modeling is a dimension reduction technique.
(b) Bag of words in a feature abstraction technique.
(c) The main challenge of NLP is handling tokenization.

Question 4
Which one of the following is not a challenge of NLP?

(a) Ambiguity
(b) Homograph
(c) Language type

Question 5
Which one of the following is not an application of sentiment analysis?

(a) Evaluate the customers' product review.
(b) Draft an empathetic email response to customers.
(c) Classify the theme of the text.

Solutions

Question 1

Solution: Option **c** is correct.

Image recognition mainly makes use of deep learning techniques.

Question 2

Solution: Option **c** is correct.

Refer to the differences between lemmatization and stemming.

Question 3

Solution: Option **c** is correct.

Refer to the challenges of NLP.

Question 4

Solution: Option **c** is correct.

The NLP techniques for different language are similar.

Question 5

Solution: Option **c** is correct.

Sentiment analysis is only able to differentiate the sentiment of the text, not the theme of the text.

Part C: Blockchain Programming and Design Thinking

Chapter 6

Blockchain and Digital Currency Advanced

6.1 Blockchain and DLT Advanced

6.1.1 *Cryptography*

Information security lies at the center of cryptography. Cryptography is a suite of algorithms based on the intractability of complex problems that cannot be solved in a reasonable amount of time. Besides the three existing key objectives of information security known as the "CIA Triad": confidentiality, integrity, and availability, two more security objectives are supposed to be followed by the security practitioner: authentication and accountability. The first objective of confidentiality covers both data confidentiality and user confidentiality. Integrity revolves around ensuring the data is not tampered with during the transition and specific tools are needed to secure data from unauthorized modifications. Integrity is closely linked with the two security objectives: authentication and accountability. As a security objective, Availability is associated with a malicious activity known as a Denial-of-Service (DoS) attack. A DoS attack has evolved to a Distributed DoS (DDoS) attack in today's time. Authentication includes both data authentication and user authentication. The former aims to verify if the origin of the data is true and the latter aims to verify that a user is who they claim to be. Accountability's objective is to thwart a user from falsely denying that a particular communication is either sent or received by them. Understanding and analyzing the possible attack strategies ensure that we enable appropriate safeguards to the system's safety and security with cryptographic techniques.

Learning Objectives
- Understand the role and the objectives of cryptography in ensuring information security.

Main Takeaways

Main Points
- Security practitioners need to address the five key security objectives: Confidentiality, integrity, availability, authentication, and accountability.
- Assessment and analysis of possible attack strategies are essential to respond effectively to information security threats.
- Cryptography is essential for security, and it is vital to have a secure cryptographic scheme.

Main Terms
- **Cryptography:** A suite of algorithms based on the intractability of complex problems that cannot be solved in a reasonable amount of time.
- **CIA triad:** Represents confidentiality, integrity, and availability, but it also includes authentication and accountability.
- **Denial-of-Service (DoS):** Attack happens when an attacker attempts to overwhelm a server with a flood of bogus requests that render the server so busy, unable to process regular traffic and becomes unavailable to other users.
- **Active Attack:** Performed aggressively and often blatant actions to affect or alter a system's operations.
- **Passive Attack:** The attacker uses covert methods to tap into a network and eavesdrop on or record communications. The objective of a passive attack is usually to gain access to a system or steal information surreptitiously.
- **Secure Cryptographic Scheme:** A cryptographic scheme that is computationally secure if no efficient attacker can break it in a reasonable amount of time.
- **Pseudorandomness:** The fact that the distribution of a string should satisfy statistical tests of randomness, even though it is not truly random.

(a) Security Objectives

The goal of cryptography is to achieve information security. Before discussing how to achieve our goal through cryptographic techniques, we first need to know exactly what we are trying to achieve. Since the inception of this field, the three main objectives of information security have been known as the "CIA triad": *confidentiality, integrity,* and *availability*. However, with the evolution of computing and technology such as cloud services and peer-to-peer networks, the CIA triad is no longer considered sufficient to protect against attacks on the data and user. Security practitioners are now also expected to address two additional security objectives: *authentication* and *accountability*. It is important to keep in mind these five objectives as they guide the design and use of cryptographic techniques. Let us look more closely at what each objective entails.

(1) Confidentiality

Confidentiality extends to both data confidentiality and user confidentiality (also understood as user privacy):

- *Data Confidentiality*: There are two primary aims of data confidentiality. First, to shield data from all unauthorized parties. This is similar to the original objective of classical cryptography and is achieved through data encryption. Second, to shield data from unauthorized parties differentiated based on access rights. For example, a patient's hospital records will contain different data types, such as identifying information, test results, diagnoses, treatments, prescriptions, and medical insurance coverage. To protect the patient's privacy, hospital employees should only have access to the records on a need-to-know basis. Doctors, nurses, pharmacists, hospital administrators, and medical social workers should all have different access rights depending on the information they need to carry out their respective roles. Therefore, the records-management system will need an authorization protocol that gives users different access levels based on their identity.
- *User Privacy*: There are two primary aims of user privacy in situations where there is reason to expect that a user remains unidentifiable. First, to ensure untraceability. We should conceal the routes of goods, money, data, and other operations so that an observer cannot follow the trail to deduce identifying information about a user. Second, to ensure unlinkability. We should be able to conceal the connection between multiple

pieces of data from the same user to appear unrelated to an observer. For example, given multiple pseudonymous transactions on the Bitcoin blockchain, it should not be possible to deduce the user's real identity who performed the transactions, nor should it be possible to deduce that the same user performed them.

High-profile cases of compromised data confidentiality have made news headlines in recent years, from the unauthorized harvesting of Facebook users' personal data by Cambridge Analytical to the data breach of SingHealth medical records in 2018. In contrast, there are almost no publicly disclosed cases of compromised user privacy, which largely remains an area of theoretical concern in academia and gaining more attention as big data, Internet-of-Things (IoT), and blockchain usage become more pervasive.

(2) Integrity

We cannot trust a message unless we know that its content has been secured because it leaves its origin to the point that it reaches its destination. Data integrity is concerned with ensuring that data is not tampered with while in transit. Though often conflated with confidentiality, integrity is a distinct objective. It is sometimes assumed that encryption is sufficient to ensure data integrity because since encryption conceals the actual content of a message, the content cannot be modified in any meaningful way. This is a false assumption as it is possible to manipulate a piece of encrypted data in ways that simply invalidate its content. In this case, the recipient has no idea if the encrypted data is received with errors or was maliciously modified. We, therefore, need tools specific to integrity protection to secure data from unauthorized modifications.

Integrity is achieved using the hash function, message authentication codes, and digital signature. Integrity is closely associated with authentication and accountability — two security objectives have evolved above and beyond the traditional "CIA triad". It is important to distinguish the subtle differences among all three.

(3) Availability

Data and online services are of no use if they are not available when authorized users need them. Availability as a security objective is closely associated with a malicious activity known as a DoS attack. As its name suggests, a DoS attack is when an attacker attempts to overwhelm a server with a flood of bogus requests that render the server so busy that it cannot process normal traffic and becomes unavailable to other users.

In this IoT era, a DoS attack has evolved to a DDoS attack, which uses a network of distributed devices connected to the Internet to carry out the attack. An attacker first injects malicious software (or malware) into any vulnerable devices connected to the Internet in a DDoS attack. These devices could be mobile phones, routers, personal computers, network printers, and Internet Protocol (IP) cameras. Once infected with malware, these devices become bots that can be remotely controlled to send bogus requests to the target server, even down to a stipulated date and time. Availability is usually addressed through good system design, such as intrusion detection or intrusion prevention systems. It is also important to note that provision of availability is closely related to how susceptible a system is to a single point of failure, i.e., how decentralized it is.

(4) Authentication

Authentication extends to both data authentication and user authentication:

- *Data Authentication*: The aim is to verify that the origin of a piece of data is what it claims to be. One of the most common ways of ensuring data authenticity is through message authentication codes and digital signatures.
- *User Authentication*: The aim is to verify that a user is who they claim to be. It can be achieved by providing authentication factors to a login system based on what you know (e.g., username and password), what you have (e.g., access card), or who you are (e.g., biometric information). Similarly, the cryptographic techniques involved are message authentication codes and digital signatures, where users are required to demonstrate something they know (i.e., the secret/private key).

(5) Accountability

Accountability aims to thwart a user from falsely denying that they have sent or received a particular communication. It is analogous to the concept of non-repudiation. Imagine that we have ensured data integrity and authentication; that is, we have secured a piece of data from tampering while in transit. We have verified the origin of the data. Accountability goes a step further by creating a digital artifact that makes it impossible for the sender to deny having sent the data. It draws an undeniable link between the data and the users who have processed it, ensuring accountability for actions performed on the data. This is achieved through the use of a digital signature. With the rise of "deepfakes" and disinformation and eroding public trust in news media, ensuring accountability is increasingly becoming a matter of social and political stability.

(6) Attacks
"Know thyself, know thy enemy, and in every battle, you will be victorious".

— *Sun Tzu*, The Art of War

To respond effectively to a threat to information security, we must know what we are up against. Understanding possible attack strategies enable us to put the appropriate safeguards to ensure the security of a system and its cryptographic techniques. We will briefly look at two types of attacks here:

- *Active Attack*: The attacker performs aggressive and often blatant actions to affect or alter a system's operations. Examples include email phishing, modifying data in transit between users, mounting a DDoS attack, and mounting a brute-force attack (trial and error) to guess a username and password combination. An active attack is easy to detect but difficult to defend, involving a thorough analysis to close all loopholes in a system or cryptographic technique. By the time an attack is detected, the damage may already have been done or underway.
- *Passive Attack*: The attacker uses covert methods to tap into a network and eavesdrop on or record communications. The objective of a passive attack is usually to gain access to a system or steal information surreptitiously. Examples include surveillance, man-in-the-middle attacks, and keystroke logging. Designed to avoid detection, passive attacks are challenging to detect but easy to prevent. One of the most straightforward methods is to encrypt communication between users.

(b) Cryptography
Earlier, we briefly discussed what is considered secure enough in cryptography. We said that cryptography is a suite of algorithms based on the

intractability of complex problems that cannot be solved in a reasonable amount of time. This section will examine the concept of security in cryptography in greater detail and identify the key properties of a secure cryptographic scheme.

Key Terms: Bit, Scheme, Algorithm, Function
A bit (short for binary digit) is the smallest unit of computer data. Each bit has one of two binary values, either 0 or 1. 4 bits of data therefore have 2^4 or 16 possible combinations:

0000	0100	1000	1100
0001	0101	1001	1101
0010	0110	1010	1110
0011	0111	1011	1111

In the following sections, we use specific terms to talk about parts of a security system. A cryptographic *scheme* is an overall description of how a security system works. Schemes consist of one or more *algorithms*, which are sets of instructions defining a sequence of operations carried out by a computer. For example, an encryption scheme may consist of a secret key generation algorithm, an encryption algorithm, and a decryption algorithm.

A *function* is a process or relation between values that takes some input and produces some output. For example, the secret key generation algorithm has a KeyGen() function that takes as input the security parameter n and produces a secret key k of n bits. The encryption algorithm has an Enc() function that takes as input a secret key k and a plaintext m and produces a ciphertext c. The decryption algorithm has a Dec() function that takes as input a ciphertext c and a secret key k and produces a plaintext m.

Cryptographic techniques cannot be proven unconditionally secure, as that would require breakthroughs in the analysis of computational complexity that are not yet within our reach. Almost all cryptographic techniques can be broken given enough time and computing power. We still consider them secure because what is "enough" is generally not achievable in our lifetime or several lifetimes. Instead of unconditional security, we aim for cryptographic techniques to be *computationally secure*.

Refining our earlier statement, we say that *a cryptographic scheme is computationally secure if no efficient attacker is able to break it in a reasonable amount of time*. An "efficient attacker" can be understood as an attacker with a reasonable amount of computing power. In contrast, "a reasonable amount of time" can be understood as a time frame during which the ability to solve a problem has ceased to be useful or interesting. Cryptographic techniques that meet these conditions have a negligible probability of being broken.

For example, to break a secret key of 4 bits, an attacker needs to try only 2^4 combinations, with the probability of guessing the right key being $1/2^4$. This is easily done through a brute-force attack. A 4-bit secret key is therefore not computationally secure. In contrast, if the key is of 256 bits, mounting a brute-force attack to try 2^{256} combinations would take an attacker several lifetimes, even with a supercomputer. That makes a 256-bit key computationally secure.

Intuitively, it seems that we could make cryptography schemes more secure by setting the highest requirements, such as assuming an attacker with unlimited, rather than reasonable, computing power. Indeed, the study of information-theoretic security (or perfect security) produces security systems that even an attacker with unlimited computing power would not be able to break, as the encrypted message provides no information about the original message. The one-time pad, or Vernam cipher, is an example of an information-theoretic secure scheme.

We can think of computational security as a practical balance between security and *efficiency*. All computationally secure cryptographic schemes rely on the provision of *pseudorandomness*. This refers to the fact that the distribution of a string should satisfy statistical tests of randomness, even though it is not truly random. Ciphertexts (encrypted texts) are not truly random; in certain conditions, when enough information is known, a user can know what ciphertext an algorithm will produce. However, to all other users who do not have enough information, the ciphertext is just a pseudorandom string.

Pseudorandomness is important because it prevents a ciphertext from inadvertently disclosing information about the statistical distributions of the secret key or the original message. It does this by ensuring that an attacker cannot distinguish one ciphertext from another. Using the example of an encryption scheme, where an encryption algorithm is denoted as

Enc(), *m* is a message in plaintext, *c* is the encrypted ciphertext, and *k* is the encryption key:

$$c \leftarrow \mathrm{Enc}_k(m)$$

A computationally-secure encryption scheme requires that given two ciphertexts c_1 and c_2, or:

$$c_1 \leftarrow \mathrm{Enc}_k(m_1)$$
$$c_2 \leftarrow \mathrm{Enc}_k(m_2)$$

Both c_1 and c_2 are indistinguishable from an efficient attacker. In other words, both c_1 and c_2 have pseudorandom distributions and do not reveal any information about the statistical distributions of k, m_1 or m_2.

6.1.2 *Consensus*

Consensus algorithms are highly essential to ensure consistency and accuracy on a blockchain and distributed ledger. PoW, and PoS is the most commonly used consensus algorithms. Besides these two, many other consensus algorithms have been proposed and implemented into the live blockchain-based applications, assets, and investments, and informed decisions. The goals of the network implementer help in deciding consensus algorithms. It could be for a decentralized public system that needs to be self-governing or an enterprise consortium blockchain which needs to handle sensitive transactions. None of the nodes are considered trusted in trustless blockchains.

The incentives must be aligned to encourage the right actions. Emergence of multiple use cases of blockchain has increased the expectation of more variety of use cases emerging from the blockchain. With the multitude of blockchain solutions, any blockchain network may also be required to communicate with several others; interoperability will become a key consideration.

Learning Objectives
• Understand and learn about the different types of consensus algorithms.

Main Takeaways

Main Points
• Consensus protocols for blockchain networks where nodes are trusted and less trusted are different.

- Consensus algorithms for trustless blockchain include PoW, DpoS, PoB, PoSpace, PoI, and Proof of Burn.
- Consensus algorithms for trusted blockchains include PoA, PoR, PoET, PBFT, FBA, and RAFT.
- The hybrid of the two types of algorithms also existed like dPoW, DAGs, Tangle, Hashgraph, and SPECTRE.

(a) Consensus Protocols Used in Blockchain and DLT

Other than PoW, many consensus algorithms were proposed and implemented onto live blockchain networks. Some of these variations are driven by the need to overcome the shortcomings of PoW by reducing the amount of energy consumed or improving the amount of decentralization on the network. Others are proposed to overcome the scalability issue that Bitcoin is experiencing, aiming to process more transactions per second. Then, some are specifically created for use in permissioned blockchain networks where nodes are considered trusted, and there is less need for incentive mechanisms to ensure behavior.

(b) Consensus for Trustless Blockchains

In trustless blockchains, none of the nodes are considered trusted. We need to rely on the consensus algorithm and the appropriate incentives like mining rewards to ensure that the network members behave correctly. The incentives must be aligned to encourage the appropriate actions. Some general guidelines to consider:

(1) Doing the right thing gets rewarded.
(2) Rewards from continuing to do the right thing should outweigh the potential net benefits from doing bad things — the costs of doing bad things should be high.

In addition to the most widely used consensus algorithms, PoW and PoS, introduced in Level 1, below are several other common ones.

(1) Delegated proof of stake

In Delegated Proof of Stake (DPoS), as the name implies, the staking is delegated. Owners of coins (or stakeholders) can elect and choose leaders who will stake/vote on their behalf. Since there are less stakers to coordinate, this is faster than PoS.

EOS[1] Utilizing DPoS, 21 leaders (or witnesses) are elected at a time in EOS, and there is a pool of standby nodes in case one of the existing witnesses drops out or turns out to be malicious. The witnesses are paid a fee (the stakeholders set that) for producing blocks. The 21 witnesses produce blocks one at a time in a round-robin fashion. Thus, a witness cannot produce consecutive blocks, making double-spending attacks by the witness impossible. A witness is skipped if it cannot produce a block within the allocated time slot. Stakeholders can vote out witnesses that continue to miss blocks or publish invalid transactions.

DPoS is collaborative instead of competitive, as everyone has a turn. This method allows faster blocks and scales better than PoW or PoS. Other than EOS, Steemit, Bitshares, and Lisk also use DPoS. However, this method is also more centralized than PoW and PoS. The control over the network falls mostly on the 21 witnesses. If a stakeholder has sufficient coins, it can vote itself to be a witness and control the entire network.

(2) Proof of weight

Proof of Weight refers to a large class of consensus algorithms where the chance of being chosen to validate or mine the next block is based on a weighted score. This consensus class usually aims to make it more costly to lose the acquired weighted score, thus ensuring validators continue to be good. Proof of Weight is generally energy-efficient, but incentive mechanism design is important, and maybe hard to ensure that incentives are aligned to the outcomes. Proof of Believability, Proof of Space, and Proof of Importance are forms of Proof of Weight.

(3) Proof of believability

Proof of Believability is used by IOST[2] and utilizes several factors to compose a believability score. With Proof of Believability (PoB), IOST aims to encourage decentralization in the network. Central to this is the reputation-based sub-token system called Servi. Servi tokens serve as a measurement of a user's contribution to the network and a way to encourage members to contribute to the development of the network. These

---

[1] https://eos.io/.
[2] https://iost.io/.

non-tradeable tokens are awarded to good actors within the ecosystem and factor heavily into choosing the next validator. Servi tokens are non-tradeable. Only the awardee can use the tokens. Once it is used, the balance is cleared. Thus one cannot accumulate the tokens to gain more advantage. All nodes will have a fair chance at validating a block. Its creation and issuance are also embedded into the protocol. A user's account will be credited after certain contributions to the network.

PoB divides all validators into a believable group and a normal group. The believable group validates the transactions in the first phase, and the normal group samples and verifies transactions in the second phase. The chance to be elected into the believable group is determined by a believability score, calculated by multiple factors such as token balance, contributions to the community, and reviews. Believable validators are formed into smaller groups (one validator per group), and transactions are randomly distributed to these groups for validation, thus improving the transaction speed.

This poses a security issue if the validator node is malicious. Thus, the normal group samples the transactions to detect inconsistencies. A malicious validator is also at risk of losing its believability (including all the tokens and reputation) if detected. The costs of being caught should outweigh the benefits of entering the bad transactions into the ledger. As a believable validator is unlikely to misbehave, the single validator approach for the transactions makes PoB very fast.

(4) Proof of space

Proof of Space (PoSpace) was first proposed by Dziembowski, Faust, Kolmogorov and Pietrzak (2015). Also called Proof of Capacity (PoC), where one dedicates a certain amount of disk space to participate in validating a block. It is similar to PoW as the miner needs to provide a mathematical proof to demonstrate that the resources (computational power or disk space) have been committed. This is implemented through the use of hard-to-pebble graphs. The prover needs to build a labeling of a hard-to-pebble graph and commits to the labeling. To verify the commitment, the prover has to open several random locations in the commitment. PoSpace is seen as fairer (disk space is general-purpose compared to specialized mining machines) and greener (uses less electricity). PoSpace is also suitable for preventing spam and denial of service attacks. Burstcoin and Spacemint are projects that are utilizing PoSpace.

(5) Proof of importance

Proof of Importance (PoI) is the consensus algorithm adopted by NEM.[3] It pays out to members participating in PoI based on their importance which depends on various factors, such as notoriety (based on the purpose-designed framework), balance, and the number of transactions made to and from that position. This "importance" calculation aims to measure the "helpfulness" of a network member.

Like PoS, to be eligible to participate in PoI, a network member needs to have a minimum stake of coins (10,000 XEM). Importance is calculated using a specific algorithm and determines the chance to win the PoI reward. It aims to be a fairer system where anyone contributing to the network gets to be rewarded. Due to its construct, PoI is also resistant to arbitrary manipulation, Sybil, and loop attacks.

(6) Proof of burn

In Proof of Burn, you "burn" your coins by sending them to an address where they are irretrievable. In exchange, you earn a privilege to mine on the system based on a random selection process. In most implementations, you "burn" cryptocurrency from an alternative chain such as bitcoin. The more you burn, the higher the chance of being selected to mine the next block. Over time this probability declines, so you will need to keep burning more coins to retain the same chance. Although the network itself does not exhaust much energy to run Proof of Burn, the cryptocurrencies required to be burnt also expand resources. This method also does not address the fairness issue. Those with money to "burn" have higher chances of mining. Slimcoin and TGCoin (Third Generation Coin) use Proof of Burn.

(c) Consensus for Trusted Blockchains

In trusted blockchains, all nodes are known. Thus, malicious acts can be identified. Since the nodes have been vetted before being allowed on the network, they are generally assumed to be trusted to validate transactions. Thus, consensus for trusted blockchains is focused on preventing crash faults rather than byzantine faults in general.

---

[3] https://docs.nem.io/ja/gen-info/what-is-poi.

(1) Proof of authority

In Proof of Authority (PoA), validation is done by approved accounts called validators. The validators validate the transactions and blocks that are recorded on the blockchain. Validators run software that automates this process and need not constantly monitor their computers. However, the validators need to ensure that their computers are not compromised or attacked. The general conditions to approve a node as a validator are:

(1) Verified identity that links the node to a real-world identity. Ideally, this identity can be cross-checked on a publicly available domain. Identity must be formally verified on-chain, with a possibility to cross-check the information in a publicly available domain.
(2) It must be difficult to become a validator. This ensures that the right to validate transactions is valuable to the validator. The validator should view this value highly such that it would not risk losing validator status by acting maliciously. An example is requiring a node to be an authorized notary to be a validator.
(3) There must be complete uniformity in the checks and procedures for establishing authority.

By attaching a reputation to identity, validators are incentivized to uphold the transaction process. They do not wish to have their identities attached to a negative reputation, thus losing the hard-earned validator role. This method is centralized as there needs to be an authority that vets and admits validator nodes. Therefore, it is usually used in private and permissioned blockchains. PoA is much faster than PoW as no computation is required. VeChain is an example that uses PoA.

(2) Proof of reputation

Proof of Reputation (PoR) is similar to PoA. It depends on the reputation of the participants to keep the network secure. A validator risks financial or brand consequences if they attempt to be malicious. Thus, the validator also needs to have a reputation important enough that the consequences are costly. A potential validator needs to pass verification and proof their reputation to be admitted into the network. Existing validators may vote on the eligibility of the new entrant, or a weighted matrix may be used to decide. Besides choosing the validator, PoR operates like PoA once the validators are admitted into the network. Due to its similar nature to PoA,

PoR is also more suitable for trusted and permissioned blockchains. GoChain[4] uses PoR.

(3) Proof of elapsed time

Proof of Elapsed Time (PoET) was invented in early 2016 by Intel. It is used in permissioned blockchains to decide who gets to mine the next block. It is based on the principle of a fair lottery system where every node is as likely to be the winner. It relies on specialized hardware, which cannot be universally adopted by a public network.

PoET algorithm works as follows:

- Each participating node is randomly assigned a period to wait and goes to sleep for the specified period.
- The first node to wake up (with the shortest waiting time) gets to mine the next block and commits it to the blockchain network.
- The same process repeats for the next block

The PoET network consensus mechanism needs to ensure two important factors:

- First, participating nodes must be given a waiting time that is indeed random and not a shorter duration chosen purposely by the participants to win.
- Second, the winner must complete the waiting time.

To achieve this, Intel utilizes its SGX technology to execute trusted code in a protected environment. This prevents any attempt to alter the code and ensures that the results are verifiable by external parties. PoET is used by the Hyperledger Sawtooth project, which Intel leads.

(4) Practical byzantine fault tolerance

Practical Byzantine Fault Tolerance (PBFT) was one of the first solutions proposed for the Byzantine General's Problem. There is a leader node in a PBFT system, and all other nodes are backup nodes. Every node will communicate with each other to agree on the state of the system using majority

---

[4]https://gochain.io/proof-of-reputation/.

voting. For PBFT to work, the number of malicious nodes cannot exceed one-third of the system. There are four phases in a round of PBFT consensus:

- A request to add a transaction to the network is sent to the leader node;
- The leader node broadcasts this to all the other nodes;
- Each node executes the request and sends a reply to the requestor;
- The requestor waits until $n+1$ nodes return the same result, where n is the maximum allowable number of malicious nodes.

The leader node is alternated and can be changed if a certain amount of time has lapsed or the other nodes determine that the leader node is faulty. PBFT is usually only used in a permissioned network as there is no incentive mechanism to prevent untrusted malicious nodes from joining the network and making up the majority. The benefit of PBFT is that it is fast and scalable. It is used in Hyperledger Fabric V0.6 and Zilliqa (Zilliqa, 2017).

(5) Federated byzantine agreement

Federated Byzantine Agreement (FBA) is another class of solutions to the Byzantine general's problem of currencies like Stellar and Ripple. Nodes are known and verified ahead of time. The nodes choose who they trust, and eventually, quorums of nodes emerge from decisions made by the individual nodes making up the FBA network. A quorum is the minimum number of nodes required for a solution to be correct. After a quorum form, the block is validated and included on the blockchain. FBA uses "quorum slices", which are subsets of quorums that can convince specific nodes operating on the network to agree with them. In Ripple's FBA, transactions are grouped into sets and are validated in four rounds, starting with 50% agreement and working its way up to 80% quorum in the fourth round. This ensures that the transactions are not double spent.

(6) RAFT

RAFT[5] is named after Reliable, Replicated, Redundant, and Fault-Tolerant. RAFT is not byzantine fault-tolerant and is usually used in permissioned networks. It is a way to ensure each node in the network agrees upon the same transactions. It arrives at consensus via an elected leader. Nodes in a RAFT network can be the leader or a follower. A follower can also be a

---

[5] http://thesecretlivesofdata.com/raft/.

candidate if the leader becomes unavailable. The leader replicates the ledger to the followers. The followers know that the leader exists from a heartbeat message sent by the leader. If no heartbeat is received in a stipulated amount of time, the follower switches to a candidate and initiates a leader election. RAFT is used in Quorum and later versions of Hyperledger Fabric.

(d) Hybrid Blockchain Networks
(1) Delayed proof of work
Delayed Proof of Work (dPoW) is a hybrid consensus method. It utilizes a secondary blockchain's hashing power to provide additional security for the primary blockchain. The primary blockchain can either be a public or permissioned blockchain.

Komodo[6] makes use of dPoW by attaching itself to the Bitcoin blockchain. A group of notary nodes adds data from the primary blockchain to the secondary blockchain. Komodo allows PoS or PoW to run on the primary blockchain and only works for PoW secondary blockchains. To tamper with a transaction on the primary blockchain, one must also change the data on the secondary blockchain. Thus, Komodo can rely on the security of the larger Bitcoin blockchain to keep its data immutable.

There are two types of nodes within the Komodo dPoW system: notary and normal nodes. Sixty-four notary nodes notarize and add confirmed blocks from the primary dPoW blockchain to the attached secondary blockchain. DPoW blockchain stakeholders elect notary nodes. The notarization process requires a majority (33 nodes) to sign the transaction. Notary nodes do this in a round-robin fashion, reducing the competition for rewards. Normal nodes partake in the usual consensus on the primary blockchain, PoS or PoW. If the secondary blockchain network goes down, the primary network can go on as usual without the additional security of the attached blockchain.

This concept of piggybacking on a stronger network allows for increased security without high energy usage. It also allows for chains of blockchain to be formed. For example, another blockchain network can attach itself to Komodo, which is attached to Bitcoin. This allows the Bitcoin blockchain to add value to other dPoS blockchains. It also creates incentives for other networks to support larger networks like Bitcoin without being entirely reliant on its functionality.

---

[6]https://komodoplatform.com/security-delayed-proof-of-work-dpow/.

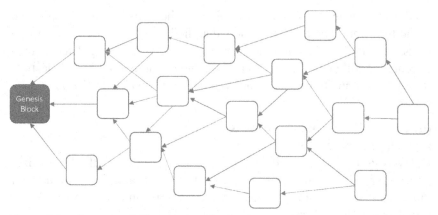

Figure 6.1:   Example of Directed Acyclic Graph network (arrows are pointing from parent to child).

(2) Directed acyclic graphs
Directed Acyclic Graphs (DAGs) are generalized forms of blockchain and can be applied to both trusted and trustless networks. DAG structure allows transactions to be added in a parallel fashion, making it highly scalable. See Figure 6.1 for an example. Most blockchain systems we have looked at have a linear structure. Blocks are added one by one to the blockchain. This makes blockchains inherently slow. In DAGs, each block or transaction confirms a number of previous blocks. Although deemed to be the next-generation blockchain structure, one of the main issues of DAGs is that smart contracts are usually implemented via oracles and not be directly deployed on-chain.

A number of variations depend on the algorithm for choosing which previous blocks to verify, the ordering of transactions, and how transaction finality is reached. We introduce three such algorithms below. Other consensus using DAG structure includes Holochain, Block-Lattice, ByteBall, and Mokka.

(3) Tangle
Tangle[7] is the DAG consensus algorithm used by IOTA.[8] Tangle adopts a pay it forward type consensus. To send a transaction, one needs to validate

---

[7] https://blog.iota.org/the-tangle-an-illustrated-introduction-4d5eae6fe8d4.
[8] https://www.iota.org/.

two previous transactions. As more transactions are added to the network, the validity of the transactions is strengthened. Technically, if one can generate one-third of the transactions on the network, it would be able to convince the rest of the network that its invalid transactions are valid. Thus, transaction volume needs to be large enough for it to be infeasible to do so. IOTA has implemented a centralized node called "The Coordinator" to double-check all of the network's transactions and remove them once the network is large enough.

(4) Hashgraph

Hashgraph is a gossip-protocol consensus developed by Baird (2016). Known transactions are shared with other nodes at random such that all transactions have eventually gossiped to every node. Hedera Hashgraph[9] is a public blockchain network that combines the hashgraph gossip protocol with a Proof of Stake consensus and promises a transaction rate of 10,000 transactions per second. Hashgraph consensus protocol has also been implemented in permissioned distributed ledgers.

(5) SPECTRE

Serialization of Proof-of-work Events: Confirming Transactions via Recursive Elections or SPECTRE (Zohar, 2016) is a proposal to scale Bitcoin that combines PoW and DAGs. Each block mined in SPECTRE points to multiple parents such that the network can support multiple blocks simultaneously. SPECTRE is not implemented yet in reality but can be an interesting solution to scaling cryptocurrency networks.

(e) Summary

Consensus algorithms are an important part of ensuring consistency and accuracy on a blockchain or distributed ledger. Developing an understanding of how the types of consensus algorithms work would give us an appreciation of blockchain-based applications, assets, and investments and make informed decisions. Ultimately, the choice of consensus depends on what the network implementer wants to achieve. It could be for a decentralized public system that needs to be self-governing or an enterprise consortium blockchain which needs to handle sensitive transactions.

---

[9]https://www.hedera.com/.

The area of consensus algorithms is still evolving as we learn more about how network participants react to different incentives (especially for cryptocurrencies). With various use cases emerging for blockchain, we would expect much variety in the type of consensus used. With the multitude of blockchain solutions, any blockchain network may also be required to communicate with several others; and interoperability will become a key consideration.

6.2 Cryptocurrency Advanced

6.2.1 *Bitcoin Script Language*

Reverse Polish Notation (RPN), also referred to as postfix notation, is placing the operation function at the end of a sentence. Reverse RPN is used by script expressions and is processed using stacks and postfix algorithms. A linear data structure can be thought of as an actual physical stack or pile known as a Stack. For stacking and execution of spending ScriptSig and ScriptPubKey is essential.

Learning Objectives
• Understand the application of the RPN for bitcoin transactions.

Main Takeaways

Main Points
• Script expressions use the RPN and are processed using stacks and postfix algorithm.
• Using RPN, the Bitcoin script pushes operands onto the stack first, followed by the operator, which triggers the evaluation.
• The operator will be popped out of the stack, followed by the operands, and the expression gets calculated, and the result will be pushed back onto the stack.

Main Terms
• **Reverse Polish Notation (RPN):** Placing the operation function at the end of a sentence.
• **Stack:** A linear data structure and can be thought of as a real physical stack or pile.

Script expressions use the RPN and are processed using stacks and postfix algorithm. RPN, also known as postfix notation, is a method of placing

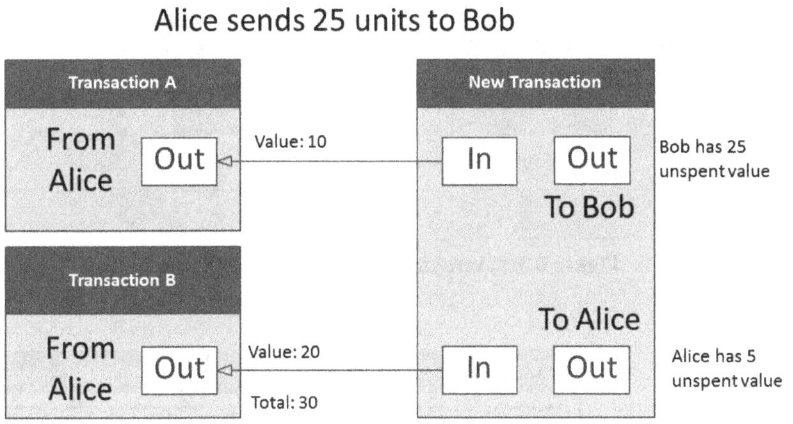

Alice sends 25 units to Bob

Figure 6.2: Spending bitcoins.

the operation function at the end of a sentence. For example, adding 5 and 6 in Script must be written as "5 6 +" rather than "5 + 6".

A stack is a linear data structure and can be thought of as a real physical stack or pile. Items at the top of the stack can be added (pushed) or removed (popped) in a "Last In, First Out (LIFO)" order. Using RPN, the Bitcoin script pushes operands onto the stack first, followed by the operator, which triggers the evaluation. Specifically, the operator will be popped out of the stack, followed by the operands, and the expression gets calculated, and the result will be pushed back onto the stack.

In a bitcoin spending transaction, the output can only be spent in discrete value (Figure 6.2). For example, Alice wants to send 25 units to Bob. Assume Alice only received two transactions previously, where she received ten bitcoins in one transaction and 20 bitcoins in the other. Both the two previous transactions' outputs (the two UTXOs) will be referenced as inputs for the new transaction to Bob. The latest transaction to Bob will have two outputs: one is to send Bob 25 bitcoins, the other is to send the balance of 5 bitcoins (or slightly less than five if we consider the transaction fee) back to Alice herself.

From earlier discussion, we also know that for Alice to spend the UTXOs successfully, she will need to provide ScriptSig (the unlocking script, based on her private key) in the new transaction (see Figure 6.3). This ScriptSig is combined with the ScriptPubKey (the locking script, based on her public key) in the previous transactions and executed. If the returned result is TRUE, it proves that Alice does indeed own the private key paired with the public key, and the spending is successfully executed.

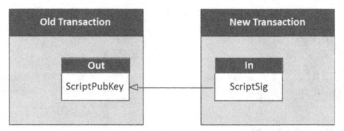

Figure 6.3:   Verifying expenditure of UTXOs.

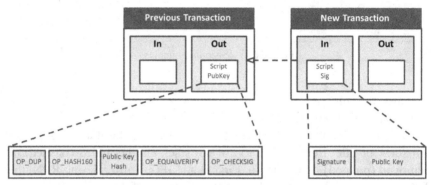

Figure 6.4:   Spending bitcoin at the script level.

Figure 6.4 illustrates how spending is executed at the script level. ScriptPubKey consists five components as shown in Figure 6.4.

(1) OP_DUP
(2) OP_HASH160
(3) <pubkeyHash>
(4) OP_EQUALVERIFY
(5) OP_CHECKSIG

ScriptSig contains two components: Signature and Public Key.

(1) <sig>
(2) <pubkey>

When ScriptPubKey and ScriptSig are combined, the two components from ScriptSig are appended at the front of ScriptPubKey's components

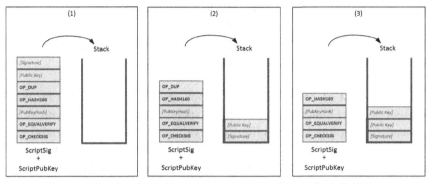

Figure 6.5:   Stacking of components of ScriptSig and ScriptPubKey.

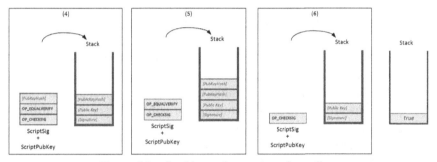

Figure 6.6:   Stacking and execution of spending.

(i.e., in front of OP-DUP) and pushed onto the stack in turn for calculations (see Figures 6.5 and 6.6).

Step 1: Signature is pushed onto the stack, and then Public Key is pushed onto the stack (see Figure 6.5);

Step 2: Operator of Duplicate [OP_DUP] is pushed on the stack: duplication operation is triggered and results in two [Public Key]s on the stack;

Step 3: Operator of Hash160 is pushed onto the stack: this operation returns the 20-byte hash value of the public key [PubKeyHash] (see Figure 6.6);

Step 4: [PubKeyHash] from the scriptPubKey is pushed onto the stack;

Step 5: The operator [OP_EQUALVERIFY] is pushed on the stack, and it verifies if the two [PubKeyHash] currently on the stack are the same. Note that the first one [PubKeyHash] is from scriptSig, and the second is from scriptPubKey;

Step 6: Once step 5 returns true, the last operator [OP_CheckSig] will be pushed onto the stack. It verifies if the public key is generated by the private key used to sign the signature. If the returned result from step 6 is true, the spending is successfully executed.

Below is a list of commonly used script opcodes (see Table 6.1). With these opcodes, functions other than spending can be achieved, e.g., instead of sending a transaction to a wallet address, one can publish a transaction on the network and send bitcoins to anyone who can return a specific hash value. Any user who can return such hash value will be able to unlock the transaction and receive the bitcoins.

(a) Issues in Blockchain

Four issues and concerns associated with blockchain should be noted:

1. Application suitability. Is blockchain superior to current solutions? What are the benchmarks? Can blockchain reduce cost, improve service quality or enhance the user experience? All these questions are relevant. The immutable public ledger, standardized contracts, accounting, and transactions may seem too idealistic. The different nature of businesses and changing needs of the organization will impede the establishment of a single standard. To succeed, blockchain applications need to create true value for the users.

2. Consolidation and allocation of research resources. With issues on the consolidation and allocation of resources, how should research resources be allocated? Can related or similar resources be consolidated to create synergies? What solutions and which industry domains should receive the most funding? These are only some questions.

3. The likelihood of reducing costs. In reality, by contrast, ensuring security and immutability of data may drive up the cost. To ensure the immutability of data implies incurring huge storage and electricity cost. Low storage efficiency is due to (a) the huge amount of copies and (b) blockchain size cannot be reduced (expired and useless data will also be stored). Moreover, rebooting of data is time-consuming. New content times the number of copies, coupled with distance and bandwidth, will all be time-consuming. These issues affect user experience, e.g., high-volume trading, processing huge databases.

Table 6.1: List of commonly used script opcodes.

Word	Opcode	Hex	Description
NA	1–75	0x01-0x4b	The next opcode bytes are data to be pushed onto the stack.
OP_PUSHDATA1	76	0x4c	The next byte contains the number of bytes to be pushed onto the stack.
OP_NOP	97	0x61	Does nothing.
OP_VERIFY	105	0x69	Marks transaction as invalid if top stack value is not true.
OP_RETURN	106	0x6a	Marks transaction as invalid. A standard way of attaching extra data to transactions is to add a zero-value output with a scriptPubKey consisting of OP_RETURN followed by precisely one pushdata op. Such outputs are provably unspendable, reducing their cost to the network. It is currently considered non-standard (though valid) for a transaction to have more than one OP_RETURN output or an OP_RETURN output with more than one pushdata op.
OP_DROP	117	0x75	Removes the top stack item.
OP_DUP	118	0x76	Duplicates the top stack item.
OP_EQUAL	135	0x87	Returns 1 if the inputs are exactly equal, 0 otherwise.
OP_VERIFYEQUAL	136	0x88	Same as OP_EQUAL, but runs OP_VERIFY afterward.
OP_RIPEMD160	166	0xa6	The input is hashed using RIPEMD-160.
OP_SHA256	168	0xa8	The input is hashed using SHA-256.
OP_HASH160	169	0xa9	The input is hashed twice: first with SHA-256 and then with RIPEMD-160.

(Continued)

Table 6.1:   (*Continued*)

Word	Opcode	Hex	Description
OP_CODESEPARATOR	171	0xab	All of the signature checking words will only match signatures to the data after the most recently executed OP_CODESEPARATOR.
OP_CHECKSIG	172	0xac	The entire transaction's outputs, inputs, and script (from the most recently executed OP_CODESEPARATOR to the end) are hashed. The signature used by OP_CHECKSIG must be a valid signature for this hash and public key. If it is, 1 is returned, 0 otherwise.
OP_CHECKSIGVERIFY	173	0xad	Same as OP_CHECKSIG, but OP_VERIFY is executed afterward.
OP_CHECKMULTISIG	174	0xae	Compares the first signature against each public key until it finds an ECDSA match. The subsequent public key compares the second signature against each remaining public key until it finds an ECDSA match. The process is repeated until all signatures have been checked or not enough public keys remain to produce a successful result. All signatures need to match a public key. Because public keys are not rechecked if they fail any signature comparison, signatures must be placed in the scriptSig using the same order as their corresponding public keys were placed in the scriptPubKey or redeemScript. If all signatures are valid, 1 is returned, 0 otherwise. Due to a bug, one extra unused value is removed from the stack.
OP_ CHECKMULTISIGVERIFY	175	0xaf	Same as OP_CHECKMULTISIG, but OP_VERIFY is executed afterward.

4. Over-regulation. Concerns include illegal activities, e.g., money laundering, financing terrorism, fraud, and impersonation. A decentralized framework may not meet regulatory requirements. Early intervention and overregulation by regulators may impede blockchain developments, and the potential benefits of blockchain may not realize. Other challenges include block size, storage, transactions per second, privacy, legality, and Oracle issues.

(b) Use Case: Application of Blockchain in Supply Chain
Digital product traceability is not new, but blockchain technology has accelerated the adoption. A useful purpose of the blockchain is to enable stakeholders to seamlessly trace the flow, the quality, the temperature, the characteristics, and any other measurements that will affect the value of the tracked products with ease. The implementation is without any trusted third party and in a user-friendly manner.

If designed successfully, the distributed digital ledger can minimize waste, improve quality and safety, lessen resources for insurance claims, and empower easier access to cheap capital. Blockchain may not solve all the problems of the supply chain, but it is a game-changer in product traceability that improves efficiency and enhances sustainability.

With blockchain, there is scope to improve the supply chain by faster and more efficient delivery of products, enhancing collaboration among partners, and empowering access to financial and insurance services. The trend is towards an emphasis on the digital economy powered by blockchain traceability.

(1) Benefits of using blockchain in the supply chain
• Better Product Quality — blockchain traceability system ensures accountability and transparency. Therefore, manufacturers or product providers can focus more on importing the quality of their products to meet the customers' needs.
• Sustainability — traceability benefits sustainability cause in two ways. First, it traces the produce to ensure that it is sustainably sourced. In addition, traceability via blockchain can better account for the greenhouse gas emitted through the entire supply chain.
• Efficiency — should the upstream producers not guarantee the safety of their supply, it falls upon the distributors to halt the distribution. This

time efficiency does not merely mean lesser manpower hours, it also distinguishes between life and death during a food pandemic outbreak. The faster Walmart can retrieve a contaminated food, the more life it can save.

- Inclusiveness — blockchain traceability system, when implemented with adequate capital financing support and sufficient investments into bridging the infrastructure gap, will have the capability to allow rural producers to gain access to a much larger market and higher productivity.

(2) Challenges of employing blockchain
In practice, some challenges stop blockchain from wide adoption globally. Some main limitations and risks are summarized as follows.

- Digital literacy: People who do not know how to use smart devices and do not understand technology may find it challenging to adopt new technology like blockchain.
- High costs: To apply blockchain technology to existing industries and manage the transactions, high implementation and operation costs may be involved. Therefore, blockchain will be infeasible for more impoverished regions and less developed countries.
- Inequality risks: The technology gap and access to advanced technology may exacerbate the inequity among individuals or organizations.
- Application constraints: Blockchain technology may not be applicable for all kinds of products. For example, blockchain may not have good performance in tracing them for the ones with complex production.
- Privacy issues: The use of blockchain may cause the private information of some companies to be transparent and accessible to the players in the system if it is a public blockchain. This is a concern of using blockchain technology, and it needs to be considered carefully before any application.

It is a good time to adopt the blockchain technology for supply chain industries because of mainly two reasons: (a) the blockchain technology is at a stage for mass adoption, and (b) given the interest in Central Bank Digital Currencies and the development of stable coins such as those by Libra Association and many others. The Value of Everything Economy will take off with blockchain via tokenization. With the use of blockchain, the increased transparency will release the value of the previously untraded or inseparable and processed products because the quality is usually unknown due to the uncertainty of the supply chain in transit.

With more data, monitoring, and trading, the awareness of quality, brand, and accountability will increase. The two-way enhancement raises the value of the supply chain to the primary stakeholders and eradicates inefficient intermediaries. New business models will emerge alongside new jobs. The principal beneficiaries of this blockchain revolution will be economies with a large agriculture sector where trust is lacking when products are in transit. With more transparency, the discovery of pricing will be much more apparent, and among the stakeholders, the weaker and least informed will derive the most benefits.

If one views blockchain as essential public infrastructure, the openness of the architecture will empower the financially weaker stakeholders such as the farmers who are always affected by climate change. Private-public-partnership is a good starting point for building a gateway for an agriculture economy to reach the world with transparency in quality, transit data, and safety.

Other considerations are education and standardization. There are enough education materials that can help with technology transfer. International standardization, however, is still at an early stage, especially in regards to smart contracts and Oracles. The lack of standards for these decentralized digital contracts and data agencies outside the blockchain is, on the contrary, a reason why there will be less resistance in adoption because blockchain is just an add-on rather than a disruption to the system. Blockchain in the supply chain is a systematic game-changer rather than creative destruction.

With the development over time, the digital supply chain employing blockchain will see the agriculture economies having a much firmer grip on the supply chain and financing process, thus leveling the playing field and enhancing inclusion and sustainability.

6.3 Ethereum and Smart Contracts

6.3.1 *Introduction*

Smart contracts are the means to embed contractual clauses into a digital asset, and a useful smart contract, transparency, and trust between the contractual parties are essential. The emergence of Bitcoin reignited the discussion of smart contracts as an application for blockchain. Application of Smart contracts also includes issuing tokens, eCommerce, and Lotteries. The Ethereum Virtual Machine (EVM) is software that runs on every computer on the Ethereum network. It allows an individual to run any program despite different programming languages given enough time and money. Ethereum's global computer (or the EVM) processes code in a decentralized way, relying on the resources of the nodes on the block-chain network. In Ethereum, smart contracts are stateful decentralized applications stored in the Ethereum blockchain for later execution by the EVM.

A token on Ethereum is just a smart contract that follows some common rules — namely, it implements a standard set of functions that all other token contracts share, such as transferFrom(address _from, address _to, uint256 _ tokenId) and balanceOf(address _owner). Smart contracts on Ethereum can be implemented in various Turing complete scripting languages.

Learning Objectives
• Understand the applications of smart contracts and the role of Ethereum in a blockchain network.

Main Takeaways

Main Points
• Smart Contracts can be helpful for a digital asset given there is transparency and trust between the related parties.
• The contracts run exactly as programmed with no possibility of downtime, censorship, fraud, and third-party interference.
• Smart contracts have different applications on the blockchain.
• Ethereum's global computer (or the EVM) processes code in a decentralized way, relying on the resources of the nodes on the blockchain network.
• ERC-20 has mainly been used for raising funds through a mechanism called Initial coin Offerings (ICOs).

Main Terms
• **Ethereum Virtual Machine (EVM):** Software that runs on every computer on the Ethereum network.
• **ERC:** Ethereum Request For Comments and 20 stands for a unique ID number to distinguish this standard from others.

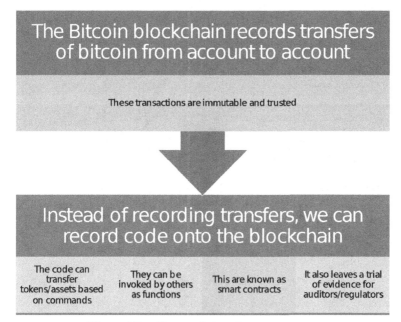

Figure 6.7: Characteristics of smart contracts.

The concept of smart contracts was first discussed in Nick Szabo's (1997) paper, "The Idea of Smart Contracts". He proposed smart contracts to embed contractual clauses into digital assets.

For smart contracts to be useful for digital assets, there needs to be transparency and trust between the contractual parties. The emergence of Bitcoin reignited the discussion of smart contracts as an application for blockchain. It serves as a system that aids the trustworthy execution of smart contracts. They run exactly as programmed without any possibility of downtime, censorship, fraud, or third-party interference. Instead of recording bitcoin transfers on the blockchain, smart contracts are stored (see Figure 6.7).

For example, the sale of original music online (see Figures 6.8 and 6.9). Suppose Billy wants to buy the song. Using the smart contract, Billy will go through the following steps (see Figure 6.10):

(1) He sends $1 from his blockchain wallet to the smart contract.
(2) The song will be available for Alice to download.
(3) The smart contract assigns the rights to download the song to Billy's wallet.

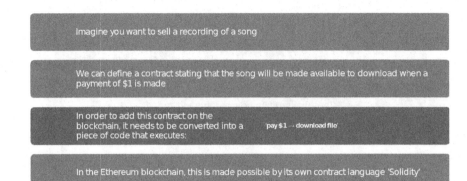

Figure 6.8: Smart contract for music.

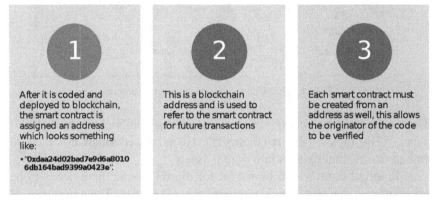

Figure 6.9: Assignment of smart contract to a blockchain address.

(4) $1 is distributed to the song creators (the smart contract can even keep part of it as a fee).

There is no middleman (like a record label or a music platform) in the above process. The smart contract will always act as it is programmed. Other ways that smart contracts are used on blockchain include:

(1) Issuing of tokens. Tokens can represent the virtual currency or physical assets. These tokens can be used for fundraising. ICOs is a good example. Other types of assets that can be tokenized include property, gold, or even fiat currencies like the USD.

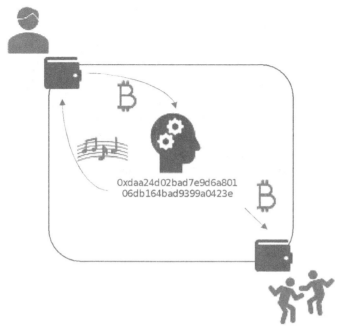

Figure 6.10: Buying a song via a smart contract on the blockchain.

(2) eCommerce. To reduce the need for middlemen to sell virtual goods such as the music example above in Figure 6.9. Another excellent use case for eCommerce is escrow contracts. Escrows hold custody of payment between a buyer and seller until the transaction is completed. Instead of having a trusted middleman (such as PayPal) hold the payment, a smart contract holds the funds (in token form).

(3) Lotteries. A smart contract can act as a lottery. Users can buy the lottery by sending funds into the contract. After the results are determined, the smart contract will be paid out to the winners. The process is transparent and cannot be changed.

(a) Ethereum

Ethereum's global computer (or the EVM) processes code in a decentralized way, relying on the resources of the nodes on the blockchain network (see Figure 6.11). Invented in 2013, the first version of Ethereum was released in 2016 (see Figure 6.12).

Ethereum is a decentralized   Ethereum is like a
platform that runs smart contracts   **"decentralized** global computer"

Figure 6.11:   Characteristics of Ethereum.

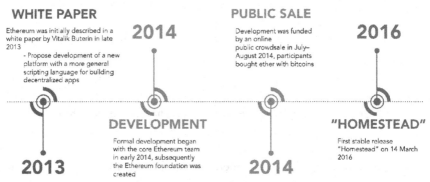

Figure 6.12:   Ethereum's timeline.

Before Ethereum was conceptualized, blockchains had limited ability to process code. Ethereum is different. Rather than giving a set of limited operations, it allows developers to create whatever operations they want. This means developers can build thousands of different applications that go way beyond anything we have seen before. Ethereum aims to be "Turing complete". Anything that can be mathematically represented can be programmed and put into a smart contract. Ethereum is a decentralized global computer that processes smart contracts.

The EVM is software that runs on every computer on the Ethereum network (see Figure 6.13). This allows one to run any program, regardless of the programming language given enough time and memory. The EVM makes the process of creating blockchain applications much easier and efficient than ever before. Rather than build and deploy a new blockchain

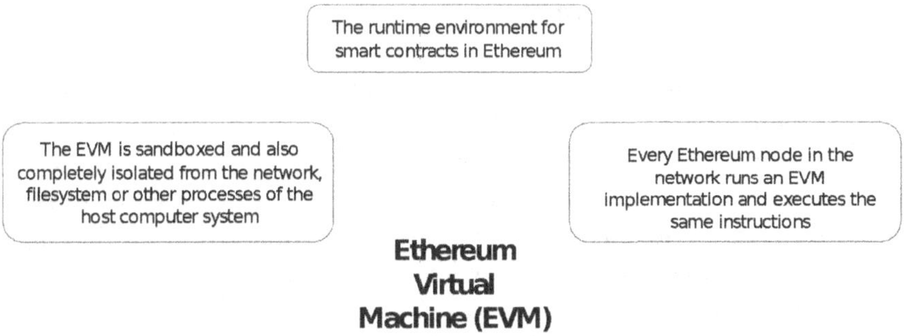

The runtime environment for smart contracts in Ethereum

The EVM is sandboxed and also completely isolated from the network, filesystem or other processes of the host computer system

Every Ethereum node in the network runs an EVM implementation and executes the same instructions

Ethereum Virtual Machine (EVM)

Figure 6.13: Ethereum virtual machine.

for each application, Ethereum allows for the development of potentially thousands of different applications all on one platform.

In Ethereum, smart contracts are stateful decentralized applications that are stored in the Ethereum blockchain for later execution by the EVM. One pays the network for executing the instructions embedded in Ethereum contracts with ether (or more technically "gas"). Ether or ETH is the native currency on the Ethereum Blockchain (similar to how bitcoins or BTC is native on the Bitcoin blockchain). It is used to pay for transactions, including deployment and invocation of smart contracts. Smart contracts on Ethereum can be implemented in various Turing complete scripting languages.

(b) ERC-20

One of the key uses of the ERC-20 contracts is to raise funds through a mechanism called ICOs. Thus, Ethereum is also known as the ICO Crowdfunding Machine. One of Ethereum's smart contract systems' easiest applications is to create a simple token that can be transacted on the Ethereum blockchain instead of Ether. This kind of contract was standardized with ERC-20. Ethereum became the host of a broad scope of ICOs.

The concept of funding projects with a token on Ethereum became the blueprint for a new and highly successful generation of crowdfunding projects. To invest in tokens on top of Ethereum, you simply transfer ETH to the ICO smart contract from your wallet. The token appears in your account, and you are free to transfer them as you want. A set of smart contracts written specifically for this purpose is termed "Token Sale" contracts.

In "ERC-20", ERC stands for Ethereum Request For Comments, and 20 stands for a unique ID number to distinguish this standard from others.

A token on Ethereum is just a smart contract that follows some common rules — namely, it implements a standard set of functions that all other token contracts share, such as transferFrom(address _from, address _to, uint256 _tokenId) and balanceOf(address _owner). So basically, a token is just a contract that keeps track of who owns how much of that token and some functions so those users can transfer their tokens to other addresses. Since all ERC-20 tokens share the same set of functions with the same names, they can all be interacted with in the same ways. An application capable of interacting with one ERC-20 token is also capable of interacting with any other ERC-20 tokens.

Another example of this would be an exchange. When an exchange adds a new ERC-20 token, really, it just needs to add another smart contract it talks to. The exchange only needs to implement this transfer logic once. Then when it wants to add a new ERC-20 token, it is simply a matter of adding the new contract address to its database. The ERC-20 standard can also be used to represent physical assets. For example, a physical asset like property can be fractionalized and traded.

6.4 New Forms of Digital Currency

The true potential of the 4th industrial revolution can only be achieved when innovation and technology become a key element of the existing financial system. The technology would enable every citizen to have an unbiased, sovereign right to a fair world. Central Bank Digital Currencies (CBDCs) and stablecoins are emerging solutions to solve challenges such as transparency, security, convenience, inclusion, and stability.

Learning Objectives
- Understand the basic types and design of CBDCs.
- Understand the benefits, challenges, and enabling factors of CBDCs.
- Understand the fundamental concepts and different types of stablecoins.

Main Takeaways

Main Points
- The design of CBDCs can be categorized based on operations, distribution, and ledger design.
- Stablecoins offer means to retain value and price stability in the cryptocurrency world.

- A stablecoin is pegged to a target currency or asset such as the U.S. dollar to maintain a stable value.

Main Terms

- **Central Bank Digital Currency:** A digital currency issued by the central banks and a digital form of legal tender. It can be CBI or CBA.
- **Stablecoin:** A stablecoin is pegged to a target currency or asset

6.4.1 *Central Bank Digital Currency*

In this age of digitalization, several industries are undergoing the 4th revolution, which has altered several aspects of people's lives. Specifically, the way in which people make payments has been evolving rapidly. As the demand for digital currency rises, there is a clear need for innovation in the payment system amongst corporations and economies. This trend has been further accelerated by the thriving cryptocurrency market. Although digital money, electronic money, or electronic currency are sometimes used interchangeably with digital currency, the meaning and scopes of the terms vary. Digital currency is known currency in the digital or electronic form. Electronic money refers to the fiat money stored in banks and transferred between parties.

The Central Bank Digital Currency (CBDC) is the sovereign digital currency launched by the central banks or monetary authorities and is a legal tender. However, the digital currencies that are not directly issued, but are authorized by the central banks are known as central bank-authorized CBDC or aCBDC. The two types of CBDCs that are legal tenders are iCBDC (issued by the central bank) and aCBDC (authorized by central banks). The digital currencies not issued by the central banks but by private corporations and are not legal tenders are called non-central bank digital currencies (NCB).

CBDCs have great potential in accelerating financial inclusion to serve the unserved and and bank the unbanked. Knowing the benefits and challenges of CBDCs will help in understanding this new form of digital currency and its usage. For the mass adoption of CBDC and the formation of an augmented action plan, aspects such as the design of CBDCs and which aspects to invest in need careful and thorough consideration and evaluation. Therefore, this section introduces the different design choices of CBDCs, its benefits, challenges, and enabling factors.

(a) Benefits and Risks of CBDC

The benefits of CBDC are summarized as follows.

- Lower costs of issuing money, as physical currency has high issuance, storage, and management costs.
- Greater convenience through hassle-free online and offline transactions using cellphones, cards, QR codes, and NFC.
- Financial inclusion enabled by the provision of financial services to the unbanked in remote areas with no digital literacy using CBDCs
- The effectiveness of monetary and fiscal policy can be ensured as transactions and activities can be traced with the use of CBDCs. This helps in clear measurement of policy impact through the reflection of economic transactions.
- Financial stability can be ensured by CBDCs as the sovereign digital currency, alleviating the potential threat posed to the stability of the financial system by NCBs such as Diem and cryptocurrencies.
- CDBCs have enhanced security compared to NCBs because they are issued by the central bank. As such, CDBCs are not subject to credit risk.
- Managed anonymity as the design of CBDCs allows for payments and transactions to be traced without revealing the identity and personal information of the merchants or receivers.

There are also a few challenges posed by CBDCs which are listed as follows.

- Disintermediation of the financial institutions can occur as CBDCs may disrupt the conventional financial system.
- Bank runs may occur, as the chances of a bank run on the collapse of the financial system are more extensive. Additionally, more widespread negative impact can be expected as CBDCs can be in use across many geographies at any time.
- Infrastructure for CBDCs needs to be developed and ready as the existing hardware and software in the conventional financial system need to be upgraded to provide the services related to CBDC.
- User literacy can hinder the government while designing and implementing CBDCs as these concepts are relatively new and complicated to understand. This may also affect the public acceptance of CBDCs.

- Technical issues related to the application and operations of digital currencies cannot be neglected and need to be addressed to successfully launch a CBDC.
- Regulations for running CBDCs are not in place in the legal system, and thus it is vital to upgrade the existing regulatory framework to ensure smooth operations of CBDCs.

(b) Design Choice

There are three possible models in terms of the designs of CBDC: a direct or a one-tier model, a two-tier model, and a hybrid model. As per the direct model, CBDC is directly issued by the central banks, and its payment and circulation are also the central bank's responsibility. However, in a two-tier model, commercial banks and financial institutions perform the payment and circulation functions. The hybrid model is a mix of the two aforementioned models. Based on the distribution model, the CBDCs can be categorized as wholesale CBDC or retail CBDC, where wholesale CBDC is for wholesale transactions between financial institutions and retail CBDC is for transactions amongst the public.

Based on ledger designs, CBDCs can be classified as account-based CBDC and token-based CBDC. In an account-based CBDC design, the transactions are connected to another account used to verify the identity of the sender or payer. It is similar to a traditional bank transfer or payment. By contrast, the token-based design relies more on cryptography as the transactions are verified by a private key in an asymmetric key infrastructure. In this case, a digital signature is used to prove legitimacy.

(c) Enabling Factors

The following are the enablers of CBDCs.

- Digital identification — A protected digital identification should be a membership criterion to be a part of the CBDC network. Both the Self Sovereign ID and the CBDC must have standards for convenient interoperability.
- Data privacy protection — Using AI and big data as a feature of CBDC, ensuring anonymity of the user and privacy of transactional details for participants will enable data privacy protection.

- Interoperable value transfer gateway — To ensure ownership transfers, just like cash, across payment systems and networks to ease payment and settlement is needed. The design of the currencies needs to ensure that the regional payment network is also considered.
- Talent, knowledge, and skills — Well-equipped and skilled talents, as well as training and educating resources, are essential for the initiation and steady development of the CBDC ecosystem. Local sourcing of talent, regional training programs, and incentive systems should play a significant part in upgrading skills and increasing the talent pool in the field.
- Open source and trust distribution governance — The uninterrupted network improvement occurs because an unbiased or property source code encourages community participation. The risk gets distributed due to distributed trust.
- Easy compliance — CBDCs decrease the dependency on the third party for audit and validation and reduce the risk of a single point of failure. This also allows for low-cost compliance and therefore, lower barriers to entry.
- Comprehensive data and oracle ecosystem — Using AI and big data, trends can be generated to analyze sustainable finance and consumer waste reduction to ensure a sustainable and energy-efficient ecosystem.
- Fast, stable, and 24/7 available network — CBDC will enable stable connectivity and efficient speed such that the financial system's transactional volume demand is met.
- Robust security framework — CBDC will ensure the development of tough infrastructure to fight cyber security threats.
- Digital literacy and user experience — Ensuring extended awareness and education will further ease financial inclusivity through CBDCs. Lowering the restrictions to become a member by providing tangency in suitable technologies for less digitally proficient users will aid as well.

6.4.2 *Stablecoins*

As of April 11, 2021, the total market capital of stablecoins has reached more than $65 billion, representing about 3.15% of the cryptocurrency market. The stablecoin trading volume per day is more than a few hundred billion dollars. Stablecoin plays a crucial role in the digital currency market because it combines the best of both worlds: the instant processing and permission-less payment of cryptocurrency as well as the valuation stability of the classical fiat currency.

Essentially, a standard mean of payment should reserve a relatively stable value, in the long run, to be accepted by the public. In contrast to the wild volatility in the price of many popular cryptocurrencies like bitcoin, stablecoin offers a means to retain value and price stability in the cryptocurrency world.

(a) Taxonomy

The taxonomy of stablecoins is based on the design architecture, generally specified by the pegging target and the type of underlying collateral.[10] A reserve asset backs a stablecoin as collateralization, and its price is pegged against specific assets. The underlying collateral asset and pegging asset can be either the same or distinct.

(b) Pegging Target

A stablecoin is pegged to a target currency or asset to maintain a stable value. Since the values of these pegging targets are stable due to their scarcity or trustfulness, the value of stablecoin will be stable as well if its value is constantly matched with the asset price. The most common choice of pegging target is fiat currency. There are stablecoins pegged against most of the major currencies in the world. The majority of the currently active stablecoins in the market are pegged against USD. In addition, it is also possible to peg against commodities. For example, the stablecoin Digix[11] and HelloGold[12] are pegged against fine gold. Similar to the portfolio concept, the pegging target can also be a bundle of currency and/or commodity instead of a single asset.

(c) Type of Collateral

This is related to why stablecoin can maintain stability in its value. Like the reserve policy of legal tender, one type of stablecoins reserves an

---

[10]Moin, A., Sirer, E. G., & Sekniqi, K. (2019). A classification framework for stablecoin designs. arXiv preprint arXiv:1910.10098.

[11]Eufemio, A. C., Chng, K. C., & Djie, S. (2016). Digix's whitepaper: The gold standard in crypto assets. White paper.

[12]HelloGold Foundation Technical Whitepaper (2017). https://www.hgfoundation.io/wp-content/downloads/HelloGold-Technical-Whitepaper-27-Aug-17-Final.pdf.

underlying asset as collateral. As a result, customers can always request to redeem the underlying asset using the stablecoin at a 1:1 ratio. As a result, the monetary value and purchasing power are retained. The stablecoin with the underlying collateral asset is called the collateralized stablecoin. The collateralized stablecoins are further divided into three categories, namely the fiat-collateralized stablecoin, the crypto-collateralized stablecoin, and the commodity-collateralized stablecoin, depending on the type of the underlying collateral assets.

Fiat-collateralized stablecoins are backed by one or multiple fiat currencies as the underlying collateral. For example, Tether (USDT),[13] which is collateralized using USD, guarantees that there will be one USD deposited in the vault as collateral for every single Tether coin released. A coin is destroyed when the collateralized fiat currency is claimed.

Crypto-collateralized stablecoins use other cryptocurrencies as the underlying reserve assets. To avoid being "over-collateralized", instead of a 1:1 ratio, a larger proportion of cryptocurrency is needed as the collateral for a smaller amount of stablecoins due to the nature of cryptocurrency price volatility. For example, to issue $100 crypto-collateralized stablecoins, a reserve of $150 or $200 worth of Ether coins are needed to counteract the potential fluctuation in Ether coin price. Regular monitoring is necessary to adjust the reserve ratio constantly.

Commodity-collateralized stablecoins use commodities like the precious metal gold as the underlying collateral since it is impossible to mine a large amount of gold in a short period. Owners of commodity-backed stablecoins can give up their stablecoins at the conversion rate to take possession of the underlying commodity. For example, the owner of Digix Gold Tokens (DGX) is eligible to exchange the coin for gold bars. Nevertheless, the drawback is that those commodities need to be stored and safeguarded physically. This will incur a non-negligible amount of cost.

There is another type of stablecoin that is not collateralized by underlying assets. These are called non-collateralized stablecoins. It maintains price stabilization through a well-designed mechanism or protocol. For instance, similar to how a central bank retains valuation of the fiat currency, the issuers of the stablecoins can take reactive action to control the supply of the currency in the market based on the demand. The fundamental

---

[13] White Paper (2016). Tether: Fiat currencies on the Bitcoin blockchain. https://tether.to/wp-content/uploads/2016/06/TetherWhitePaper.pdf.

mechanism of this approach is to increase supply when the price of stablecoin is high and to contract supply when the price is low. The users of stablecoin in the market are theoretically rational and self-interested. They will, therefore, automatically react and eventually reach the supply-demand equilibrium. In contrast to central bank control, the price of stablecoin is stabilized by implementing a series of smart contracts on a decentralized platform that can run autonomously.

6.4.3 *Summary*

The rapid growth and breakthrough in digital currency have reformed everyone's lifestyle. Soon, paying and transferring money to anyone, anywhere in the world, can be as easy as sending a chat message to a friend on social media within seconds. The rapid development and vast adoption of the WeChat ecosystem in China may serve as a way for us to imagine how the future payment system may look like. In particular, it provides a one-stop integrated payment solution for almost all aspects of daily life, such as shopping in stores, transferring money across institutions and individuals, paying utility bills, making investments, taking loans, and many more.

As the potential candidate for the future means of payment, stablecoins possess attractive features such as low cost, fast transaction speed and convenience in cross-border payments, security, and open architecture. Many governments have already started developing pilot central bank digital currency (CBDC) [Lee2020],[14] for example, the People's Bank of China, Bank of England, Bank of Canada, central banks of Thailand, Sweden, and Singapore. Pegged against each country's fiat currency, CBDC may become the future means of payment, the unit of account, and store of value.

If we expand our imagination, what if the whole world will embrace one or two global stablecoins that are not limited by the border of countries? How will that change the entire world? The growth of the global economy would be further promoted. Many small enterprises that were previously excluded or had limited access to financial services due to the high transaction cost may identify new opportunities. Nevertheless, there are also challenges to be addressed. For example, how to protect the

---

[14][Lee2020] Lee, D. K. C., & Teo, E. G. (2020). The New Money: The utility of Cryptocurrencies and the need for a New Monetary Policy. Available at SSRN.

privacy of personal data, how to avoid money laundry, how to prevent the local fiat currency from being threatened by strong stablecoins. This will be an ongoing research topic.

6.5 Privacy and Security

It is challenging to modify or tamper with the data stored in a ledger because of the design of bitcoin and its blockchain. The application of cryptography ensures the same. Incentive mechanisms embedded in the consensus protocol helps to align all validators to be good. The security of the blockchain network comes with its decentralization and distribution. This section discusses the 51% attack, denial of service attacks, software flaws and crypto currency exchange hacks. The blockchain network is more prone to 51% attacks if the network size is small. Major networks such as Bitcoin and Ethereum enjoy greater resilience to these attacks as the costs make it difficult to achieve, both monetarily and logistically.

Owners of bitcoins enjoy some amount of anonymity when they transact on the Bitcoin blockchain as they are identified only by their public address. However, all transactions are transparent on the blockchain. Coin mixing services prevent users' addresses from being tracked by mixing coins from multiple senders before sending them to the recipients. Privacy on blockchain extends beyond cryptocurrency transactions. In many business applications, sensitive business data is involved. This data needs to be shared appropriately with the members of the blockchain network.

Learning Objectives
- Understand the different types of attacks to privacy, privacy technologies used in blockchain, privacy design, causes of data leaks, and Privacy Considerations for Blockchain.

Main Takeaways

Main Points
- The security of the blockchain network comes with its decentralization and distribution.
- A blockchain network, in principle, is meant to be immutable.
- The risk of different attacks must be considered when trading in cryptocurrencies and deploying a blockchain network.

- All transactions are transparent on the blockchain. Privacy technologies used in Blockchain range from Coin Mixing to Anonymous signatures and State Channels. Privacy on blockchain extends beyond cryptocurrency transactions.
- Privacy is not just about the technology but its design and policies that restrict what humans can do. Most government regulations include obligations in terms of where data processing can take place.
- In the current data economy, many services like social media or messaging platforms are offered free to users in return for their data. This landscape is now changing due to increased user protection from various governments.

Main Terms

- **Coin mixing services:** Prevent users' addresses from being tracked by mixing coins from multiple senders before sending them to the recipients.
- **Group signature:** A cryptography scheme proposed in the 1990s. With this scheme, any group member can sign a message for the group using her secret key.
- **Ring signature scheme:** Achieves anonymity with a group of users. However, a group admin is not required.
- **Homomorphic encryption:** A cryptography method that allows certain operations to be performed on encrypted data.
- **Trusted Execution Environment (TEE):** An isolated computing environment, other applications within the machine will not be able to access or tamper with the computation.

6.5.1 *Security of Blockchain Networks*

The design of Bitcoin and its blockchain ensured that the data stored in the ledger is tough to change and tamper with. The use of cryptography in blockchain ensures this. Incentive mechanisms embedded in the consensus protocol helps to align all validators to be good. The distributed network checks the validity of the transactions to ensure that no fraudulent transaction goes through.

The security of the blockchain network comes with its decentralization and distribution. As these features diminish, someone could gain control of the network and compromise the security of the network. Some common network attacks are hard to execute on a blockchain network.

For example, a Sybil attack is an attack where someone attempts to take over a network by creating multiple accounts on the system. This would mean running multiple nodes on a blockchain network on a blockchain network. If the attacker can access enough nodes, he can block transactions (from other users) and disconnect you from the public network. He can double-spend or block your transactions by separating you from the main network.

Consensus algorithms make it hard to carry out a Sybil attack. One usually has to expend resources (such as computer power or tokens) to become a node on the blockchain network. This makes an attack expensive and difficult. Miners have a strong incentive to keep mining honestly as extensive resources are needed to mine coins. However, this sort of attack happens in real life to weaker/smaller blockchain networks. In large-scale Sybil attacks, where the attackers manage to control the majority of the network computing power or hash rate, they can carry out a 51% attack.

(a) The 51% Attack

In blockchain networks running Proof of Work (PoW) consensus, nodes are usually programmed to look for the blockchain with the most blocks as the correct version of history. Miners with more than 50% of the network hashing power can take advantage of this. This miner (let's call it Miner X) can send funds to one address (Wallet A) on the main chain and double-spend the same funds to another address on a forked copy of the blockchain that they are secretly mining with more hashing power than the main chain.

Other miners will continue to mine on the "Main Chain" while the secret fork is not revealed (see Figure 6.14). Thus, they will recognize the 100 BTC transferred to Wallet A as valid. Cryptocurrency exchanges may pay out in fiat currency as a result.

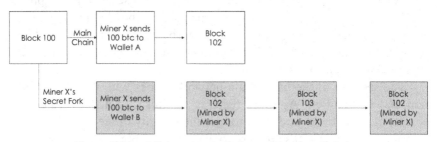

Figure 6.14: Mining process, forks, and creation of chains.

With more hashing power, Miner X can mine faster on the secret fork. Miner X can reveal it once it has more blocks than the main chain. The rest of the miners will mine on the longer fork when it is revealed. The secret fork will be recognized as the main chain, and the 100 btc in Wallet A will become invalid. However, if someone (like an exchange) has paid out fiat money or goods and services based on the receipt of the 100 btc in Wallet A, this may not be recoverable. This is also known as a "double spend" attack.

Ethereum Classic (ETC) fell victim to a 51% attack on January 5, 2019.[15] This went on for three days, finally halting on January 8, 2019, with estimated losses of US$1.1 million. On January 7, digital asset exchange Coinbase reported that its systems had detected unusual activity on the ETC blockchain. As a result of the suspicious activity, the trading platform suspended all ETC trades to protect user funds.

According to Mark Nesbitt (Security engineer at Coinbase),[16] the platform's systems had detected this activity as early as January 5, a couple of days before the reports began in the media. At that time, ETC developers contended that the unusual activity detected by Coinbase could be attributed to the testing of new mining machines. They denied any double spends or any losses stemming from the activity.

However, more reports and evidence began to trickle in from blockchain analysis firms and other digital asset trading platforms. Gate.io was the first exchange to corroborate Coinbase's findings.[17] Gate.io Research confirmed that the ETC 51% attack happened successfully. The analysis detected seven rollback transactions (invalid transfers due to a block becoming invalid). Four of them were created by the attacker, and 54,200 ETC were transferred. Gate.io further corroborated Coinbase's findings that the attack was not just an innocent deep chain reorganization.[18]

Revealing the attacker's wallet addresses and other information pertinent to the malicious transactions, Gate.io also explained the attack had resulted in losses amounting to US$40,000 for the exchange. However,

---

[15] https://cointelegraph.com/news/ethereum-classic-51-attack-the-reality-of-proof-of-work.

[16] https://bravenewcoin.com/insights/etc-51-attack-what-happened-and-how-it-was-stopped.

[17] https://www.gate.io/article/16735.

[18] This can happen in certain circumstances as the blockchain network is asynchronous and some machines mine faster than others.

the exchange said it would not pass on the losses to its users. It also raised the confirmation number for ETC transactions and called on the ETC developers to change the consensus mechanism for the blockchain to avoid another attack. Following the Gate.io revelation, more exchanges began to either limit ETC trading activity on their platforms or increased the confirmation limit. Some of these include CoinCheck, Bitflyer as well as the mining pool Etherchain. Concurrently, ETC developers finally confirmed the presence of a 51% attack, referencing a report that a single party had been able to acquire over 50% of the networks' hash rate.

On January 9, SlowMist published a report with an in-depth analysis of the attack.[19] The firm found the first attempted malicious transaction on the trading platform, Bitrue. The attacker executed a double spend worth US$14,000. Appearing to confirm Coinbase's estimate of $1.1 million loss as a result of the attack, Slow Mist said that the attacker halted its activities due to exchange actions. "Based on continuous tracking, we found that, because of the increase in block confirmations and the ban on malicious wallet addresses by exchanges, the attacker's 51% attack on ETC has stopped after that".

Coinbase was able to protect its users by halting trading of ETC. Given that ETC was one of the top 20 digital assets by market capitalization, the 51% attack reverberated throughout the cryptocurrency community. It was easy for machines mining ETH to switch to mining ETC as ETC uses the same mining algorithm as Ethereum. Since the ETC network was much smaller than ETH's, it was easy to gain the majority hash rate. The rise of cloud-based mining has made "hash rate for hire" a norm in the industry. And for relatively small blockchain networks, it became attractive for bad actors to launch such attacks. Crypto 51[20] lists the estimated costs of renting the necessary hash power for some popular cryptocurrencies. It is surprising how low the costs of launching such attacks were.

An hour-long attack on ETC, for example, could be done for around US$6,000. A Litecoin hijack would cost around US$16,000 an hour. Even Ethereum could be attacked at the cost of approximately US$120,000 an hour.

---

[19] https://medium.com/@slowmist/the-analysis-of-etc-51-attack-from-slowmist-team-728596d76ead.

[20] https://www.crypto51.app/.

Figure 6.15: Number of nodes in Bitcoin Gold.[22]

In May 2018, Bitcoin Gold (a Bitcoin Fork) was also attacked.[21] Bitcoin Gold's hash rate was significantly lower than Bitcoin, making it vulnerable to attacks. The cost of the attack on Crypto 51 was only US$400. In Figure 6.15, we compared the number of nodes on both networks in February 2019. Bitcoin Gold's nodes make up less than 2% of Bitcoins. Thus, we can see that a blockchain network is more vulnerable to 51% attacks if the network size is small (Figure 6.16). Larger networks like Bitcoin and Ethereum enjoy more resilience to such attacks as the costs make it harder to achieve both monetarily and logistically. This factor needs to be considered for anyone looking to invest in cryptocurrencies or run their applications on their blockchain networks.

---

[21] https://qz.com/1287701/bitcoin-golds-51-attack-is-every-cryptocurrencys-nightmare-scenario/.

[22] https://status.bitcoingold.org.

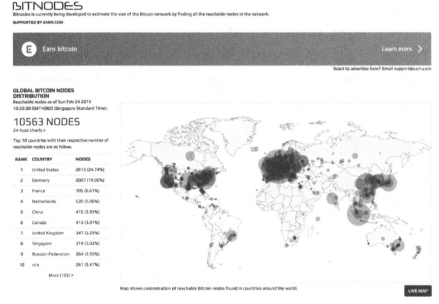

Figure 6.16:   The number of nodes in Bitcoin.[23]

(b) Denial of Service Attacks

A DoS attack aims to make a system or network inaccessible to its users. This is done by constantly sending traffic or information to the target, causing it to crash. A DoS attack blocks legitimate users from accessing the service. High-profile organizations such as financial institutions, media, or government, are usually susceptible to these attacks. DoS attacks usually do not result in loss of information or assets, but the downtime it causes can also be costly. For example, if a bank gets attacked, it may not process financial transactions.

The decentralized nature of blockchain makes for strong protection against DoS attacks. If certain nodes on the network have gone offline, the blockchain network can continue to validate transactions and create blocks. When the nodes come back online, they can sync up with the network and resume from the current block. However, in blockchain networks with distributed computing such as Ethereum, DoS attacks are possible if there are vulnerabilities in the code.

---

[23] https://bitnodes.earn.com.

In 2016, the Ethereum network experienced such an attack.[24] On 22nd September, the first day of Devcon (Ethereum foundation's annual conference), nodes running the geth client (an implementation of an Ethereum node in the Go programming language) started to crash due to lack of memory. The crash only affected clients based on the Go language, and Ethereum created a hotfix the next day.

Vitalik Buterin (Ethereum's founder) released a statement[25] in the post-mortem. The underlying problem involved Ethereum's EXTCODESIZE attribute, which is included in each transaction by design. An attacker could use this attribute to ask for additional checks against the Ethereum network database, up to 50,000 at a time. This causes the clients to crash as they run out of memory. It causes a two to three times reduction in the rate of block-creation. As stated by Vitalik, there was no consensus failure, and neither the network nor any client at any point fully halted.

(c) Software Flaws
Although the flaw (which allowed the DoS attack) in Ethereum was patched, this event also revealed the vulnerability of more complex blockchain networks. In particular, networks with applications or smart contracts running on them are susceptible to flaws in the code or bugs. Smart contracts are only as good as the humans who write them. Code bugs or oversights can lead to unintended adverse actions. Smart contracts on the blockchain are meant to be immutable. This means that there is no easy way to prevent this when the code gets exploited. Various software bugs, decentralized apps (dApps), or smart contracts have led to tens of millions in damages over the years.

One of the first significant incidents with smart contracts was the DAO (Decentralized Autonomous Organization) hack.[26] "The DAO" was a project by a team behind a startup called Slock.it. The aim was to create a decentralized venture capital firm where investors can make decisions to invest through smart contracts. It was funded through a token sale that raised US$150 million. Shortly after the fundraiser was completed in 2016, The DAO was hacked by an unknown attacker who stole US$50 million worth of ether. This was possible because of a backdoor in the code.

---

[24] https://cointelegraph.com/news/ethereum-is-under-ddos-attack-miners-are-alerted.
[25] https://blog.ethereum.org/2016/09/22/transaction-spam-attack-next-steps/.
[26] https://blockgeeks.com/guides/ethereum/.

As a large amount of money was involved, the Ethereum foundation stepped in and the community voted to roll back the blockchain and executed a hard fork. ETC (Ethereum Classic) resulted from this event, being the original blockchain where the hack happened. ETH (Ethereum) is the blockchain where the majority agreed to rewrite a small part of the blockchain and return the stolen money to the owners. Both blockchains are identical up to the point where the fork was implemented. This move was intensely debated and controversial. A blockchain network, in principle, is meant to be immutable. A dangerous precedent has been set that goes against blockchain's spirit by executing the rollback.

As such, any smart contract that is to be deployed into a blockchain network should go under intense review and testing. Smart contracts and code should be reviewed and audited by external parties. The application should undergo penetration testing. It is advisable to have good security practices in place as flaws may remain hidden for a while. No matter how experienced the programmer, mistakes can be made.

(d) Cryptocurrency Exchange Hacks

The final blockchain security issue is not an issue with the actual blockchain network and its technology. It has to do with cryptocurrency exchanges. Exchanges are very attractive to hackers as they hold massive amounts of cryptocurrencies and sometimes do not have very good security practices. Most exchanges operate in a centralized manner; thus, they do not have the benefits of the decentralized blockchain. Private keys and wallets containing the cryptocurrencies of investors were not well protected, allowing hackers to steal these keys and transfer the assets out of the wallets.

The most famous exchange hack was that of Mt. Gox in 2014,[27] where around 850,000 bitcoins worth US$470 mil (at that time) were stolen by a hacker. Mt. Gox was the industry leader who processes about 70% of all bitcoin transactions. All the affected users were unable to get the money back. Exchange hacks are still prevalent. Hackers stole hundreds of millions. It is always good practice to transfer your crypto holdings to self-managed secure wallets (such as a hardware device). If you have significant amounts of cryptocurrencies, consider using custodian services with high levels of security.

---

[27] https://www.wired.com/2014/03/bitcoin-exchange/.

The situations describe above cast light upon the fact that blockchain networks are still vulnerable to exploitation by bad actors despire their "secure" design. The risk of such attacks needs to be considered when trading in cryptocurrencies and deploying a blockchain network. However, security considerations go beyond hackers. In the next section, we look at protecting user data privacy.

6.5.2 Ensuring Privacy of Users on Blockchain Networks

Owners of bitcoins enjoy some amount of anonymity when they transact on the Bitcoin blockchain as their public address only identifies them. However, all transactions are transparent on the blockchain. Forensic analysis can bundle addresses and find patterns. When you transact with exchanges, the regulation requires that the exchange collects your identity and information. Even if you only transact on a peer-to-peer basis, your IP address can be logged in nodes and linked to your bitcoin address. When you purchase something online with bitcoin, your physical address and other information can also be linked to your bitcoin address. This means that a bitcoin user's privacy is not entirely protected when they transact on the blockchain. Privacy is an essential element when it comes to digital payments. With paper money, however, you have the freedom to use it without being tracked.

(a) Ensuring the Privacy of Cryptocurrencies
The crypto community has been working to improve the privacy aspects of cryptocurrencies. Figure 6.17 provides an overview of the technologies.

One commonly used method is coin mixing. Coin mixing services prevent users' addresses from being tracked by mixing coins from multiple senders before sending them to the recipients. The ownership of coins

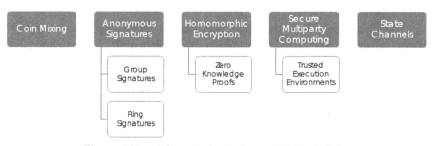

Figure 6.17: Privacy technologies used in blockchain.

is obfuscated with coin mixing. Some examples are Mixcoin, CoinJoin, SharedCoin, and CoinShuffle. The solutions differ in the amount of security they provide.

Another method is to anonymize signatures. The two most commonly used signature schemes to achieve this are "group signatures" and "ring signatures". Group signature is a cryptography scheme proposed in the 1990s. With this scheme, any group member can sign a message for the group using her secret key. The digital signature can be validated by the group public key. The verifier can only know that the signature came from the group but not the identity of the actual signer. The group signature scheme requires an administrator or authority to add and remove group members. By the nature of its design, this is suitable for consortium blockchains.

Ring signature scheme also achieves anonymity with a group of users. However, a group admin is not required. With ring signatures, one cannot determine who the actual signer within the group is. Any users can arbitrarily form the group without any additional setup. Thus, such schemes are suitable for public blockchains. Examples of public blockchains with ring signature schemes are Monero and Ethereum.

Another important method to protect data privacy is homomorphic encryption. It's a cryptography method that allows certain operations to be performed on encrypted data. This means one can perform a calculation without having to decrypt the data. For example, one can determine if a wallet has a sufficient amount for a transfer without knowing the actual amount of funds in the wallet. This technique can be used to store data on the blockchain without changing the properties of the blockchain. It allows public blockchain to operate without having to store transactional data publicly. Ethereum smart contracts can provide homomorphic encryption on data stored on the Ethereum blockchain. Zero-Knowledge Proofs are one form of homomorphic encryption and are used by blockchains such as ZCash.

Another widely discussed privacy protection technique is Secure Multi-Party Computation (SMPC). This technique allows multiple parties to each compute part of the input data in a way that does not compromise the input's privacy. Many real-world problems (where inputs need to remain anonymous) such as voting and bidding can be solved with SMPC. SMPC eliminates a need for a trusted authority to count votes or check bids. In 2015, a decentralized (blockchain-based) SMPC platform called Enigma was proposed. Enigma provides autonomous control and protection of personal data while eliminating the necessity and dependency of a trusted third party.

Enigma utilizes a trusted execution environment (TEE). TEE is an isolated computing environment. Other applications within the machine will not access or tamper with the computation. One notable type of TEE technology is the Intel Software Guard eXtensions (SGX). It forms the basis for secure and privacy-preserving smart contracts on Enigma. One use case is for a decentralized credit scoring algorithm. Multiple inputs for a person's credit score, such as account information, transactions, payments, and credit history, can be stored in an encrypted manner on the blockchain. When required, the credit score is calculated within the TEE, and only the credit score is returned to the requestor (without exposing the raw data). Blockchain provides additional trust for the encrypted raw data as it cannot be tampered with once stored.

Another method of ensuring privacy on permissioned blockchain is the use of state channels. These are private channels between two or more users. These users exchange the signed transactions without broadcasting them to the blockchain. We can imagine state channels as mini blockchains within the main blockchain network. State channels can be configured to have a limited lifespan, and the channel can be closed by updating the latest state of transactions to the blockchain.

(b) Privacy Considerations and Design for Blockchain Applications
Privacy on blockchain extends beyond cryptocurrency transactions. In many business applications, sensitive business data is involved. This data needs to be shared appropriately with the members of the blockchain network. Global regulations around user privacy are also evolving rapidly and becoming stricter. The implementation of the EU's General Data Protection Regulation (GDPR) in May 2018 changed the landscape of technology. When personal data is collected, companies have to indicate what it will be used for and cannot use it for anything else. They need to minimize the amount of data they collect and keep, limiting it to only what is necessary for the purpose intended. When requested, companies have to tell users what data they hold and alter or delete the data.

The largest causes of data leaks are human-related (see Figure 6.18). Thus, privacy is not just about the technology but its design and policies that restrict what humans can do. Data privacy is concerned with the proper

Figure 6.18: Causes of data leaks.[28]

handling of data. There are three key considerations: consent, notice, and regulation. Specifically, practical data privacy concerns often revolve around:

- Whether or how data is shared with third parties?
- How is data legally collected or stored?
- Regulatory restrictions such as GDPR and PDPA

Most government regulations include obligations in terms of where data processing can occur, also known as transfers of personal data to third countries. The Indonesian data protection bill guarantees that the personal data of Indonesians will exist only within Indonesia and will be protected by the government. The GDPR specifies that personal data can generally only be transferred to third countries if deemed "adequate". This presents an interesting problem for decentralized blockchain networks. It may be necessary to border off the blockchain network to ensure that the data does not leave the geographical constraints of the country.

Another consideration is how the data is being stored. Some amount of processing could increase the privacy of the data. Various techniques can be used for this purpose.

---

[28] *Source*: https://www.dataprivacymonitor.com/cybersecurity/deeper-dive-human-error-is-to-blame-for-most-breaches/.

Pseudonymization can hide personal data by replacing information that links the data to particular individuals with artificial identifiers. One can mask the data by hiding parts of the data by replacing it with random characters or other data. Data blurring is one form of pseudonymization. Pictures and videos containing faces can be blurred out to protect the identity of individuals captured by the camera. In pictures of identity documents such as passports, the sensitive information can also be blurred out.

Encryption converts data to another form that is only readable to someone with access to a key or password. There are two categories of encryption, symmetric and asymmetric. There is only one password in symmetric encryption, and anyone with the password can decrypt the data. In asymmetric encryption, there are sets of keypairs (public and private keys). The keypairs are required to encrypt and decrypt the data. Asymmetric encryption is widely used in the design of blockchain systems. Data should be encrypted while it is being moved and also while it is in storage.

As its network can read data in a blockchain, we need to consider two types of risks when storing sensitive data on the blockchain. "Reversal risks" are the likelihood that the data can be decrypted, such as when someone can gain access to the keys. Reversal risks exist as long as the keys exist. Many encryption techniques may one day be cracked. Thus, it is not sufficient to just store encrypted data. "Linkability risks" occur when one can link the data to an individual by analyzing patterns.

Hashing techniques that are used in blockchain applications are non-reversible. Whether personal data is hashed is widely debated. It also comes down to whether there are potential reversibility and linkability risks. It may be possible to reverse a hash using brute force if the data comes from a known set of possibilities (e.g., numbers from 1 to a million). This can be mitigated by salting or peppering the data, where extra data (only known to the hash generator) is added before creating the hash. Transactional data on blockchain may be linkable if you use an application to perform actions on your behalf and is linked to your address. This can be mitigated by using the anonymous signature schemes described above.

When designing a blockchain network that will store user data, one needs to consider the following points (see Figure 6.19).

One should pick the appropriate techniques and apply them to the design of the network. "Privacy by Design" is an approach to systems engineering

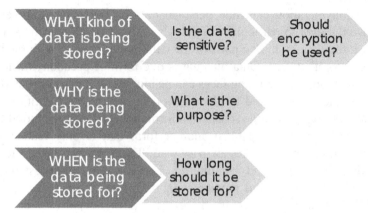

Figure 6.19:   Privacy considerations for blockchain data.

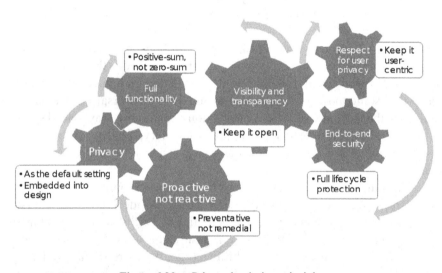

Figure 6.20:   Privacy by design principles.

that requires privacy to be taken into account throughout the engineering process. It is based on seven "foundational principles" (see Figure 6.20).

In the current data economy, many services such as social media or messaging platforms are offered free to users in return for the use of their data. This landscape is now changing due to increased user protection from various governments. However, this does not mean that users cannot choose to share aspects of their data in return for free services.

Blockchain networks can potentially help manage users' consent concerning their data. New developments in applied mathematics around cryptography, blockchains, and machine learning can allow for data-driven business models. By solving the privacy concerns, we may create a decentralized data economy where the market can all share and trade data. With tools like secure multiparty computing and zero-knowledge proofs, data can train machine learning algorithms without revealing the raw data. Users can contribute to their data and get paid for it. Data from humans, devices, applications, and algorithms can be agglomerated and analyzed.

6.6 Scalability

In BFT Systems, Authentication plays a crucial part. Most distributed consensus protocols are inversely proportional to scalability and performance. The protocol generally cannot scale very well when it can cater for high-performance. Ricardian Contracts is another trend taken up by some start-ups to ensure enforceable "Smart Legal Contract" in bridging the on-chain and off-chain contracts. These contracts are proposed for bond instruments originally to be issued as contracts that are both human and machine-readable. When the system does not behave the way it is expected to, termination of the agreement becomes difficult. This occurs due to different faults such as Fail-Stop Fault and Byzantine fault. The consensus protocol depends heavily on the ability of the system to keep time. It was proven that if the nodes of a distributed system have not bound on the time to time, it takes for a message to be sent across to another node or that relative difference in processing speed between two nodes. There is always a possibility that the system cannot converge in consensus.

Learning Objectives
- Understand the types of faults in a network and the importance of Authentication, Scalability, and a synchronous environment.

Main Takeaways

Main Points
- Authentication plays an important role in BFT systems.
- If the protocol can scale very well, it will not achieve high performance.
- In a synchronous environment, as long as the number of failures is less than the resilience level that the consensus protocol is designed to tolerate, it is possible to find solutions that can guarantee consensus.

- However, it is not possible to find a solution that can guarantee consensus even with a single failure in an asynchronous environment.

Main Terms

- **Ricardian contracts:** Proposed for bond instruments originally issued as contracts that are both human and machine readable, is another trend taken up by some start-ups to create enforceable "Smart Legal Contract" in bridging the on-chain off-chain contracts.
- **Fail-stop fault:** A type of fault that will stop the system when it runs into an error.
- **Byzantine fault:** Describes the super class of all faults that includes fail-stop faults and malicious faults.

6.6.1 *Authentication and Non-Repudiation*

Authentication plays an important role in BFT systems. According to Lamport (1982), it is shown that a consensus can converge for any number of Byzantine nodes as long as they are authenticated and the messages are unforgeable (non-repudiation). Without these conditions, no solution exists that can only tolerate more than 33% of Byzantine nodes. This is because the effect of a Byzantine failure is more severe when the erring node cannot be identified from the messages.

6.6.2 *Scalability and Performance*

Most distributed consensus protocols are inversely proportional to scalability and performance. The protocol generally cannot scale very well when it can cater for high-performance. If the protocol can scale very well, it will not achieve high performance (Vukolic, 2015). Scalability and performance is a popular topic for researchers in the field of consensus protocols.

- Bitcoin blockchain has a performance bottleneck from consensus latency of 60 minutes. It also has a throughput of seven transactions per second (TPS) based on a block size of 1MB, which is a far cry from global credit card transaction average throughput (VISA, 2015) of 2,000 TPS (with a peak of 56,000 TPS). Properly speaking, Bitcoin does not cater for consensus finality because there is no way to tell in theory if the block will reshuffle on the chain due to forking. Bitcoin networks requires six blocks for the transaction to be confirmed because the probability of reversing or changing of records is extremely small. Blockchain latencies arise as a result of this consensus latency by design. One can overcome this performance bottleneck in the short term by increasing the block generation frequency for 10 minutes to a shorter time or use a larger block size than 1MB. Yet, the performance increase will trade off against security risks, and the benefits are largely incremental — there will be a lot to the debate on the correct block size.

- The traditional approach of consensus protocol such as PBFT is initially designed for use in cases around distributed databases or filesystems at a relatively small scale of 10–20 nodes based on State Machine Replications. It is unproven to work at large scales like Bitcoin. It requires the nodes to be authenticated and identified ahead of time and not designed for use cases like Bitcoin or other public blockchains. Participating nodes can join or leave at will without any permission. In this way, it can achieve high performance and some in tens of thousands of TPSs and limited by network latencies only. Yet, since all nodes must participate in the consensus, when the number of nodes increases, the number of resources required for coordination and increase in message size may substantially impact, especially when operated over the public Internet. At this very moment, such protocols are applicable to scale only within physically near premises.

Ricardian Contracts, proposed for bond instruments originally to be issued as contracts that are both human and machine-readable, are another trend taken up by some start-ups to create enforceable "Smart Legal Contract" in bridging the on-chain off-chain contracts.

Smart contracts are essential for a private blockchain to be useful.

- This is because the need for business logic processing for enterprise usage is a lot higher than for public individuals.
- Enterprise businesses also rely heavily on off-chain enterprise applications such as accounting, human resources, payroll, and other enterprise resource planning systems to support the business's operations. Besides, most business enterprises may also have in-house developed proprietary applications used within their business processes.
- As a result, there is little utility value for the use of blockchain unless business processes can operate across on-chain and off-chain logic. This is where private blockchains start to behave a lot more like a middleware than a database for enterprise applications integration.

- However, this is not a straightforward affair because to maintain a consistent state of the blockchain, the smart contract logic must be deterministic. All nodes must converge at the same result from execution using the same input parameters. This is why individual nodes cannot pull data directly from external sources. Every node will receive a different result even though they make the same call with the same input at the same time if the external source happens to be non-deterministic, for example, a service that returns a random number after each call.

6.6.3 *Types of Fault*

All consensus protocols are designed to help the system of nodes to agree on one single value. This is not an issue under normal conditions. However, the system may become difficult to terminate in agreement when the nodes are not behaving the way they are expected. This is why understanding the types of fault and trade-offs available is essential for choosing the required consensus protocol. Two main types of faults that are generally concerned by people are Fail-Stop Fault and Byzantine Faults.

Fail-Stop Fault. It is the most basic type of fault. A fail-stop fault is a type of fault that will stop the system when it runs into an error. This is a less difficult problem to deal with because it is relatively easy to detect. This type of fault does not include data corruption fault nor node collusion, which on the other hand, fall under the Byzantine category.

- **Paxos** (Lamport, 1998) is the most well-known consensus protocol for this type of fault. It is a leader-based consensus protocol developed more than 15 years ago. It is notoriously complex to implement as it is designed to handle all cases of non-Byzantine faults. Paxos always converge to one value (no forks), and the value will eventually reach all nodes, which means that it will always guarantee safety. However, in asynchronous systems, Paxos cannot guarantee to make progress continuously with more than 50% failures. Google's Chubby service (Burrows, 2006) and Microsoft's Autopilot cluster management service both employ Paxos.
- **RAFT** is a more modern consensus protocol. It is also leader-based, and it is gaining popularity due to its simpler implementation and fewer moving parts than Paxos. One of the key differences between Paxos and RAFT exists in the leader selection process. RAFT only selects the

leaders among the recent servers, whereas Paxos allows the selection of leaders across all nodes.

Byzantine Fault. Describes the super class of all faults that include fail-stop faults and malicious faults. In these types of faults, results can be arbitrary due to data corruption, code error, node collusion, and other attacks. This is the hardest type of fault because it is difficult to identify an honest node from an adversary node based on the result from one single node.

The solutions to deal with Byzantine Faults are the Byzantine Fault Tolerance (**BFT**) systems. BFT is typically very costly, and it is often applied in aircraft and submarine systems and applicable in low network latency environments.

- The traditional approach to solving Byzantine Fault involves the use of **State Machine Replication** (Lamport, 1978). One popular implementation of this technique is **Practical Byzantine Fault Tolerance** (PBFT), introduced by Castro and Liskov in 1999 (Castro & Liskov, 1999). Since BFT systems were costly to build, it was only useful in critical real-time systems where Byzantine faults can result in expensive failures (e.g., Aircraft, submarine, space craft, etc.). PBFT shows that a solution can only exist in a more conventional setting utilizing commodity hardware over the Internet with acceptable performance, guaranteeing liveness and safety up to 33% resiliency.
- The Bitcoin blockchain is designed to address Byzantine faults, specifically. Bitcoin Proof-of-Work (PoW) is commonly assumed to require 50% of adversary nodes for the network to be subverted (also known as 51% attack). However, it was shown that only 25% is actually required (Eyal & Sirer, 2013). Yet, because of the sheer scale of Bitcoin compared to traditional systems, the resiliency is robust enough, as demonstrated in practice.
- A number of PoW type, token-based, or blockchain-inspired consensus protocol hybrids have been developed after Bitcoin. For example, BitShares created the first Proof-of-Stake consensus protocol.
- Tendermint is a token-based BFT consensus protocol developed by combining Proof-of-Stake consensus protocol with DLS algorithm, which assumes partial synchrony of network.
- Hyperledger is a token-less BFT consensus protocol developed by combining PBFT design with blockchain.

- Ripple Protocol Consensus Algorithm (RPCA), a token-based BFT consensus protocol that does not depend on the blockchain design, has a resiliency of 20% but provides a strong safety guarantee.

6.6.4 *Synchrony*

The consensus protocol depends heavily on the ability of the system to keep time. It was proven that if in a distributed system the time it takes for a message to be sent across to another node or the relative difference in processing speed between two nodes are not bound, there is always a possibility that the system cannot converge in consensus. This is because it is impossible to tell whether it is due to process failure, slow processing, or network latency. This is called the FLP Impossibility Proof, named after its inventors Fischer, Lynch, and Patterson, who published a paper in 1985 called the "Impossibility of Distributed Consensus with One Faulty Process" (Fischer, Lynch, & Paterson, 1985). This breakthrough resolved a long debate in the distributed systems circle on how consensus can be achieved in a fully asynchronous environment.

In conclusion, we can say that:

- In a synchronous environment, as long as the number of failures is less than the resilience level that the consensus protocol is designed to tolerate, it is possible to find solutions that can guarantee consensus.
- However, it is not possible to find a solution that can guarantee consensus even with a single failure in an asynchronous environment.

Since the Impossibility Proof cannot be circumvented, it is a matter of relaxing the asynchronous requirement and finding the condition for achieving consensus with the number of failure nodes it can tolerate.

- By controlling the block frequency and timestamp, Bitcoin PoW achieves a weak form of synchrony. The block timestamp is considered valid if its value lies between the median timestamp of the last 11 blocks on the chain and two hours after the network-adjusted time. The block will not make it onto the chain if it is not valid. It was also shown that the PoW protocol could provide a strong and consistent guarantee in an asynchronous network under known conditions (Pass, Seeman, & Shelat, 2017).
- A paper published by Dwork, Lynch, and Stockmeyer in 1988 titles "Consensus in the Presence of Partial Synchrony" (Dwork, Lynch, &

Stockmeyer, 1988) illustrates a way known as the DLS algorithm to circumvent the impossibility proof by assuming a partial synchrony environment. DLS is adapted by Tendermint's consensus design (Kwon, 2014) for use with blockchain with Proof-of-Stake. Synchrony is not required to guarantee PBFT's safety. However, it is necessary to provide liveness. This means that each node will constantly resend messages upon timeout, and the message will eventually be received by the other node, as long as less than 33% of the nodes are malicious. PBFT is adapted for use by Hyperledger.

- By requiring all validator nodes to submit a candidate set of transactions within 2 seconds, RPCA maintains a strong synchrony for the set to be proposed for committing into each validator's ledger. If the validator does not receive any submission, the wait time will be extended to 20 seconds.

6.7 Types of Blockchains

6.7.1 *Introduction*

Few other types of blockchains that utilize distributed consensus protocols besides PoW exist, and they can be classified into token-based or token-less. In this section, Token-Based Consensus Protocol Blockchains with Mining and without Mining, Token-Less Blockchain Technologies, and Smart Contract Oracle are discussed. PoW uses the help from friendly nodes to secure it through mining. At the same time, it makes it extremely costly for malicious nodes to launch an attack. Token-less consensus protocols are used mainly in private blockchains. It uses classical State Machine Replications, which are traditionally used in replicated database design.

Learning Objectives
- Understand the different types of token-less and token-based blockchains and their features and applications.

Main Takeaways

Main Points
- Not all token-based consensus protocols use tokens for incentive purposes. Some protocols, such as Ripple, use a token for servicing transactions of transaction fees. And Ethereum for Ether is to provide the gas necessary for operating smart contracts.

- The security aspect of Smart Contract Oracle is more manageable since the Oracle is authenticated and permissioned.
- Distributed database designs are based on the precondition that all the participants are authenticated, and numbers of participants are known beforehand.
- Tendermint built a class of its own by blending traditional State Machine Replication algorithm (DLS algorithm) that assumes partial synchronicity of the network with a deposit-based Proof-of-Stake incentive model.

Main Terms
- **Ripple Protocol Consensus Algorithm:** Developed by Ripple Lab in 2014. It is another token-based consensus protocol without the use of mining. Strictly speaking, blockchain is not used in Ripple's design.
- **PBFT:** A distributed consensus protocol that works by requiring all clients in the network to be authenticated and authorized to send transactions to the validators.
- **Corda:** A distributed ledger platform for recording and processing financial agreements developed by R3 (Brown, 2016) with a design geared towards enforceability by human laws, where "distributed ledgers are those reliant on legal institutions".

This section explores a few other Blockchains that utilize distributed consensus protocols besides PoW, by classifying them as either token-based or token-less. This section is not exhaustive, as the evolution of consensus technology is advancing at an incredible pace nowadays. This section illustrates the purpose of exploring the differences between the various consensus protocols, both old and new, to identify the characteristics and conditions where one may work better than the other.

(a) Token-based Consensus Protocol Blockchains (with mining)
PoW uses the help from friendly nodes to secure it through mining. At the same time, it makes it extremely costly for malicious nodes to launch an attack. This creates an incentive model that makes token-based consensus protocols suitable for application in the public blockchain space. However, unlike Bitcoin, not all token-based consensus protocols use tokens for incentive purposes. Some protocols, such as Ripple, use a token for servicing transaction fees. And Ethereum for Ether is to provide the gas necessary for operating smart contracts.

(b) Smart Contract Oracle

Hence, the need for Oracle as a gateway to provide a single view emerges. Ecosystems can be created around Oracles such as Oraclize in a public blockchain like Ethereum. However, it creates a trust dependency on Oracle on a public blockchain by doing so, which potentially contradicts the original zero trust intent. The security aspect is more manageable for a private blockchain since the Oracle is authenticated and permissioned. Microsoft's implementation of a private blockchain called Bletchley (at this point), making use of off-chain code components called "Cryptlets", which runs in a secure container and data is accessed by smart contracts via event hooks.

Due to the above reasons, several variants of Proof-of-Stake design are currently in existence or development, and it is impossible to validate their theoretical pros and cons at this moment:

- Peercoin (King & Nadal, 2012) uses PoW for bootstrapping in its initial design called "ppcoin" and Proof-of-Stake, which combines the number of unspent digital tokens with the number of days it is held by the node called the *"Coin Age"*. The probability of successfully mining a digital token is based on the Coin Age.
- Bitshares (BitShares, n.d.) uses a variant of Proof-of-Stake called the *Delegated Proof-of-Stake (DPoS)* that relies on the concept of "witnesses", which are voted in by stakeholders to prevent network centralization on regular intervals.

(c) Token-based Consensus Protocol Blockchains (without mining)
- Tendermint

Tendermint (Kwon, 2014) built a class of its own by blending traditional State Machine Replication algorithm (DLS algorithm) (Dwork *et al.*, 1988) that assumes partial synchronicity of the network with a deposit-based Proof-of-Stake incentive model.

The protocol requires validators to put up a bond deposit that determines the validators' voting power to participate in the consensus process. Since Tendermint requires at least 2/3 majority of validators' combined voting power for a block for it to be committed. Hence, a fork can only happen when some nodes are double-signing a block. If they perform a double sign, validators are disputed by having their bond deposit forfeited.

When compared against PBFT, another State Machine Replication implementation, Tendermint has slightly lower performance but better security. This is because of the use of Round-Robin-based leader election over every round compared to PBFT's design of the Sticky-Leader approach. The leader of the Sticky-Leader approach is only elected upon failure. Tendermint is designed with peer-to-peer in mind. It can cater to nodes joining or leaving at will, and it uses Bittorrent-based message broadcast algorithms.

• Ripple Protocol Consensus Algorithm (RPCA)

Ripple Lab developed the Ripple Protocol Consensus Algorithm in 2014. It is another token-based consensus protocol without the use of mining. Strictly speaking, blockchain is not used in Ripple's design. Yet, it is frequently considered as part of the blockchain family. Ripple uses a distributed record-keeping system that only keeps track of the final ledger balance. Unlike blockchain, which tracks the entire transaction history, it adopts its native token called XRP in this case. It is not meant for incentive purposes and was initially used to facilitate transaction payment and as a bridging currency between fiat currencies in illiquid markets. RPCA has made some highly explicit design choices optimizing it for speed and real-time cross-border remittance, clearing, and settlement.

RPCA consensus is based on all validators proposing a set of transactions it receives in its open ledger to all the validators it is connected to within a two-second window. Several rounds of voting are executed to identify transitions that show up in each validator's proposal. It is often enough until the transaction achieves 80% of votes to be confirmed into the Validators ledger.

(d) Token-less Blockchain Technologies

Token-less consensus protocols are used mainly in private blockchains. It uses classical State Machine Replications, which are traditionally used in replicated database design.

One important reason behind this is that private blockchain is governed by business agreements established between identified parties' networks and do not require using a token as a defense mechanism against Sybil attack. This is also why most private blockchains do not need to rely on mining or PoW consensus protocols to keep the system safe.

Distributed database designs are based on the precondition that all the participants are authenticated, and numbers of participants are known beforehand. This fits in the private blockchains' context because members must be authenticated. However, one may wonder why we do not simply use distributed databases instead? That is because distributed databases are typically designed to be centrally-owned or administered where blockchain provides the option for decentralized administration, even though there is a centralization of membership. One of the most important aspects of private blockchain is that the newer generations of blockchains can generally support the use of smart contracts.

- Practical Byzantine Fault Tolerance (PBFT)
PBFT is a distributed consensus protocol that requires all clients in the network to be authenticated and authorized to send transactions to the validators. The validators have access to a public key infrastructure supporting identity and digital certificate management. Each validator is a replicated state machine, with a leader being chosen as the primary and the rest of the replicas as backups. The clients can only send transactions to the primary, and only the primary can broadcast messages to the backups. The primary is replaced when it is suspected to have failed (consecutive timeout). Upon processing the messages, each backup will send the result to the original client. When it receives 33% of the same result from all the nodes, the transaction is confirmed to be complete by the client.

- Hyperledger
The Linux Foundation's Hyperledger Project combines the codebase from IBM, Digital Asset Holdings, and Blockstream to create a fabric to support different implementations of distributed ledger technologies. It aims to go beyond financial use cases. Like most modern private blockchain, Hyperledger is designed to decouple core blockchain features in mind. It supports the pluggability of different distributed consensus protocols such as PBFT. With support for other languages like Java in the pipeline, It also supports the creation of smart contracts called chaincode written in Golang. Hyperledger supports using the Unspent Transaction Output (UTXO) approach adapted from Bitcoin, where balance is derived from past transaction records. The other approach uses the account model, which keeps track of the account balance directly. One important aspect central to Hyperledger design is the support for complex identity management with built-in certificate authority systems.

- R3 Corda
Corda is a distributed ledger platform for recording and processing financial agreements developed by R3 (Brown, 2016) that has a design geared towards enforceability by human laws, where "distributed ledgers are those reliant on legal institutions" (Swanson, 2015). Unlike Hyperledger but

similar to Ripple, Corda is specialized for use cases applicable to the financial sector only. Here are some notable high-level features of Corda. Unlike most smart contracts, inspired by the Ricardian Contract (Clark, Bakshi, & Braine, 2016), Corda is designed to be both executable by programming logic and enforceable by human law. Traditionally, consensus protocol involves validation at the ledger level, whereas Corda maintains transaction privacy by which validation is only performed by parties involved in the same transaction. Supervisory observer nodes such as financial authority participation can be included for carrying our audit activities. Corda is designed to work with universal financial messaging standards such as ISO20022 to work in a bank setting. Readers can refer to the Non-Technical White Paper called "Corda: An Introduction" for more details.

References/Further Readings

Baird, L. (2016). The Swirlds Hashgraph Consensus Algorithm: Fair, Fast, Byzantine Fault Tolerance. Swirlds, Inc. Technical Report SWIRLDS-TR-2016, 1.

Dziembowski, S., Faust, S., Kolmogorov, V., & Pietrzak, K. (August, 2015). Proofs of space. In *Annual Cryptology Conference* (pp. 585–605). Springer, Berlin, Heidelberg.

Lamport, L., Shostak, R., & Pease, M. (2019). The Byzantine generals problem. In *Concurrency: The Works of Leslie Lamport* (pp. 203–226).

Zilliqa (2017). The Zilliqa Design Story Piece by Piece: Part 2 (Consensus Protocol). Retrieved from https://blog.zilliqa.com/the-zilliqa-design-story-piece-by-piece-part-2-consensus-protocol-e38f6bf566e3.

Zohar, A. (2016). SPECTRE: Serialization of Proof-of-Work Events, Confirming Transactions via Recursive Elections. Retrieved from https://medium.com/@avivzohar/the-spectre-protocol-7dbbebb707b5.

CBDC

BIS (2020). Central Bank Digital Currencies: Foundational Principles and Core Features. Retrieved from https://www.bis.org/publ/othp33.pdf.

Raphael, A., Giulio, C., & Jon, F. (2020). Rise of the Central Bank Digital Currencies: Drivers, Approaches and Technologies. Monetary and Economic Department. BIS Working Papers. Retrieved from https://www.bis.org/publ/work880.pdf.

IMF (2020). A Survey of Research on Retail Central Bank Digital Currency. IMF Working Papers. Retrieved from https://www.imf.org/en/Publications/WP/Issues/2020/06/26/A-Survey-of-Research-on-Retail-Central-Bank-Digital-Currency-49517.

DC/EP
Gu, M. (2021). China's National Digital Currency DCEP/CBDC Overview. Boxmining. Retrieved from https://boxmining.com/dcep/#How_to_buy_DCEP.
Fanusie, Y. J. & Jin, E. (2021). China's Digital Currency: Adding Financial Data to Digital Authoritarianism. Center for a New American Security (CNAS). Retrieved from https://s3.us-east-1.amazonaws.com/files.cnas.org/documents/CNAS-Report-Chinas-Digital-Currency-Jan-2021-final.pdf?mtime=2 0210125173901&focal=none.

Project Bakong
National Bank of Cambodia (2020). Project Bakong: Next Generation Payment System. Retrieved from https://bakong.nbc.org.kh/download/GUIDE_ BOOK_FA_7.pdf.
Global Blockchain Business Council & SORAMITSU (2020). GBBC Open-Source Ideas Series: Digital Money. Retrieved from https://gbbcouncil.org/ wp-content/uploads/2020/12/GBBC-Open-Source-Ideas-The-Rise-of-Central-Bank-Digital-Currencies-Spotlight-on-Project-Bakong-4.pdf.

Project Ubin
Dalal, D., Yong, S., & Lewis, A. (2017) The Future is here — Project Ubin: SGD on Distributed Ledger. Retrieved from https://www.mas.gov.sg/-/media/ MAS/ProjectUbin/Project-Ubin--SGD-on-Distributed-Ledger.pdf.
MAS (2021). Project Ubin: Central Bank Digital Money using Distributed Ledger Technology. https://www.mas.gov.sg/schemes-and-initiatives/Project-Ubin.

6.8 Sample Questions

Question 1
Which of the following is NOT one of the key security objectives?

(a) Availability
(b) Integrity
(c) Accuracy

Question 2
Which of the following statements is true?

(a) Script is a programming language used by Ethereum.
(b) A smart contract can act as a lottery.
(c) Delegated Proof of Stake (DPoS) is a widely used consensus algorithm used by many major cryptocurrencies such as Ethereum.

Question 3
Which of the following is NOT a correct categorization of CBDCs?

(a) Token-based CBDC and NCB
(b) aCBDC and iCBDC
(c) Retail CBDC and wholesale CBDC

Question 4
Stablecoin is a type of digital currency

(a) Whose value remains unchanged
(b) That is sovereign
(c) Whose value is pegged to fiat money or an asset

Question 5
Which of the following features is not one of the main factors that ensures the security of blockchain?

(a) Decentralized
(b) Distributed
(c) Anonymous

Solutions

Question 1

Solution: Option **c** is correct.

Security practitioners need to address the five key security objectives: Confidentiality, integrity, availability, authentication and accountability.

Question 2

Solution: Option **b** is correct.

Option a is wrong because Script is a programming language used by Bitcoin. Option c is wrong because Ethereum does not use the DPoS algorithm.

Question 3

Solution: Option **a** is correct.

NCB is not CBDC.

Question 4

Solution: Option **c** is correct.

The value of stablecoin may change as the pegged currency or asset changes.

Question 5

Solution: Option **c** is correct.

The security of the blockchain network comes with its decentralization and distribution.

Chapter 7

Token Economics, Blockchain Ecosystem, and Design Thinking

7.1 Token Economy and Valuation

This section introduces the key concepts in token economy and the various methods for fintech valuation.

Learning Objectives

- Understand the key elements, design thinking, and types of an effective token economy.
- Understand the role of tokens.
- Understand the different approaches to value Fintech companies and projects.

Main Takeaways

Main Points

- Three essential elements make a token economy effective: tokens used as reinforcers to exchange for other reinforcers, back-up reinforcers that act as rewards, and specified target behaviors.
- Factors that may influence the token's value such as the motive, market demand and supply, and dissemination significantly affect the economy

Main Terms

- **Token economy:** An innovative system and a network that utilizes tokens.
- **Token economics:** A discipline that studies token economies.

7.1.1 *Token Economy*

Bitcoin and the blockchain technology it introduced have made it possible to have a feasible system that is decentralized, distributed, and open. It also brings a potential solution to address trust in the conventional business environment. Cryptocurrencies can function as a unit of account, a medium of exchange, and a tool to pay for services and goods on the platform.

The others without these functions are known as non-currencies or crypto-tokens. Both cryptocurrencies and non-currencies fall under the category of tokens, which have a more general meaning than blockchain and cryptocurrencies. Within the token economy, token can be used in various scenarios.

The token economy is an innovative system and a network that utilizes tokens. It is rapidly capturing attention in the present world because of the emergence of various technologies such as blockchain, big data, AI, cloud, and IoT. In a token economy, people receive tokens as a reward for certain actions, and these tokens can be further used for exchanging goods and services or specific rights in the future. Using a decentralized peer-to-peer system and design thinking ideas, tokens help reward good behavior and vice versa. This will help improve the system as people will pursue good behavior and avoid destructive behavior.

Three essential elements make a token economy effective:

- Tokens in the digital form that are used as reinforcers to exchange for other reinforcers
- Back-up reinforcers that act as rewards. Possible forms include things, services and privileges
- Specified target behaviors that are clearly defined

Tokens do not have any intrinsic value. Hence, the potential to earn tokens by displaying good behavior can encourage good behavior.

Additionally, to run a token economy, two things are needed: target behavior criteria should be lucid and specific, and the reward should be clearly defined. People need to know clearly what to do to earn tokens, how to use the tokens earned, how many tokens they have earned, and how they can redeem the rewards (or back-up reinforcers). All these aspects need to be specified clearly.

Token economics guides the exploitation of technology after the intersection of blockchain technology, economic theory and cryptographic algorithms. It explains the structure of a particular ecosystem in the blockchain sphere by considering the creation and distribution of value, consumption and circulation.[1]

Further evolution of tokens built on blockchain technology has led to the creation of a token economy (Xu, 2019). A token could symbolize two things: value or right. When token is an embodiment of value, it is also usually the core of the entire economic model; and the token economy is centered upon the creation and distribution of the value, the consumption, and the circulation. Alternatively, when token functions as a symbol of right, it represents a kind of incentive. The token economy then is more gravitated towards researching different types of suitable organizations, and ways to design captivating economics models to embrace partners, suppliers, or competitors. The benefit of this research is that analytical findings and observations will contribute to the entire ecosystem in addition to observing changes in the governance model.

A huge difference lies between the logic of token economy and that of the present-day tech giants such as Amazon, Google, and Facebook. The latter's key operational logic is driven by user traffic and accurate match. Details of several relevant economics will be covered in the following section.[2]

7.1.2 *Tokens and Design Thinking*

As suggested by its name, Token is a critical element of token economics. In token economics, multiple issues related to tokens such as their issuance, supply, demand, validation, usage, behavior, and their effect on other things in the ecosystem are addressed. Both broader topics such as the entire ecosystem and the functions as well as other detailed issues such as the technical parameters and individuals are studied under token economics. Generally, digital tokens tend to have the following functions (see Table 7.1).

Functions of the tokens need to be conceptualized thoroughly while designing a token economy to ensure the smooth functioning and sustenance of the ecosystem. Well-developed tokens in a successful token economy have the following features (see Table 7.2).

---

[1] https://applicature.com/blog/blockchain-startups/what-is-token-economics.
[2] What is a Token Economy? (with picture) (wise-geek.com).

Table 7.1: Functions of digital tokens.

Type	Detail
Transactional	Transactional tokens provide a form of payment
Utility	Utility tokens facilitate transactions, sometimes meaning the ability to use the platform itself
Operation	The token is a determinant of important decisions related to operations in the ecosystem
Profit	Token holders get a portion of revenues or profits, like shares of a company in some sense
Asset-backed	Asset-backed tokens are linked to real-world or virtual assets such as gold, fiat currency, or property

Source: Lee and Teo (2020), Smith + Crown, and Authors.

Table 7.2: Features of tokens.

Facilitating the ecosystem	High value
To have usefulness and utility in the economy to well facilitate the economy	To have high value so that it is worthwhile to earn tokens and people will have the incentive to do good behavior.
Listed on exchanges	**Resist to inflation**
To be listed on exchanges so that people can trade it and the value can be seen	To be relatively stable and have resistance to inflation so that it can serve as a good incentive and will not affect its function
Social and technical scalability	**Potential to growth**
To be socially and technically scalable to ensure the value of token in the future	To have potential to increase in usage in the future so that its value is expected to increase

Source: Hlebiv (2018) and Authors.

Besides the roles and functions of the tokens, their future trends and values are of equal importance. The entire ecosystem would be erratic if the tokens have restricted use cases, are not freely exchangeable, cannot resist inflationary pressure in the short-run, do not have long-term worth, or cannot meet the legal and technical expectations. Due to these reasons, the users would not have any motive to earn and use the tokens, and the whole ecosystem will become untrustworthy.

There is a need for the designers to adopt suitable monetary policies and identify the role of a token to address price volatility and the stabilization mechanism of the token as they are important matters for any economy. The consensus algorithm is required in a decentralized economy to identify how new tokens are created. A surge in the supply of the tokens will lead to inflation or a reduction in the prices (supply increases when the demand remains unchanged) which is a notable supply and demand problem for tokens. Various actions are taken to mitigate the negative impacts on the token's value. For example, many cryptocurrencies, Bitcoin included, set an upper limit for the supply of tokens, implying that the maximum number of tokens that can ever be created in the ecosystem is constant.

We have highlighted a lot on the significance of tokens and how they can be utilized to initiate transactions, self-govern business models, and encourage good practices by giving incentives. The following question is how to accomplish these objectives. Token economics goes beyond just making the tokens into creation of the entire ecosystem. This means that the designers need to be prepared for the future and ensure users are spurred to consistently enter and remain with the platform, with the support of tokens.

Most importantly, the network effects need to be studied. The term refers to the fact, which is fundamental in economics and business, that development in the number of users will improve the value of goods and services and thus the entire platform and ecosystem. Therefore, users should benefit from the network effects in a good token economy due to its open, shared, and decentralized nature. The value of products, services, or the platform can develop with more individuals being a part of the ecosystem.

There are two categories of network effects and two corresponding strategies to improve (Tönnissen, Beinke and Teuteberg, 2020):

- Direct network effect — A new user will increase the value of goods/services. Offering customized services addresses the direct network effect.
- Indirect network effect — A new user from one user group will increase the value of goods/services in a different group. Motivating satisfied users to make recommendations will improve indirect network effect.

To meticulously design the tokens utilized in the ecosystem is critical. Things that may influence the token's value, such as the motive, the

Table 7.3:   Key elements of token economics.

Purpose	The token is more than just investment vehicles or financing tools. Its purpose and utilities need to be thought through for the ecosystem to function well.
Supply and Demand	The supply and demand will affect the token's value, so the relationship needs to be considered when designing the functions of the token and the supply.
Distribution	Token distribution considerations like when and how many to distribute initially and subsequently affect the performance and effectiveness of the system significantly.

market demand and supply, and dissemination, significantly affect the economy (see Table 7.3). Engineers should design the tokens such that the tokens are worth retaining in the future and individuals value the utilities or advantages in the system or network and not just for speculation.

Based on the different categories and functions of the token, there are two kinds of token economy design: dual and simple; the former uses two tokens, of the same or different kinds, and the latter uses a single token. Although a straightforward design can be successful and have multiple use cases, it accompanies several issues. The token's value tends to rise if the people use a particular token to exchange goods and services on a platform or pay the transaction fees to access the platform. On one hand, it is attractive for the ecosystem because people would be motivated to join the network, hold the tokens and pursue good behavior. On the other hand, some token holders, such as investors and speculators that buy or earn the token, not for its utility or function but the potential price increase, may sell the tokens in exchange for profits. This will reduce the prices of tokens, and consequently increase the volatility in prices and destabilize the monetary utility of the token economy.

Hence, to address the problem where two tokens with non-identical roles are introduced in the system to set apart the token utilities or functions and eliminate the value of tokens, dual architecture comes as a solution. As per this scheme, two different tokens with different utilities can be used (e.g., one to use as a transaction fee to facilitate transactions and gain platform access and the other to use as "currencies" that can be exchanged for goods or services). Also, a single token can be used in the network while the others are used as securities, stores of value, or collateral that can be traded with other tokens (Brouwer, 2018).

There are seven key factors that need to be considered while deciding the architecture (Hlebiv, 2018):

1. alignment of interest between users and investors;
2. real goal of the project and token;
3. reserve estimation and rules of reserve release;
4. cost of development;

Key elements of token evaluation:
5. projected demand;
6. token velocity;
7. estimated price volatility.

What determines successful token economics is the incentivized desirable behavior and the ability to stabilize the network operation. On the contrary, inappropriate token economics may cause a death spiral if the loss of value in the token economy is discerning. The good and bad examples of token economics are as follows.

7.1.3 *Good and Bad Examples*

To begin with, let us consider Bitcoin, the very first decentralized cryptocurrency that dominates the market today. It has proven to be a safe and thriving ecosystem that aims to solve double-spending by incentivizing nodes to participate in the network without validating transactions required by a third party. Miners verify transactions following the consensus protocol and are rewarded for the work, which includes the reward of a new block generated and the transaction fees (all paid in the token, bitcoin). Hence, a greater number of miners will join the network for the return, which will further secure the network and increase the speed of the transactions.

The duties of specific nodes are greater than others. For example, the miners who mine new blocks and validate the transactions and some participants in the ecosystem have less heavy duties like those who make transactions using bitcoins. The importance of the Bitcoin network and the token itself will rise because of an increase in the number of miners and related lower costs, increased transaction speed, and higher safety in the network. Therefore, the design makes it a win-win-win strategy for all parties: miners get a reward, investors get returns, and developers get fame. As the token's value rises, the network tends to become more secure and efficient. A significant characteristic that ensures steady growth of the token's value is the absence of conflict of interests amongst the stakeholders and users.

The complicated designs consist of consensus protocol and algorithm in practice, and many additional measures are taken to guarantee efficiency in the Bitcoin network. We will not go deep into the details as we hope to give a fair idea of the issues faced when designing an excellent token economy. These issues are non-negligible and need to be carefully thought through before launching the token as it may result in unacceptable results due to faulty design. One popular example of poor token design is FCoin.

Launched in May 2018, FCoin is a cryptocurrency exchange that reached a peak daily trading volume of over 10 billion in June 2018 and was much greater than any of the cryptocurrency exchanges at that time. However, there was a steep decline in the trading volume soon after, and it defaulted in early 2020. All the unissued tokens and the ones held by the team were destroyed and burnt, and it left millions' worth of bitcoins unpaid to the token users (Wan, 2020).

The critical reason behind the failure of FCoin was the fundamental flaws in its token economics design, "Trans-Fee Mining" — a new business model brought by the team that paid out 80% of the platform's revenue, including trading fees paid by traders and collected by FCoin which was distributed to FT holders as dividends (He, 2018). It served an extraordinary motive and appeared to be engaging at the beginning.

However, the coin's value depends heavily on the volume of its trade, and paying dividends will normally prompt a price drop, consequently triggering selling exercises of the tokens since it might imply that the token is losing value. What is worse — new tokens are being mined when these exchanges happen, making the cost of the tokens drop further (think about the market interest relationship). In other words, the token's value is affected by inflation and lacks growth potential. (Sounds familiar? Yes, these are key features of a well-developed token in the ecosystem). Once the users started to understand, the imploding of the token was very quick.

7.1.4 *Token Valuation*

(a) Considerations for Token Valuation
To examine the value of a token or a Fintech startup, it is essential to study the characteristics of crypto-tokens and the token. The value of cryptocurrencies, the value of the token, and its function in the architecture play a pivotal role. (Cong, Li, and Wang, 2020). Besides the valuation mentioned earlier, given below are some key conceptual frameworks that are also essential for evaluating the tokens and token economies.

Table 7.4:   4Es.

Economies of Scale	It refers to the ability to produce a product for less cost the higher level of production. This helps scale the product as you are spending less money per unit to produce more.
Economies of Scope	In the crypto world, it can be defined as the benefits to scaling when the product is extended to different industries. For example, Ethereum can be said to have higher economies of scope than Bitcoin as the programming language allows for more varied smart contracts compared to Bitcoin's limitations to largely financial functions.
Economies of Integration	If any resource can be used for multiple purposes, it can be said to have economies of integration. A real life example would be electricity derived from burning fossil fuels. Heat generated from this process is used to turn a steam turbine which in turn produces more electricity. This is also known as co-generation. If the resource generated from using cryptocurrencies can be used back into the cryptocurrency system (such as tokens that serve as mining reward), it creates a positive cycle of generation results.
Economies of Convergence	Emphasis and rapid development of any emerging technology will promote the development and innovation of other technologies. Companies that put great emphasis on technology will likely be the leading ones that benefit from the technology convergence trend, which will also lead to the convergence of profits and social goals.

(1) 4Es

The 4Es refer to Economies of Scale, Economies of Scope, Economies of Integration, and Economies of Convergence. These are significant four aspects to estimate Fintech companies' value (see Table 7.4). As the cost and production relationships of the tokens are different, it may be quite contrasting to value the products and the services provided by fintech companies compared to the traditional companies because the tokens and the products are both digital. Specifically, the marginal costs of additional units of products are very low. The 4th E (economies of convergence) becomes significant as the convergence of technology is accompanied by the convergence of profit and social objectives, which is why leapfrog economies may achieve mass adoption before others.

(2) 3Cs

The 3Cs represent characteristics of an environment (geological or institutional) that are desirable nurturing grounds for successful fintech companies, and by extension, cryptocurrencies.

Community:

The idea of clustering in economics depicts how companies in similar industries tend to converge together in geographical concentrations. This raises the industry's overall productivity as it encourages productive competition amongst business peers. Similarly, a strong community has a high tolerance for failure and promotes innovative thinking, which is extremely important for a technology company or product like cryptocurrency to succeed.

Compassion:

Another factor that spikes technological advancement in technologies is empathy to failures. The mindset of individuals existing in these communities is that failure is not the end of the world. It is essential learning for the next attempt. This kind of thinking is a must in fintech start-ups and specifically for the cryptocurrency market where the failure rate is high, and competition is tough.

Creativity:

Keeping in mind the first two characteristics, it is not surprising that creativity can be fostered in such a community as innovation is encouraged verbally and backed by economic action.

(3) LASIC principles

Outlined in the LASIC principles are five characteristics that cryptocurrencies should have to increase the chances of success and reduce the risk of government or social media resistance. Therefore, they are necessary for evaluating the tokens.

Low margins:

Low margins are meant to avoid competition and attract users to achieve critical mass in terms of a sticky user base. Economies of scale can occur, and monetization tends to be easier with low margins. Compared to conventional businesses, low margins are an essential feature for cryptocurrencies and fintech companies.

Asset light:
Asset light companies can maintain low fixed costs and stay nimble and flexible. Scaling an asset-light company is a lot easier in this case.

Scalable:
As mentioned above, the product's future profitability depends majorly on the product's ability to scale directly. Another key factor in monetizing the product and estimating its value is the number of sticky users. For example, cryptocurrencies that can scale well will handle more business transactions and thus enhance the value of the token economy.

Innovative:
Like the Creativity in the 3Cs rules, businesses should keep making their products innovative. It is essential to identify future trends and tap on the opportunities lying ahead to maintain a competitive edge. Leading the trend is also another way, just like Apple and Bitcoin and its blockchain technology.

Compliance easy:
Finally, providing services or products that are compliance easy will minimize the risk of regulators restricting their use and jeopardizing its prospects for a fintech startup. The costs of fintech companies and thus its profitability and value of fintech companies are majorly affected by the changes in the regulatory environment and compliance process.

(4) 6Ds
The First Industrial Revolution involved steam and coal power to operate machinery. The Second revolved around electricity. The Third involved electronics as well as information technology to automate production. Currently, we might be in the midst of the Fourth Industrial Revolution, which aims to use AI and IOT technology to transform the physical and digital world further. This transformation will take the form of 6Ds: Digitalization, Disintermediation, Democratization, Decentralization, Diminishing Oneself, and Data Privacy Protection (see Table 7.5).

First, the discussion of the digital economy is entangled with the concept of "Digitization." The meaning of the two terms digitization and digitalization are very different. However, they are sometimes used interchangeably. Digitization refers to converting information from physical format to digital

Table 7.5: 6Ds.

Digitalization	**Digitalization** involves the usage of digital technologies to change a business model. We see how firms are beginning to explore advertising opportunities using social media and increase their customer base through e-commerce. Cryptocurrency can tokenize assets to bring physical assets into the digital space for transactions and secure ownership.
Disintermediation	**Disintermediation** refers to the removal of the middlemen in transactions to reduce costs on the transacting parties and increase efficiency. Ethereum is an example of a cryptocurrency with potential disintermediation applications with its smart contract capabilities.
Democratization	**Democratization** is the process in which digital technology allows people who are currently underserved or unserved to have access to the technology at an affordable cost to them. With cryptocurrency, micro insurances and micro lending can be secured and provided for customers with risk profiles that may be deemed as too risky for traditional financial institutions.
Decentralization	**Decentralization** refers to the process where control is distributed amongst the users without any centralized third parties to control the network. Cryptocurrencies like Bitcoin and Ethereum are by nature decentralized.
Diminishing Oneself	**Diminishing Oneself** refers to the process of having the creators of the coin to step down from a leading role in the continued development of the product. The purpose of this factor is to allow creators to function like a facilitator instead to minimize single points of failure. Satoshi Nakamoto, the creator of Bitcoin, is the premier example of this trait as he faded away after he published the paper on the cryptocurrency.
Data Privacy Protection	**Data Privacy Protection** refers to the growing emphasis on privacy in an increasingly transparent world where information is stored for eternity on servers and is accessible by anyone everywhere.

format, where the vector and form of information changes. "Digitization" is the change of physical conversion into numbers that can be understood as information digitization.

The way of work and workflow will experience qualitative changes when the information exists in a digital form. Therefore, Digitalization implies using digital information to improve business processes and change business and business models. That is, the Digitalization of business processes and business models means Digitalization. There is a big difference between digitization and digitalization. Digitalization will significantly impact the economy, and it can solve many existing economic imbalances.

At the same time, in the virtual world, once such a trust has been attacked by invasions or illegally controlled, the loss will be incalculable. Therefore, in the long run, to promote the establishment of distributed trust mechanisms, sequential, gradual "decentralization" is advocated for. The gradual, appropriate distribution of trust is the most important foundation to achieve sustainability and stability. Decentralization and data privacy are two important pillars of the digital economy. Additionally, along with technology, one must abandon self-centered thinking — diminishing oneself.

In general, the 4th — decentralization has not been done yet by many eCommerce or fintech companies that have done the first three Ds. Diminishing is also important as this may not create extra barriers when bringing the services and products abroad. Accomplishing the last 3Ds makes the companies the most valuable compared to others by protecting users.

(5) 7Ws

The 7 Dimensions or 7Ws (维度) are the seven key characteristics a fintech company possesses that can make it highly valued: Open, Altruistic, Global, Crowdsourcing Wisdom, Crowdsourcing Contribution, Encompassing Interest of All, and Beneficial to All. The idea was first mentioned by Shen (2015).

Open:

Openness refers to how open a project or company is. For example, suppose the source code is open and publicly available, like Python and Bitcoin. In that case, it becomes easier for developers to implement the codes, build additional layers on them, revise them and develop them. This gives assurance to the stakeholders such as users and investors regarding the design and the function of the network.

Altruistic:
The founding team and managing team of fintech companies should also be altruistic. The value of the firms gets limited if they only think about their interests as it becomes difficult to see that the stakeholders' interests will be valued in the long run.

Global:
As mentioned earlier, the user base plays a vital role in any businesses' success, more so for fintech companies. Due to the absence of geographical restrictions compared to traditional business, it is easier for fintech companies to target Global as they provide digital services or products. Besides, as decentralized and distributed as many cryptocurrencies are, the security and reliability of the system depend on the number of people that use it. The more, the better. Hence, fintech companies should consider catering to a global audience instead of merely focusing on its local jurisdiction.

Crowdsourcing wisdom:
Crowdsourcing wisdom will utilize the wisdom of the crowd or the network. A minor breakthrough from various sources leads to a huge breakthrough when brought together.

Crowdsourcing contribution:
As mentioned above, a decentralized cryptocurrency can crowdsource contributions to attain supercomputers like processing speeds and power. For instance, Mesh technology can lower the average costs if an increasing number of users contribute to the network. The crowd-sourcing concept is critical in a token economy to benefit from the economies of scale.

Encompassing interest of all:
Considering every stakeholder group is necessary. This is especially so for a peer-to-peer network where every stakeholder is vital as they play key roles in developing the project and determining whether a token economy can be well-functioning.

Table 7.6 summarizes the conceptual frameworks to consider when valuing fintech companies we have discussed.

7.1.5 *Future Considerations*

The overall ecosystem and underlying blockchain design thinking cannot be ignored to understand token's value better. The governance, economic

Table 7.6:　Summary of conceptual valuation frameworks.

4Es	3Cs	LASIC	6Ds	7Ws
• Economies of Scale • Economies of Scope • Economies of Integration • Economies of Convergence	• Community • Compassion • Creativity	• Low Margin • Asset Light • Scalable • Innovative • Compliance Easy	• Digitalization • Disintermediation • Democratization • Decentralization • Diminishing Oneself • Data Privacy Protection	• Open • Altruistic • Global • Crowdsourcing Wisdom • Crowdsourcing Contribution • Encompassing • Interest of All • Beneficial to All

incentives, and scalability dimensions should be considered from the business perspective to ensure trust and increase the cost of hacking constantly. Considering just one project or company is insufficient, as out of 100, 95 may not be useful in building the capabilities for the entire ecosystem. Without ladder projects, the ecosystem can never be built. Therefore, we may need to consider the value of the whole ecosystem — something that traditional bankers and fund managers find difficult to reconcile and explain to shareholders and investors, especially when the individual or too many projects fail before the last few succeed.

With better design of the token economics, projects like FCoin would have been successful. Therefore, factors such as the role and functions of the tokens, the architecture, and the monetary policy discussed here are extremely important. It is very likely that the winner takes all if no token exists. That is why tokens, along with token economics, are needed. The company, platform provider, or developer will control all the data and earn most of the profits, which is not what we aim to do. Many of the topics are already covered under traditional economics. Token economics is just an expansion to include the knowledge on the cryptocurrencies and tokens as well as the new business models.

We look forward to various token applications in a more inclusive ecosystem, and the emergence of widely accepted and successful token valuation methods.

In the future, it is highly possible that the majority of companies will use tokens to raise funds, similar to what ICOs did before but with various schemes and/or names. Many blockchain start-ups failed with

ICO because they treat tokens as securities or financing instruments without thorough considerations about the token utilities and economics. Tokenization is a process and alternative that can be much more powerful — it can give legal status to the things that do not have legal status previously, such as live stocks. For instance, previously, only the ownership of a cow has legal status. Still, tokenization makes assigning legal status to the trading activities or transactions of the cow possible so that customers can purchase a fraction of a cow and exchange the share with other things. It is undeniable that such a process may require delicate design and multiple parties involved, such as insurers, to finance and verify. Yet, it provides solutions to tackle many pain points in businesses today and helps achieve an inclusive and ultimate goal of maximizing values for all. Also, the value of the tokens and stocks shall not compete with each other but supplement each other to increase both. We should focus on what can be achieved in the future.

7.2 Blockchain Design Thinking

This section introduces the advanced topics in blockchain technology, such as its architecture, design thinking, token design, and the ideas of game theory.

Learning Objectives
- Understand the considerations to utilize and design a blockchain.
- Understand the token design and use of game theory in the token economy.

Main Takeaways

Main Points
- A good blockchain use case should have the following attributes: a business problem to be solved, an identifiable network/ecosystem, and requires trust that is decentralized, transparent, and secure.
- Blockchain applies game theory mechanics to protect the system, and the Nash Equilibrium is self-enforced in the blockchain with a recursive punishment design.

Main Terms
- **User:** Refers to anyone who interacts with the blockchain network.

- **Prisoner's Dilemma:** Is a famous game with two players in the game theory. In it, equilibrium may not be the best outcome for both players.

7.2.1 *Blockchain Architecture and Design*

The world is gradually beginning to understand blockchain and its benefits as more people and enterprises are discovering and experimenting on various use cases. The obvious Bitcoin use case for peer-to-peer payments has evolved into a big world of decentralized finance; stable-coins, decentralized exchanges, lending platforms, prediction markets, and more. In traditional finance, banks have explored beyond cryptocurrencies and have established solutions using blockchain for trade finance (letters of credit in particular); central banks such as the Monetary Authority of Singapore have experimented with interbank clearing and settlement. The use cases for blockchain are not restricted to finance space. There are government and enterprise efforts in identity, personal records, retail, trade, and manufacturing (see Figure 7.1).

It is exciting to think about applying blockchain in your business or use case as an emerging technology. However, it is good to remember that blockchain is not a solution to every problem. A good blockchain use case should have the following attributes, as shown in Figure 7.2.

The business problem (or any other problem statement) should make sense for blockchain. A more mature technology can solve the existing inefficiencies in the industry arising due to a lack of digitization or coordination. The network of participants, assets (that need to be held and moved within the network), and transactions (or rules which define how these assets can be moved) need to be clear and identifiable. For instance, lack of trust between stakeholders can lead to creating a good blockchain use case. The need for the essential features (as described in Figure 7.3) of blockchain to solve a business problem justifies its application.

Blockchain technology can solve the trust issue for a network of participants whose objectives may not be aligned. Also, decentralization can help ensure that there is no one point of failure, and the consensus protocol ensures internal network alignment. The network accepts the validity of the transactions that are written onto the ledger. Additionally, blockchain is transparent to its participants (to some degree), making it easy to audit. Due to these features, the ledger is secured as the data is fixed and

Blockchain Use Cases: Selected Industries

Figure 7.1: Blockchain use cases.

A Good Blockchain Use Case

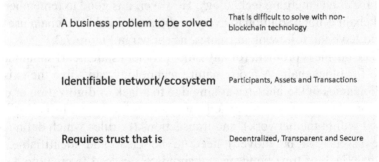

Figure 7.2: Attributes of a good blockchain use case.

cannot be easily changed or hacked. This helps in creating a layer of trust for the network participants.

7.2.2 *Planning Your Blockchain*

Suppose you have established that you have a good blockchain use case and want to develop the application. Blockchain applications can be put together in many possible ways and are based on multiple considerations.

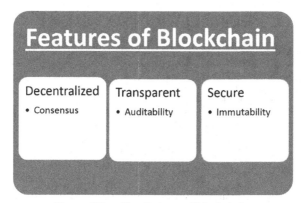

Figure 7.3: Key features of blockchain.

To begin with, it is essential to understand the fundamental use case to decide what kind of technology and network should be used. The essential steps are outlined in Figure 7.4.

First, identify and define the primary purpose of applying blockchain in the use case. Are there various stakeholders involved in the process causing a lack of trust, resulting in manual checks and bottlenecks? Is there a need to store evidence or audit trails in a decentralized way such that any centralized party cannot manipulate the data? Or is the use case for a decentralized economy with digital tokens or assets? Next, we dive deeper to understand your use case and outline the requirements by considering its users, assets, participants, and network.

(a) Define Users

User refers to anyone who interacts with the blockchain network. This includes administrators, auditors, node operators, and end-users. Types of questions to ask include:

(1) What types of actions do they need to take? Is it view only, or do they need to interact with the blockchain?
(2) Are they part of an organization? What are their roles in the organization? Is there an organizational hierarchy to consider?
(3) User actions include the ability to transact and hold assets. Does this ability depend on their role?
(4) How would they usually interact with the system? e.g., mobile phones or laptops.

Planning Your Blockchain

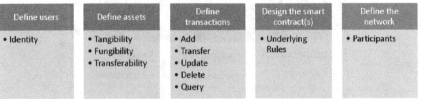

Figure 7.4:   Planning your blockchain.

Another important consideration is the user's identity (or account). Two kinds of identity are considered. Firstly, consider whether a blockchain-based identity or account is needed. When users are assigned a blockchain account (or address), they can transact and hold assets using their assigned blockchain account (or address). If this is required, the following consideration is the management of user keys. Are your users technically savvy enough to manage their own private keys (i.e., Manage their own blockchain wallet)? Do you need a mechanism for key recovery? Is it better to run a key management service? In this case, what are the security considerations?

Considering that a user's profile is the second type of identity, this acts as a connecting point between the user and its real-world identity. Should your users transact only with their blockchain accounts? Pseudo-anonymous blockchains like Bitcoin do not require verification of the user identities.

Certain forms of identity are required in most business use-cases because of legal or business considerations. If required, you also need to consider how the identity verification needs to be done, and the kind of identity information is required. Does it include name, email, identity documents, or more? A gateway or controller makes sure identity is verified before credentials are issued to the user in private or permissioned blockchains. After collecting this information, you will need to store and manage the user data securely. Users' identities can also be collected on your servers and link them to blockchain accounts while using a public blockchain. For example, exchanges that are legally obligated to store KYC information. Identity oracles that are linked to a trusted database are alternatives in public blockchains. Uport, which worked with the city of Zug to issue government verified identities on the Ethereum blockchain, is an example.

(2) Define Assets

Digital assets can be broadly defined as any type of information where ownership can be assigned. Cryptocurrencies are the most familiar type of asset on blockchain networks. Cryptocurrency is an on-chain asset as they are generated through algorithms that run on the blockchain, like bitcoin mining. This type of asset only exists on the blockchain.

Rights over physical property such as real estate, vehicles, or precious metals are another category of assets that can potentially be digitized on a blockchain. A trusted party acts as an issuer of the digital title in these cases. To ensure the redeemability of the asset, a legal process needs to exist behind its issuance. The benefit of such types of digitization is fractionalizing the asset. This makes the asset more accessible to the mass market and allows the asset owners to issue tokens to the asset for financing purposes.

On the blockchain, intangible digital assets can also be issued. Entities that are a part of the network can generate them digitally. Generally, these parties need to be trusted for the network to acknowledge the legitimacy of the asset. Letters of credit, bank guarantees, loyalty points, equity, and intellectual property rights are a few examples.

The fungibility of the digital asset/token is another attribute that needs to be considered. In addition, it affects the technology you can use to issue the asset. Cryptocurrencies like bitcoin are non-fungible, and one bitcoin is not distinguishable from another. Since each property may have distinguishing attributes and value, tokens representing properties need to be fungible. However, fractionalized tokens of a particular property can be fungible as each indicates a share of the property (which is no different from another share).

Digital assets/tokens generally should be transferable to allow for changes in ownership and trading of the asset. However, there is a class of digital assets that should be non-transferrable, and such assets are particular to an individual or entity. This consists of medical records, identity registries, education credentials, and employment records.

(c) Define Transactions

Once we decide on the types of assets on the network, we should consider the rules that govern these assets. These are the transactions that will occur on the network. These rules vary with the type of the users and the assets. Types of transactions include:

1. Add: Creating or issuing of asset
2. Transfer: Change of asset ownership
3. Update: Alteration of the asset (such as updating an expiration date or status)
4. Delete: Destruction of asset
5. Query: Look up information about the asset

(d) Design the Smart Contracts

The next step is to bundle your assets and transactions into smart contracts. The rules for your assets in code are called a smart contract. Consider what the underlying rules or conditions for the transfer of assets are? This is where an understanding of the business process comes in. How are the assets created, and by whom? Who is allowed to own and transfer these assets? Once deployed, smart contracts are tough to change. It is important to ensure that you have the necessary functions. Consider "bad" scenarios to ensure that you have an "exit" if things go wrong, particularly, if your smart contracts deal with valuable digital assets.

(e) Determine the Network

We should consider the network after having a clear idea of the participants, assets, and transactions. Who will operate and/or regulate the blockchain? Are gateways (such as exchanges or data providers) needed to connect to systems outside the blockchain network? Do you need to integrate external data sources?

There may be participants in your blockchain network that are not merely users. Additional questions related to the participants that need to be asked include: How will they access and interact with the blockchain? Are they required to be nodes on the blockchain network? Figure 7.5 and Table 7.7 depict and elaborate on the types of participants that can be part of the blockchain network. Not all types are required participants of the network, depending on the use case. So, you need to decide what types to use.

7.2.3 *Choose Your Technology*

The initial step in deciding the technology you will use is identifying if you need your blockchain network. You will require your blockchain if

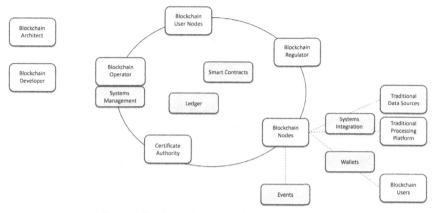

Figure 7.5:   Participants in a blockchain network.

you have a token-related use case where the token is utilized as a utility for operating the network. Another scenario where you will require your blockchain is using a unique consensus protocol designed to incentivize your network participants. That would allow you to customize the blockchain network from the protocol level. Also, you will need your permissioned blockchain network if you plan to run a permissioned blockchain network where only your partners can join. Technologies like the Hyperledger family, Corda, Multichain, and even Ethereum (Enterprise), allow you to customize and run your blockchain network.

You can put down your consensus and rules if you have an experienced blockchain development team that can code your blockchain from the protocol level. A few years ago, this would have been the only choice available. However, many tools for developing blockchain networks have become mature and can be utilized now. It is not always practical to set up and run a network independently. Blockchain as a Service provider (BaaS) like Azure, AWS, and Kaleido offer services that allow the clients to implement a blockchain network with simply a few clicks. You can choose between various technology options when using BaaS.

When deploying your blockchain, do you keep it permissioned or to make it public? Do you want others to join your network as nodes without requiring your permission? The visibility of the blockchain data is another factor that needs to be considered. A blockchain network could be written and read public, for instance. This implies that only the permissioned blockchain nodes can write to the blockchain; however, the blockchain ledger is open for the public to access.

Table 7.7: Participants in a blockchain network.

Participants of a blockchain network	
Entities, Systems, and Hardware	
Blockchain Architect	Designs the network and the software based on the system requirements.
Blockchain Developer	Develops and codes the blockchain protocol and smart contracts.
Blockchain Operator	Runs and manages the blockchain's daily operations.
Blockchain Regulator	Decides and enforces the rules. Manages the nodes. More likely in permissioned blockchains.
Certificate Authority	Issues authenticated certificates to users and provide proofs of identity.
Blockchain Node	A server on the blockchain network may or may not participate in consensus and storing of the blockchain ledger.
Blockchain Users	Individuals or entities that are using the blockchain network.
Traditional data sources and processing platforms	Third-party data sources and systems may need to be connected to the blockchain.
Software	
Wallets	For management of digital assets assigned to blockchain users.
Applications	Software that provides an interface for the user to connect to the network and interact with its functions.
Smart Contracts	Code that is deployed on the blockchain to manage assets and transactions.
Ledger	The blockchain database that records the transactions.
Events	External sources of information (or oracles) that may be used to trigger a smart contract process.
System management	Program for managing the blockchain network, such as upgrading the protocol and giving permission to nodes.
System integration	Software was written to connect the blockchain network to third-party sources of information.

Pros and cons exist for permissioned (private) and permissionless (public) blockchain networks. The industry opinions vary. It can be argued that running a highly permissioned system where the nodes can be controlled is merely opening with the same single point of failure weaknesses which blockchain originally is designed to overcome although it may be claimed by others that trusting a network that can be joined by anyone may be difficult for institutions. To answer which is a better alternative is hard as it is subjective to the use-case, company policies, and the mindset of stakeholders. No rule of thumb nor industry-standard exists to conclude which one is better. Some institutions will choose to trust permissioned systems, and on the contrary, a pro-decentralization public use case may prefer the permissionless approach.

The ability to form the network should also be considered when creating your network. If your goal is to create an industry-wide blockchain, would you be able to get most of the industry to agree to participate as nodes? Can you get the relevant authorities like trade associations or regulators to be part of your network? If participants are potential competitors, there may not be enough trust within the participants. If you are starting a public blockchain, will you be able to get nodes (or miners) to join your blockchain? How would you make them aware of this network? Are your incentives attractive enough to make them join? For this, you will need to consider network economics (see the next section).

However, there is no need to deploy your own blockchain network in many cases. Considering your use case is just focused on creating a decentralized application (dapp), you can deploy your smart contracts onto an existing blockchain network. You can also connect your dapp to the network as well. Multiple applications running on the Ethereum network are solid examples. If all you need is an application, having your blockchain network may not be necessary. If the requirement is to have an application, there is no need to create your blockchain network.

In deciding to use an existing public blockchain, you also must consider the non-functional requirements of the solution you are developing. What are the number of users, transaction volume, and speed? Is there a minimum level of service you need to provide for your users? Note that there may exist a trade-off between safety and speed. More extensive blockchain networks (like Ethereum) may be more secure but at the same time more prone to congestion and greater network transaction fees (gas) even when networks like these provide a high level of data immutability and security compared to smaller or private networks.

If you decide to use an existing blockchain network, the key considerations would be if the network is healthy (secure) and the technical features support your use case. Ethereum is the network of choice still for deploying dapps, but many next-generation blockchains networks like QTUM, NEO, Cardano, Zilliqa, EOS, Tron, and Tezos are also catching up. Ethereum 2.0 is also launching, and it aims to address scaling issues currently faced by Ethereum. Blockchain technology with built-in privacy features such as Zero-Knowledge Proofs, Secure Signature Schemes, or Private State Channels should be considered if privateness is essential.

Solely permissioned or solely public blockchains are not the sole options. In a hybrid setting, private permissioned blockchains may depend on public blockchains for maintaining immutability and trust in a hybrid setting. This involves posting the blockchain of your permissioned network to the public blockchain of choice and also provides added security (immutability) to the transactions on your blockchain. Such methods were first discussed in Komodo's Delayed Proof of Work using the Bitcoin network. However, they can also now be found in Kaleido's Ethereum's tethering service.

Figure 7.6 summarizes the process of choosing the blockchain technology/network.

7.2.4 *Designing Token Economics*

The term token economics stems from mechanism design. Mechanism design is an economics approach to design incentives (or economic mechanisms) to get a strategic outcome (where players act rationally). Bitcoin's mechanism design aims to get miners to validate transactions, ensure consistency in the blockchain ledger, and prevent double-spending of coins, which is the goal of bitcoin's mechanism design. In addition to the limited supply, incentives were used to collect bitcoins. This, in turn, gives bitcoins economic value and drives miner incentives.

The key consideration is the outcome you wish to achieve, considering if you plan to design your own token and consensus. The incentives of the network participants must align to drive towards that outcome, irrespectively of whether mining or other methods are used as an incentive. It would help if you also were on the lookout for undesired outcomes.

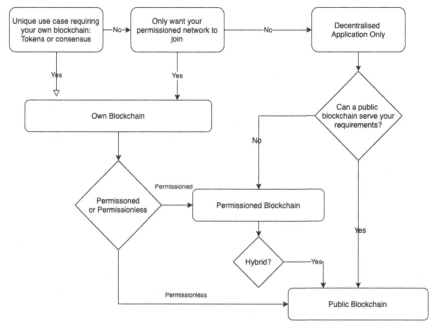

Figure 7.6:   Choosing blockchain technology.

Consolidation of miners was not expected when bitcoins were designed. Centralization of mining power and the exclusion of nodes with low computational power occurred when bitcoin prices became appealing in reality. Large use of electricity consumption for the network due to intense competition in mining was also not anticipated.

Points to note when designing your tokens are attributes such as how the tokens are created or generated, how the tokens are distributed to the network (is it competitive), and the token's utility within the network. In some instances, your objectives may also include not only just the actions that happen within your blockchain network but also the token price. External factors to your network determine the token price. Since both demand and supply are internally and externally driven, external factors to your network help determine the token price. Non-participants may trade the tokens as well as contribute to price volatility. The token design may affect the price, and investors may accredit shortage or high utility to the potential increase in prices. Price volatility in the external market needs to be examined if your aim for the token is to power the utility within the blockchain network. The volatile and speculative nature of bitcoin has prevented it from satisfying its primary intention as a payment token.

7.2.5 *Putting it Together*

Now that we have examined the various considerations. We can put it together by describing the processes within your solution. The user's end-to-end journey is mapped in a process flow diagram. The diagram should include the various users or participants, user interfaces or applications, the blockchain network, smart contracts and assets, and the interactions (transactions) between them. Figure 7.7 illustrates an example for the use case of education certificates on the blockchain. The school uses an Issuing Application to interact with the blockchain to store hashes of the certificates for verification. The Issuing Application returns the Certificate to the school, then sends it to the student. The student can share this certificate with a potential employer. Both student and employer can use the Web Application to verify the Certificate's authenticity. The Web Application queries and verifies the Certificate with the hash stored on the blockchain. If the Certificate is tampered with or fake, the Web Application will return a negative result.

To better understand the implementation of your use case, you can either sketch or draw the user interface. Create mock-ups of your website

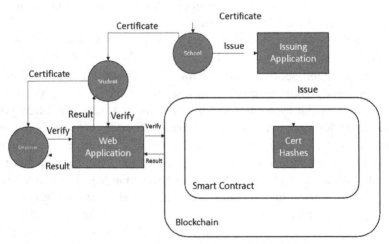

Figure 7.7:   Issuing certificates on the blockchain.

or mobile app, which should include all functions required to interact with the smart contracts and the blockchain. Decide what the user sees from the blockchain on the UI and what happens in the background. This will aid you in the development of the applications and smart contracts.

Designing and architecting a blockchain solution is an art rather than science. A deep understanding of the problem statements, use cases, and user requirements are needed, along with the appreciation of blockchain's features and how to utilize and apply them in the solution to achieve your objectives. This chapter serves as a guide to get the reader started; the rest comes with experience.

7.2.6 *Token Design and Game Theory*

(a) Cryptocurrency Game Theory

As we have learned in Level 1, game theory studies strategic decisions or interactions among multiple rational players. Nash equilibrium, in which each player has an optimal strategy for the other's strategy without being better-off by shifting the strategy, is the solution to the game. Game theory was first developed by John Van Neumann and Osker Morgenstern in 1944 (Neumann and Morgenstern, 1944). It has become a breakthrough for social sciences to apply mathematical models to simulate complex human thoughts and behaviors. It has been widely implemented in various technologies and fields.

The public blockchain, like Bitcoin, is completely decentralized and internally collusion-free. The logic behind that is from game theory (Rosic, 2017). For example, if we consider the mining process in blockchain as a game, the application of game theory is the design to keep the blockchain mining system working (Liu *et al.*, 2019).

Blockchain consists of a chain of blocks that record many transactions. The mining process starts from the genesis block, the first block of the chain. The miners use high computation power to find a block and append it into the chain with transaction records to get rewards (e.g., Bitcoins).

If the miners would like to cheat for their interest, they might ruin the system as they maintain the system. Specifically, miners could include invalid transactions and misconducts such as double-spending or simply assigning themselves extra coins. To illustrate this, let's assume a malicious miner is coming out after block 89 is created, as shown in Figure 7.8. The main chain is the upper one in dark gray that honest miners create. Suppose the malicious miner creates a fork to mimic the next

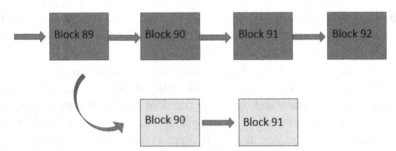

Figure 7.8:   Fork of blockchain.

block 90 (in light gray below) and includes the "fake" transactions of his/ her interest. In this case, the light gray chain would benefit the malicious miner and disrupt the system in the end if other miners do it in the same way. However, this does not happen in reality. Blockchain applies game theory mechanics to protect the system (Singh *et al.*, 2020), and the Nash Equilibrium is self-enforced in the blockchain with a recursive punishment design.

As Block 90 in the light gray chain is not created by following the rules of the main blockchain, it would be recognized as an invalid block unless most of the miners accept and append the blocks subsequently. As the number of miners is very large, it is very difficult to coordinate most of the miners. Block 90 would remain invalid, and any block appended to this invalid block would become invalid as well. Therefore, Block 91 in light gray in the figure will also be invalid. Thus, miners have no incentive to append a block on this light gray chain because there is no reward, and there is cost from computation power. So the misconduct would be punished. Under this logic, other miners would ignore the light gray one and stay on the main chain. Then the stable status of the main chain is a state with Nash equilibrium.

However, the equilibrium might be challenged in the blockchain with the proof of work consensus. The light gray chain might take over the main chain in certain situations by using a pregame strategy. We can consider the mining process as a sequential move game. The miner could have some strategic pregame moves using a smart contract to change the rules. One example given by Vitalik Buterin[3] is to make a credible

---

[3] Vitalik Buterin: Cryptoeconomic Protocols In the Context of Wider Society, retrieved from https://www.youtube.com/watch?v=S47iWiKKvLA.

promise. According to the characteristics of a smart contract, the guarantee with the smart contract is credible, observable, and irreversible.

Suppose the malicious miner makes a hypothetical smart contract for the light gray chain. The terms of the contract go like this:

(1) Any miner can send a large deposit of tokens to the contract and verify their hash power to join the game.
(2) Any miner can leave if the participants in the contract do not reach 60% of the miners in the world.
(3) When more than 60% of the miners join the game, the smart contract is triggered until 20 blocks are appended to the light gray chain, making all the light gray blocks valid.
(4) All participants would get rewarded from the light gray chain as the light gray chain is under control after the smart contract is triggered.

We can see that this contract is attractive as there is no risk of participating and possible rewards. The original main chain will become invalid if more than 60% of the miners join the game. Then the value of the token will decrease because the malicious miner enables double-spending and could change the total amount of token supply.

This threat is possible, but it scarcely happens in the real world due to a famous game theory mechanism: Grim Trigger (Engle-Warnick and Slonim, 2006) argument. Grim Trigger is a strategy in a repeated game and can lead to cooperation if players are sufficiently patient. If the light gray chain replaces the main chain, then the light gray chain would be replaced by a new one and continues these endless hard-forks. If the miners are rational and can foresee the endless hard-forks, they will not hard-fork in the first place; otherwise, their tokens could be valueless in the end. But sometimes, Grim Trigger does not work if the miners have several types of tokens to work on, and they might take over the low-value one. Grim Trigger would work well if the miners were bound and loyal to one token. Proof-of-stake is based on this logic. The miners have a stake in the tokens, and they have incentives to maintain the system.

(b) Design Thinking with Token and Smart Contract
In game theory, the Prisoner's dilemma is a famous game that we have learned in Level 1. In Prisoner's Dilemma, equilibrium may not be the best outcome for both players. To illustrate this, let us review one example first. Suppose there are two players (A and B) in the game. The strategy and the payoff are shown in the matrix as follows in Table 7.8.

Table 7.8: Game table of Prisoner's dilemma.

	B confesses	B does not confess
A confesses	(–2, –2)	(0, –4)
A does not confess	(–4, 0)	(–1, –1)

Table 7.9: The modified game table of Prisoner's dilemma.

	B confesses	B does not confess
A confesses	(–2, –2)	(–deposit, –4 + deposit)
A does not confess	(–4 + deposit, –deposit)	(–1, –1)

In this example, the equilibrium is (A confesses, B confesses) with payoff (–2, –2). However, the best outcome should be (A does not confess, B does not confess) with payoff (–1, –1). In such a non-cooperative game, players only choose a strategy according to personal benefit, so the best outcome is never in equilibrium.

In reality, to reach the best outcome, the players could have some strategic moves before the game: threat. This conveys the idea to the opponent player that if one particular action is taken, then the threat would come true later. However, to make the threat or promise credible is a problem in reality. With a token and smart contract, this issue could be easily solved. A simple way is for both players to create a smart contract with a large deposit of tokens before the game. If any player confesses, the smart contract will be triggered and incurred a huge cost to that player. The incentive would be changed, and the payoff matrix would be changed to the one in Table 7.9. Under this design, the best outcome could be achieved.

Overall, we mentioned a straightforward idea to illustrate the logic in this section. It is the foundation for many recent blockchain projects. Combining tokens and smart contracts could be widely applied with game theory for society to make the world better.

(c) Tokenization and Enterprise Development

Tokens provide incentives for the users to behave well (Tan, 2019). Without tokens, the Blockchain system might become a pure database with a recording function for transactions and rely solely on legal agreements or contracts. It might not be as efficient as the one with token design because the legislative enforcements are challenging in cross-border situations. The users are more self-disciplined in a token-based setting.

There are token-based and tokenless blockchain systems. Token-based blockchain systems usually provide public access. Therefore any party is free to reach the consensus process and transaction activities. The tokens could be used to provide incentives for the users to maintain the system and punish wrongdoings. Tokenless blockchain systems are usually private. Particular parties grant the access. Therefore all parties need to get permission to get on board. The design of this type of system is to facilitate enterprise management and business flow recording. The token function seems not remarkable. Therefore, it is optional for further development.

As more and more enterprises would like to develop their blockchain, there could be several requirements for choosing a suitable framework. The users' access could not be randomly assigned. The identification seems necessary. Besides, privacy; high volume of transactions; and volume expansion are significant concerns as the business could grow. Regarding the aforementioned two types of blockchain frameworks, the adoption of blockchain platforms for enterprise are usually private or permissioned, and the token feature might not be activated. However, it is still possible to create personalized tokens in the system for the recent development of enterprise platforms. Enterprise blockchain enables trust between users on the platform by using legal agreements and contracts to restrict legitimate users' behavior.

Under a permissioned blockchain framework, it is not entirely decentralized and transparent. The business application owner determines all the attributes, and the users need approval from the owner to get access to the application. If the owner is a sole organization, then the framework is a private blockchain. Alternatively, the owner could be an alliance including many organizations, who will jointly formulate all internal management rules and mechanisms for the application. This framework is called consortium blockchains.

Currently, popular Enterprise consortium blockchain platforms include Blockchain-based Service Network (BSN),[4] Hyperledger Fabric,[5] Hyperledger Iroha,[6] Multichain,[7] R3 Corda,[8] and Quorum.[9] We compare these inclusive blockchain projects that see mass adoption in Table 7.10.

---

[4] "BSN White Paper".
[5] "Hyperledger Fabric".
[6] "Overview of Iroha".
[7] "MultiChain White Paper".
[8] "Corda Introduction".
[9] "What Is Quorum Blockchain? A Platform for The Enterprise", Blockgeeks.

Table 7.10: Comparison of consortium platform.

	Hyperledger Fabric	Hyperledger Iroha	Multichain	CORDA	BSN	Quorum
Developer	The Linux Foundation, and has received contributions from IBM, Intel and SAP Ariba	Hyperledger member company, Soramitsu	Coin Sciences Ltd.	R3	Main six founders of BSN are: (1) State Information Center of China, (2) Union Pay, (3) China Mobile Financial Technology, (4) Beijing Red Date, (5) China Mobile Communications Corporation Design Institute (6) China Mobile Communications Corporation Government and Enterprise Service Company	JPMorgan Chase
Governance	The governing board of the Hyperledger Project consists of twenty members chaired by Robert Palatnick	The governing board of the Hyperledger Project consists of twenty members chaired by Robert Palatnick	Coin Sciences Ltd.	The control of governance is owned by R3 and the organizations participating in the transaction	BSN development association has the ultimate governance over the network. In future, BSN international will be jointly managed by world-renowned companies	JPMorgan Chase

Consensus	Supporting pluggable consensus protocols that enable the platform to be more effectively customized to fit particular use cases and trust models	YAC (Yet Another Consensus), which is based on voting for block hash	A round-robin scheme with "Mining Diversity" as the consensus protocol	The consensus happens between or among parties involved at the level of users rather than the level of system	BSN provides one uniform consensus node cluster service that is developed, built, operated, and maintained by China UnionPay and that provides services to each blockchain application within all of the city nodes	Proof of Authority (Raft, IBFT, and Clique) consensus mechanisms
Cryptocurrency	FabToken	No native cryptocurrency	built-in blockchain tokens design	Tokenless	"Localized" Tokens	JPM coins

(Continued)

	Hyperledger Fabric	Hyperledger Iroha	Multichain	CORDA	BSN	Quorum
Programming Language	Distributed applications written in general-purpose programming languages such as Java, Go, NodeJS/Java-script without depending on any native cryptocurrency	C++; Java	It itself is written in C++. It has a JSON-RPC interface that can be used with modern popular languages like C#, Go, Java, Python, Java and Java-script	The source code of CORDA is written in Kotlin. Although it is compatible with any JVM language, application developers are encouraged to write their code in Kotlin to achieve consistency	Allow developers of with absolutely no prior knowledge of blockchain development to use familiar programming language and operating environments to access the BSN. DAML serves as a standard for creating decentralized applications on the BSN	Java and Kotin

| Targeted Industry | Multinational companies (IBM, Huawei, Thales, Accenture, etc.) | Mobile payment and banking | Aims to overcome a key obstacle to the deployment of blockchain technology in the institutional financial sector | Originally conceived as a blockchain solution to issues prevalent in the financial industry. Also attracting customers from industries such as healthcare and supply chain | No specific targeted industry | Logistics, healthcare, identity, property, payments, capital markets and post trade |

Across these consortium blockchain platforms, BSN seems more inclusive than others. The networking of BSN follows a mode of Internet networking. Any entity with cloud services or data centers worldwide can apply for being a public city node and access BNS free of charge if BSN standards and specifications comply. This enables BSN to develop and expand at high speed. BSN would localize public chains in its network by making the decentralized public chains permissioned and transferring their tokens with Chinese currency to cover transaction fees on chains. The BSN users use the Internet or dedicated line to access the BSN from the nearest public city node. To ensure the security of transactions, a dedicated line is required for financial-related data transmission. All the public city nodes support local dedicated lines at a lower cost than cross-region dedicated lines.

Nevertheless, each platform has different features that would make them ideal. Depending on the industry focus and specific solution, resources are needed to adapt the platform to operations or security requirements inside the organization.

The decision of choosing a suitable blockchain platform for enterprise development is crucial as the blockchain can leverage the businesses' processes. When comparing the platforms, some key features most enterprises might consider are privacy, transparency, cost-efficiency, and adaption. However, tokenization should be an important feature to consider.

In public systems, native tokens provide an incentive mechanism for block validators to comply with predefined rules. In permissioned distributed ledger systems, validators and block-creators are contractually obligated to maintain the system. It might seem that the token design is not necessary due to its consensus design. Combining the token and smart contract technology could reward honest behavior and impose punishment on dishonest or malicious behavior, helping regulate business activities in the enterprise system.

References/Further Readings

Aguilar, F. J. (1967). *Scanning the Business Environment*. Macmillan.

Alabi, K. (2017). Digital blockchain networks appear to be following Metcalfe's Law. *Electronic Commerce Research and Applications*, 24, 23–29.

Brouwer, A. J. (2018). The Dual Token Structure Thesis. Retrieved from https://blog.goodaudience.com/the-dual-token-structure-thesis-c3a43ef54537.

Burniske, C. (2017). The Crypto J-Curve. Medium. Retrieved from: https://medium.com/@cburniske/the-crypto-j-curve be5fdddafa26.

Cong, L. W., Li, Y., & Wang, N. (2020). Tokenomics: Dynamic Adoption and Valuation (No. w27222). National Bureau of Economic Research.

Denault, J. F. (2018). *The Handbook of Marketing Strategy for Life Science Companies: Formulating the Roadmap You Need to Navigate the Market.* Routledge.

Elmerraji, J. (2020). 5 Must-Have Metrics for Value Investors. Investopedia. Retrieved from https://www.investopedia.com/articles/fundamental-analysis/09/five-must-have-metrics-value-investors.asp.

Graham, A. (2017). TAM Methodology: An Explanation and Example of Total Addressable Market Analysis. Toptal. Retrieved from https://www.toptal.com/finance/market-sizing/total-addressable-market-example.

Hayes, A. (2016). Decentralised banking: Monetary technocracy in the digital age. In *Banking Beyond Banks and Money* (pp. 121–131). Springer, Cham.

Hayes, A. S. (2019). Bitcoin price and its marginal cost of production: Support for a fundamental value. *Applied Economics Letters*, 26(7).

He, H. (2018). The Death of FCoin: A Tale of Bad Token Design. Retrieved from https://hackernoon.com/the-death-of-fcoin-a-tale-of-bad-token-design-261d64a8116f.

Hlebiv, O. (2018). What is Token Economics. Retrieved from https://applicature.com/blog/blockchain-startups/what-is-token-economics.

Jain, N. (2019). How to Value a Fintech Startup. Retrieved from https://www.toptal.com/finance/valuation/how-to-value-a-fintech-startup.

Kalichkin, D. (2018). Rethinking Network Value to Transactions (NVT) Ratio. Medium. Retrieved from https://medium.com/cryptolab/https-medium-com-kalichkin-rethinking-nvt-ratio-2cf810df0ab0.

Lannquist, A. (2018). Today's Crypto Asset Valuation Frameworks. Medium. Retrieved from https://medium.com/blockchain-at-berkeley/todays-crypto-asset-valuation-frameworks-573a38eda27e.

Lee, D. K. C. & Teo, E. G. S. (2020). The New Money: The Utility of Cryptocurrencies and the need for a New Monetary Policy. Working paper. Retrieved from https://papers.ssrn.com/sol3/papers.cfm?abstract_id=3608752.

Leilacher, A. (2019). What the Network Value to Transactions Ratio can Tell About Crypto.Cryptonews. Retrieved from https://cryptonews.com/exclusives/what-the-network-value-to-transactions-ratio-can-tell-about-3156.htm.

Lielacher, A. (2019). Digital Asset Valuation: Top 7 Metrics for Valuing Bitcoin, Altcoins, and Cryptocurrencies. Bitcoin Market Journal. Retrieved from https://www.bitcoinmarketjournal.com/digital-asset-valuation/.

Liu, K. (2019). Token Economics #2: Comparison Review of Token Economy. Retrieved from https://hackernoon.com/token-economics-1-why-do-we-need-token-economics-2c0006098aea.

Mesenbourg, T. L. (2001). Measuring the Digital Economy. U.S. Bureau of the Census.

Shen, B. (2015). 分布式资本沈波: 区块链经济价值观-开源的心态、利他的精神、全球的视野. [The Economic Values of Blockchain: Open-minded, Altruism, and Global Vision]. Retrieved from https://www.ccvalue.cn/article/78508.html.

Tönnissen, S., Beinke, J. H., & Teuteberg, F. (2020). Understanding token-based ecosystems — A taxonomy of blockchain-based business models of start-ups. Electron Markets. Retrieved from https://link.springer.com/article/10.1007/s12525-020-00396-6.

Trinh, L. (2018). Sharing Economy vs Token Economy: You Decide. Retrieved from https://kambria.io/blog/sharing-economy-vs-token-economy-you-decide/.

Wan, C. (2020). Cryptocurrency exchange Fcoin expects to default on as much as $125M of users' bitcoin. Retrieved from https://www.theblockcrypto.com/post/56191/cryptocurrency-exchange-fcoin-expects-to-default-on-as-much-as-125m-of-users-bitcoin.

Wang, J. C. (2014). A Simple Macroeconomic Model of Bitcoin. Working paper. Retrieved from https://ssrn.com/abstract=2394024.

Xu, M., Li, J., & Wang, M. (2019). *Token Economics*. CITIC Press Corporation, 1st edition.

Zhang, X. Z., Liu, J. J., & Xu, Z. W. (2015). *Tencent and Facebook Data Validate Metcalfe's Law*. Springer Link.

Engle-Warnick, J. & Robert L. Slonim, (2006). Learning to trust in infinitely repeated games. *Games and Economic Behavior*, 54(1), 95–114.

John von Neumann & Oskar Morgenstern (1944). *Theory of Games and Economic Behavior*. Princeton University Press.

Rosic, A. (2017). What is Cryptocurrency Game Theory: A Basic introduction.

Singh, R., Dwivedi, A. D., Srivastava, G. *et al.* (2020). A game theoretic analysis of resource mining in blockchain. *Cluster Comput*, 23, 2035–2046. https://doi.org/10.1007/s10586-020-03046-w.

Ziyao Liu, Nguyen Cong Luong, Wenbo Wang, Dusit Niyato, Ping Wang, Ying-Chang Liang, & Dong In Kim. (2019). A Survey on Applications of Game Theory in Blockchain. Retrieved from https://arxiv.org/pdf/1902.10865.pdf.

7.3 Sample Questions

Question 1

Which of the following is NOT an essential element that makes a token economy effective?

(a) Governance model
(b) Back-up reinforcer
(c) Specified target behaviors

Question 2
Which of the following is NOT a Fintech or token valuation approach?

(a) 5Vs
(b) 7Ws
(c) LASIC

Question 3
Which of the following statements is correct?

(a) The most important objective of token economics is to generate tokens.
(b) It is easy for an economy to function well even without any tokens.
(c) Token economy is to make the entire ecosystem.

Question 4
Which of the following is NOT a type of user in the blockchain network?

(a) Administrator
(b) Governor
(c) Auditor

Question 5
Which of the following is NOT an attribute of a good blockchain use case?

(a) A network or ecosystem that is identifiable
(b) A good business strategy
(c) Requires decentralized trust

Solutions

Question 1

Solution: Option **a** is correct.

Three essential elements make a token economy effective: tokens used as reinforcers to exchange for other reinforcers, back-up reinforcers that act as rewards, and specified target behaviors.

Question 2

Solution: Option **a** is correct.

5Vs are the features of big data, not a Fintech or token valuation approach discussed in the chapter.

Question 3

Solution: Option **c** is correct.

Token economics is something beyond just making the tokens, but to create the entire ecosystem, which means the designers need to get ready for the future and ensure users are spurred to consistently come and remain with the platform, with the support of tokens.

Question 4

Solution: Option **a** is correct.

Administrators, auditors, node operators, and end-users are all examples of users.

Question 5

Solution: Option **b** is correct.

A good blockchain use case should have the following attributes: a business problem to be solved, an identifiable network/ecosystem, and it requires trust that is decentralized, transparent, and secure.

Global Fintech Institute - World Scientific Series on Fintech

(Continued from page ii)

Forthcoming:

Applications and Trends in Fintech II: Cloud Computing, Compliance, and Global Fintech Trends
David Lee Kuo Chuen (Global Fintech Institute, Singapore & Singapore University of Social Sciences, Singapore), Joseph Lim, Phoon Kok Fai and Wang Yu (Singapore University of Social Sciences, Singapore)